Literary and Cultural Relations: Ireland, Hungary, and Central and Eastern Europe

Literary and Cultural Relations: Ireland, Hungary, and Central and Eastern Europe

Edited by Mária Kurdi

Carysfort Press

A Carysfort Press Book in association with Peter Lang

Literary and Cultural Relations: Ireland, Hungary, and Central and Eastern Europe
Edited by Mária Kurdi

First published as a paperback in Ireland in 2009 by
Carysfort Press Ltd
58 Woodfield, Scholarstown Road, Dublin 16, Ireland

ISBN 978-1-788748-95-7

Cover design by Alan Bennis

Typeset by Carysfort Press Ltd

The publication of this book was supported by the
Embassy of Ireland, Budapest

and is published with the financial assistance of
The Arts Council (An Chomhairle Ealaíon), Dublin, Ireland

Contents

CROSSCULTURAL DIALOGUE AND TRANSLATION

Acknowledgements

The papers published in this book were originally given at the first international conference of HUSIS, the Hungarian Society for Irish Studies, which was hosted by the University of Pécs in September 2007. As conference organizer and editor I wish to thank the Embassy of Ireland, Budapest, and the University of Pécs for their generous support of both the conference and the publication of this volume. Thanks are also due to my colleagues in the Department of English Literatures and Cultures and members of the Irish Studies Research Centre at UP who helped me with the work of organization, as well as to the group of Hungarian and international scholars who peer-reviewed the papers and gave me advice in the process of selection and editing. Finally, I express my gratitude to directors Dan Farrelly, Lilian Chambers, and Eamonn Jordan of Carysfort Press, who have made the publication of this book possible.

Introduction

Mária Kurdi

The papers collected in this book were originally given at the first conference of the Hungarian Society for Irish Studies (HUSIS), a small but dedicated body of scholars, which took place at the University of Pécs in September 2007. The theme of the conference, the same as the title of the present volume, was chosen with great care by those members who attended the annual meeting of HUSIS in late 2006. That meeting was generously hosted by the Embassy of Ireland, Budapest. We tried to make its topics as broad as possible to show relationships with Ireland. Fortunately, the conference managed to attract not only Irish and Hungarian scholars but also scholars from countries like the Czech Republic, Romania, France, Sweden, and the United States.

In October 2005 an unprecedented event called 'Forum on the Future of Irish Studies' was held at the European University Institute of Florence. It brought together over fifty scholars from Ireland and a range of European countries, the United States, Brazil, Canada, Japan, Australia, and New Zealand, and proved to be a uniquely fruitful opportunity to discuss ideas pertaining to the present fate and the future endeavours of Irish Studies worldwide. The plenary lectures were later published in an elegant little volume alongside reports about the sessions, in which one can read about the need for addressing topics in Irish Studies on a comparative basis in order to reshape critical paradigms and allow approaches to become more inclusive through the recognition of transnational parallels with non-Anglophone countries. Luke Gibbons, for instance, claims that 'Cross-cultural and comparativist perspectives are vital to bring Irish Studies out of centuries-old stereotypes of the insular Celts.' To this end, he explains, 'it is necessary to expand the range of reference to throw new light not just on Ireland, but on wider contemporary debates...'[1]

In a sense, the HUSIS Conference, representing scholarship concerned with relations among Ireland, Hungary, Central- and Eastern Europe, took its cue and drew encouragement from the above as well as from the realization that cross-cultural explorations lead to new insights about all countries involved. The present book is structured in two parts, each containing six papers. 'Drama and Theatre', the subtitle of the first section, demonstrates that the diversity of Irish dramatic achievements and the complex traditions of Ireland's theatre inspire a significant proportion of Irish Studies scholarship in the international context. The essays here are headed by Patrick Lonergan's 'All We Say is "Life is Crazy": Central and Eastern Europe and the Irish Stage', originally delivered as a plenary lecture at the HUSIS conference and illustrated by some well-chosen images while discussing both a delicate and far-reaching subject. Lonergan's starting point is that in recent years, especially during the Abbey centenary year, 2004, Irish theatre has been conspicuously enriched by guest performances of companies from Central and Eastern Europe. These productions, he argues, stage characters and issues in a way that, although suggesting difference from the Irish experience, can encourage the audience to feel that they face problems equally relevant to their own society in the age of globalization. Moreover, Lonergan discusses in more general terms the status of international work and multiculturalism in the Irish theatre while considering why the significance of this presence has not been better recorded so far. His argument is underpinned by references to several Irish plays, companies, and productions in Ireland which feature immigrants from Central and Eastern Europe, among others, and highlights the diversity of Irish responses to them.

A different approach is provided by Donald E. Morse's paper, which inquires into the impact of the Irish theatre abroad, namely the influence of the Beckettian Absurd on the Transylvanian-Hungarian writer and philosopher Géza Páskándi's dramaturgy. The discussion includes an analysis of Páskándi's *Todogar jaur Kvárna* [*They Are Waiting for Godot to Come Again*], in which the Gogo and Didi figures make covert references to the plight of the Hungarian ethnic minority in Romania who tried to resist cultural assimilation under the dictatorial regime before 1990. Morse also points to the differences in terms of dramatic strategy between the Absurd in Western and Eastern Europe because of respective cultural contexts. He stresses that the Páskándi play's focus is not so much on metaphysical issues as on the defeat of individuality and personal integrity under despotism. Péter P. Müller's paper complements Morse's as it briefly addresses two Central European Absurdist plays by Slawomir Mrożek and the Hungarian István Eörsi. This time the contrast is with Martin McDonagh's *The Pillowman*. In the latter the setting, although also evoking the mechanism of totalitarian police states, remains rather abstract and undefined. Müller emphasizes the multilevel, self-reflexive character of *The Pillowman* as opposed to the two other plays, and notes that McDonagh foregrounds body politics through the parental mistreatment of children and child abuse. They bring the play closer to the contemporary trend of new brutalism than to the revival of political theatre.

McDonagh also stands out as an important author in Ondřej Pilný's survey of Irish drama and theatre in the Czech Republic during 2000-2007, since his entire dramatic *oeuvre* has been translated and staged in the country. Within the period under consideration over sixty professional productions of Irish plays from Oscar Wilde to Marina Carr were mounted by the Czech theatres, a huge number in a relatively small country. Pilný, himself the translator of several Irish plays, also comments about the audience and critical reception of Irish drama in the Czech Republic in relation to cultural endeavours and events, at home and abroad, which promote the internationalisation of Irish theatre. Interestingly, the author remarks, despite the affinities between the histories of the two countries in terms of colonial/-semi-colonial subjugation, the critical analysis of Irish drama by Czech critics rarely focuses on the plays as the product of a nation. Part of the reason may be, the argument runs, that the Czechs did not lose their language although they suffered long-term Habsburg dominance and their aristocracy tended to use German. Not even the production of Friel's *Translations* in 1997 elicited Czech views about the play's relevance to the Czech audience in a postcolonial sense.

The postcolonial aspect finds an echo in Csilla Bertha's paper about performances of Friel in the Hungarian theatres. *Translations*, Bertha reports, has never been produced by any professional theatre in present-day Hungary; the Hungarian audience were allowed to see it only when a student group performed it in English at the University of Debrecen (1996) and when the Abbey Theatre took it to Budapest on its tour of the region (2001). However, two ethnic Hungarian theatres in Romania did venture to produce it. Bertha discusses the significance of these events in the context that after the abolition of the dictatorship, minorities there experienced a kind of decolonizing process more so than the population of the mother country, since they were engaged in reclaiming their right to use their mother-tongue and to call attention to their distinctive culture. Bertha herself helps this process by having translated, with Donald E. Morse, a number of Transylvanian-Hungarian plays into English.[2] The larger framework of Bertha's paper is the question of theatre adaptation with an eye to the fortunes of Friel's plays on the Hungarian stage. Friel performances in Hungary, Bertha claims, invite one to see them against present-day cultural-ideological divisions in Hungarian intellectual life, a kind of post-imperial situation after the collapse of communism. With examples, the paper then focuses on the problems of some of the Friel productions in Hungary since 1990, which, according to the author, largely derive from the inability to retain the quality and complexity of the original material in balance with the innovations of staging.

Zsuzsa Csikai's paper, where one of the Irish playwrights in analysis is also Brian Friel, while the other is Frank McGuinness, considers the reverse situation. Aware of theories of translation and cultural appropriation with the domesticating/foreignizing differentiation as a core issue, Csikai looks at the divergent linguistic strategies that the two Irish playwrights deploy in their respective renderings of Chekhov's *Uncle Vanya*. The two versions are also treated as largely part of (the Friel text) or in a way contestatory of (the McGuinness text) the practice that Nicholas Grene, referring to transpositions of Chekhov to the Irish stage, describes as follows: 'Turn-of-the-century Russia is matched by turn-of-the-century Ireland: the crumbling country houses, the frustrated artistic ambitions, the melancholy and ennui. We are on home ground in Russia'.[3]

The second section of the book contains articles which inquire into historical affinities and cultural dialogue as well as translation, this time of prose and poetry. Carla King, in her paper about Michael Davitt and Lajos Kossuth traces similarities between the ideas of the two politicians who were contemporaries and met each other during the years of Kossuth's exile from Hungary after the defeat of the Hungarian revolution and war of independence, 1848-1849. King points out that in both their thinking nationalism was combined with liberalism, yet their approaches to nationalism also diverged, in King's analysis, due to the different social and political *milieux* in which they worked. Kossuth organized the anti-Habsburg revolution in a country with many nationalities whose interests were not always recognized and integrated by the Hungarians, while in Davitt's Ireland the population was far more ethnically homogeneous, but the land question equally called for solution. In the reception of the two politicians, there is a parallel again. King concludes that the evaluation of Kossuth's work divides historians, whereas Davitt's radical thought, internationalism, and attention to class and gender were overlooked until a few recent studies – with King's book among them, let us add.[4]

The essay by Gabriella Vöő describes the Hungarian reception of Irish literature in the literary periodical *Nyugat* [West] (1908-1941), the lifespan of which indicates that history loomed large in the background. According to Vöő, there were two major ways in which *Nyugat* reflected on Irish literature and culture in interwar Hungary: it strove to generate a vivid interest in literary Modernism, while it also engaged in a kind of positive national stereotyping. On the one hand, as a promoter of high modernist principles, it familiarized readers with Irish writers like Wilde and Yeats alongside other European modernists through high quality translations and criticism. On the other hand, especially after the Trianon peace accord, as a result of which millions of Hungarians became an ethnic minority outside the borders of the dwarfed country, there was a tendency among Hungarian literati to interpret the divergence of Irish culture and literary discourse from the English using the terms 'national' or 'racial'. Vöő discusses this phenomenon citing from the reviews published by *Nyugat* of European writings about the issues of nation and race. From the early 1930s, witnessing the growth of fascist ideology and politics in Germany, Hungarian authors and critics abandoned the use of 'race' as a contaminated term. With this the perception of Irish culture as distinct from the English one suffered, and, the essay points out, made the reception of Irish literature, for example, of Joyce's *Ulysses*, rather one-sided and deprived of appropriate context for decades.

Reception as rewriting is the focus of Gabriella Hartvig's paper. The author of an essay about early-and mid-twentieth-century Swift imitations in Hungary,[5] Hartvig's contribution to the present book is a kind of sequel to that work since now she writes about a handful of contemporary Hungarian novels which are inspired by the apparently evergreen Gulliver theme and the form of the imaginary voyage. Diverse as their approaches are, the Gulliver character in them is usually led to a totalitarian or post-communist country, often recognizably Hungary or like Hungary, to be confronted with certain negative phenomena and processes in political and social life. Thus highly politicized, the new versions borrow elements of twentieth-century genres like science fiction and dystopia, which show parallels with the strategies of their usually apolitical predecessors. By way of formal novelty, a couple of the recent books display features that link them to the self-reflexive nature of postmodern fiction. Self-reflexivity, stylistic parody, and intertextuality are the sophisticated techniques that make the translation of a novel using them so difficult, as is demonstrated by Erika Mihálycsa's paper about the risks of rendering Flann O'Brien's *At Swim-Two-Birds* into Hungarian. The difficulty is confirmed by the fact that its translation has been just recently accomplished; other works by the writer are already available to the Hungarian-speaking public. As the paper elaborates, the genesis of this translation could hardly be more congenial to the spirit of the Irish author and his linguistic bravura. First of all, it is the result of the fusion of two people's efforts: one of them, Erika Mihálycsa, the author of the paper, is an ethnic Hungarian citizen of Romania, while the other, Gábor Csizmadia, lives in Hungary. Mihálycsa, who is responsible for the final shape of the translation, provides an account of how they selected idioms from the variants and registers of the Hungarian language as well as from the treasury of classical Hungarian literature, poetry especially, in their attempt to invent an eclectic, hybridized language as the best possible vehicle of Flann O'Brien's work. Besides translation theories, Mihálycsa consulted the existing Romanian and German translations of *At Swim-Two-Birds*, and also Joyce translations into Hungarian in tandem with recent critical material on the translatability of Joyce.

The two essays which close the volume address aspects of the reception of Seamus Heaney and Mahon, sharing the strategy that both write about poets and poetry in their homelands, Poland and Hungary. They show how the changing political situation in the second half of the twentieth century influenced literary production. 'The Polishing of Heaney: Seamus Heaney's Poetry in Poland: Translations, Reception, Impact' by Jerzy Jarniewicz looks at approaches to the translation of the Irish poet in Poland and introduces two directions as represented by two major poets. In the bulk of the paper Jarniewicz focuses on the differences between them with regard to selection, interpretation, technique, and the perception of Irish-Polish affinities. Jarniewicz also elaborates on Heaney's contribution to the internationalisation of Polish literature though his collaboration with Stanisław Barańczak in the translation of Jan Kochanowski's sixteenth-century sequence of elegiac poems under the title *Laments* (1995). István D. Rácz's paper about other international aspects of Heaney also under a punning title, 'Heaneys of the Mind',[6] this time addresses the journey of Irish poetry in Hungary in 'The Uses of a Disused Shed: Mahon's Poem in Hungarian'. In the comparative analysis and evaluation of the choices Derek Mahon's Hungarian translators make, Rácz works on the assumption that a translated poem reflects the cross-cultural 'liminality' of the text in the sense of bringing the process of translation into focus rather than allowing the reader to view the result as something finished and complete. Not unlike the discovery of two distinct directions in the Polish translation of Heaney by Jarniewicz, Rácz finds that András

Fodor's Mahon appears to be a traditional poet whose verse displays affinities with his own, whereas Eszter Tábor's translation of Mahon calls attention to the experimental features in 'A Disused Shed', which in turn seem to influence her own work. The introduction of Mahon to the Hungarian-speaking readers proves to be, thus, a many-sided journey.

As editor, I hope that readers will find a great many more links among the papers and their subjects, which implicitly argue for the validity of informed and enriched comparative approaches in literary and cultural studies and remind us of the artificiality of all kinds of divisions. In gratitude I warmly thank the twelve authors who have made the volume possible by writing their works in consideration of its main goal, to strengthen the growth of a relatively new but certainly rewarding line in Irish Studies.

---

1 Luke Gibbons, 'Prefiguring the Past: Re-imagining the Archive in Irish Studies' *The Future of Irish Studies: Report of the Irish Forum*, eds Christina Hunt Mahony, Laura Lizzara, Elizabeth Malcolm, John P. Harrington, Ondřej Pilný, and Catriona Crowe (Irish Forum, Centre for Irish Studies, Charles University, Prague, 2006): 77.

2 Csilla Bertha and Donald E. Morse, *Silenced Voices: Transylvanian-Hungarian Plays,* Selected and Translated by Csilla Bertha and Donald E. Morse (Dublin: Carysfort Press, 2008).

3 Nicholas Grene, 'Irish Drama and the Occlusion of Influence', *Princeton University Library Chronicle* 68. 1-2 (2006/07): 513.

4 Carla King, *Michael Davitt* (Dundalk: Dundalgan, 1999).

5 Gabriella Hartvig, 'Hungarian Gulliveriads: *Gulliver's Travels* in Faremido, Capillaria, and Kazohinia', *Reading Swift. Papers from the 5th Münster Symposium on Jonathan Swift*, ed. Hermann J. Real (Munich: Wilhelm Fink Verlag, 2008): 519-31.

6 István D. Rácz, 'Heaneys of the Mind', *Hungarian Journal of English and American Studies* 10. 1-2 (2004): 127-36.

1 | All We Say is 'Life is Crazy': Central and Eastern Europe and the Irish Stage

Patrick Lonergan

If you had visited the Abbey Theatre during 2007, you might have seen a card displayed prominently in its foyer. 'Join Us,' it says, its purpose being to convince visitors to become Members of the Abbey – to donate money to the theatre and, in return, to get free tickets for productions, to have their names listed in show programmes, and to gain access to special events. The choice of image to attract potential donors is easy to understand (Figure 1). The woman, we see, has reached into a chandelier to retrieve a letter, and we can tell from her expression that the discovery she's made has both surprised and delighted her. Why is she so happy? What does the letter say? And who is that strange man, barely visible, holding her up at such an unusual angle?

As well as being eye-catching, the image is also an interesting analogue for the experience of watching great drama. The woman's face is surrounded by darkness, as if she were an audience member in a darkened auditorium; the lights of the chandelier are like an illuminated stage at which she marvels. In other words, this image doesn't just aim to get people's attention: it is hinting to them the delights that they might experience as Members of the Abbey Theatre.

It might come as a surprise to learn that this image is not taken from an Abbey Theatre production. It isn't even taken from an

Irish play. The still comes from a production by the Polish Theatre company TR Warszawa, from their adaptation of the Danish film *Festen*.

ABBEYTHEATRE PROMOTIONAL CARD, 2007

The Abbey hosted a visit by this company in 2004, when, to celebrate Ireland's presidency of the European Union and its own centenary, the theatre welcomed visiting productions from Poland, Slovenia, and Hungary.[1] *Festen* seemed very popular while it played in Dublin, generating a lot of discussion, despite its short run.[2] The production was notable for its theatricality and its dramatic power – and, particularly, for its treatment of the theme of child abuse. Although there had been plays about sexual abuse in Ireland before, most of them had placed that issue at a distance from audiences: it was shown happening in rural Ireland in the plays of Marina Carr, such as *On Raftery's Hill* (2000), and it was suffered by a working class Dublin male in Mannix Flynn's *James X* (2003). But *Festen* confronted Irish audience with the reality that sexual abuse occurs in families that are middle class, urban, cosmopolitan, and professional – in families that are, in fact, just like those of the Abbey's audience. So although the production appeared for only four nights at the theatre, *Festen* offered Irish audiences a rare opportunity to face a difficult issue: this Polish presentation of a Danish story was allowing them to come to terms with an Irish problem.[3]

You won't uncover much of this history by glancing at the Abbey's brochure. And unless you had actually attended the production of *Festen* at the Abbey, it would be very difficult to find evidence of its significance: there were a few overnight reviews of it, and it featured prominently in reviews of the year in culture for 2004 – but no substantial treatment of its relevance to Irish life exists.[4]

The Abbey's use of this image from a Polish production thus tells us two important things about the presence of work from Central and Eastern Europe on the Irish stage. The first is that such work has actually appeared in Ireland: audiences throughout the country have been seeing productions like *Festen* not just for years, but actually for decades – often in the original language. As I discuss in more detail below, those productions have had an impact upon Irish audiences but, perhaps more importantly, they've also influenced the development of new Irish writing. And the second thing that we learn from the Abbey's use of that image is that there is a lack of documentation about many important productions. Because writing about Irish theatre continues to involve discussion of plays written by Irish authors, or plays performed by Irish companies, it is often very difficult to find accurate information about what is often the most interesting element of Irish theatrical culture – the plays that are seen by Irish audiences.

This essay aims to take a step towards resolving this problem. I want to discuss the presentation of characters from Eastern and Central Europe on the Irish stage, which tends to characterize them as abject figures who are deserving of sympathy from an audience presupposed to be Irish. This status contrasts strongly with the impact that people from that part of Europe have had on

Irish theatrical production. I conclude by broadening the discussion out to consider the status of international work within Ireland. In doing so, I aim to point out some of the gaps in our historical record of Irish theatre, while suggesting how those gaps were created – and continue to exist.

The arrival of ten new states to the European Union in 2004 has, of course, had an enormous impact upon Ireland, which has welcomed thousands of immigrants from Eastern Europe, particularly Poland, Lithuania, and Latvia. The arrival of so many people from such countries has changed the terms of debate in Ireland about immigration – and this has been reflected upon the stage to a certain extent. The change is a feature of Paul Mercier's *Homeland,* which was produced at the Abbey in 2006, and which concerns a man who returns to Ireland after being away for twenty years – as a result of which much of the play involves his being surprised at how much things have changed. His surprise is often provoked by the language that he hears spoken in contemporary Dublin. The play features Polish chambermaids and Russian shopkeepers, whose presence is used mainly for comedic purposes: we don't actually learn anything about any of these people, but simply observe the Irishman's surprise at their presence.

And if we aren't being asked to laugh at those characters, we will instead be encouraged to pity them. There is for example the young Ukrainian woman in Michael West's *Everyday,* performed in Commedia dell'arte style by Corn Exchange in 2006. Because she doesn't speak English, the only thing we learn about her is that she is mistreated by Irish people: a sleazy landlord, a neurotic mother for whom she works as an au pair, the clientele of a city centre pub where she works as a barmaid. The play offers closure for this character by having her fall in love with a failed Irish rock singer – who, conveniently enough, also happens to teach English as a foreign language.

These presentations could be seen as evidence of the development of a second phase in Irish theatre about multiculturalism. Emerging in the late 1980s and early 1990s, the genre's first phase considered that issue strictly in relation to racism and racial difference, with a strong emphasis on asylum-seeking and the status of refugees. Since patterns of migration to Ireland have changed so much since 2004, those considerations have broadened to consider language and religion as well. In both 'phases', Irish writers' attempts to address multiculturalism have often been aesthetically unsatisfying and politically unadventurous. Some are directly educational, designed for schools as theatre-in-education or, as in the case of Calypso's *Mixing it on the Mountain* (2002), devised with children from multiple racial and ethnic groups within Irish schools. Others are educational in that they set out to challenge audiences' attitudes to ethnic difference. Some do so by borrowing from the cinematic model of the (usually black) boyfriend who is brought home for dinner, to prove to a conservative father-figure (or the audience?) that he is really 'just like us'. One example of this is Ken Harmon's *Done Up Like A Kipper*, which appeared at the Peacock Theatre in 2002. Although the play principally concerns a Dublin taxi-driver's fear that he has contracted AIDS after being attacked with a blood-filled syringe, there is also a sub-plot involving the relationship of his daughter with a young black man from Coolock, a working class suburb on Dublin's north side. Kim tells her mother about this new boyfriend, Nathan. 'There's something else I haven't told you. About Nathan. Just so it doesn't come as a shock.... He's black.... Wait'll you see him. And. He's just so not an absolute wanker', she says.[5] Kim feels compelled to make the same announcement to her father: 'Just so as it doesn't come as any great surprise to you, Nathan is black'.

> **GINO.** What's that supposed to mean?
> **KIM**.He's black, Daddy, Nathan is black.
> **GINO**. He's black? Fair play to him... And what's your point? Ah, hold on. The hills are alive with the sound of music. This is what this is about. You think I'm a racist, don't you (61).

Part of the movement of the play involves Nathan's integration into this working class Dublin family, which is effected by his speaking in a working class Dublin accent (although in performance, his accent was instead from rural Cork – but the impact was intended to be the same), using standard Irish idioms such as 'Jaysus' (38), and singing Irish folk songs. In case the audience fail to comprehend the messages being conveyed by these strategies,

Nathan will conclude the play by declaring to Kim's father that 'you're the same as meself'. Not 'myself', note, but the more Irish 'meself' (85). It's interesting that whereas Nathan speaks in a Dublin accent, his girlfriend uses the syntax and intonation of American sitcom ('he's just so not an absolute wanker').

Other plays in this vein include Jim O'Hanlon's *The Buddhist of Castleknock* (Fishamble Theatre, 2002), and Roddy Doyle's *Guess Who's Coming For The Dinner* (Calypso, 2000), all stories about 'colourful' working class Dublin families, who use 'colourful' language throughout the action, which proceeds through a series of mishaps before we see the family welcoming the outsider into its arms. That such plays imitate a genre developed in Hollywood over forty years ago gives some indication of the quality of work on the subject.

Another common strategy in the first phase of Irish multicultural theatre is to present the outsider as a 'victim', often an asylum seeker whose deportation should make 'us' hang our heads in shame – a theme most successfully developed in Donal O'Kelly's 1994 *Asylum! Asylum!* Such approaches do not necessarily promote respect for difference, but may instead ask an audience presupposed to be white to sympathize with an abject other. Ethnicity is simplified as being about race, and an 'us and them' mentality is often strongly reinforced. Furthermore, it is worth asking whether an audience member who willingly chooses to attend a play billed as anti-racist, often produced by companies specifically devoted to social change, is expected to need persuasion that racism is a bad thing.

It is notable that so many of these plays share a conception of migrants into Ireland, whether they're male or female, Polish or Nigerian. The character of the immigrant on the Irish stage is typically represented as an abject figure who embodies the needs of all immigrants. The purpose of such characters is not to represent a person who happens to come from Poland, or Nigeria, or wherever it might be – but instead to act as an emblem that will remind audiences who (for the reasons I explain below) are presupposed to be white, wealthy and Irish-born of their responsibilities. Far from being an example of interculturalism or multiculturalism, such theatre instead tends to reinforce a particularly narrow conception of Irishness, allowing a culturally homogeneous group – the Irish theatregoer – to register their sense of distaste for such phenomena as racism, sex trafficking, or economic exploitation. As well as being problematic in its own right, this mode of presentation risks obscuring the contribution that people from such countries have made to our theatre, and to Irish society generally.

Probably the best example of this phenomenon is Charlie O'Neill's play *Hurl*, an exploration of how 'an Ireland of difference has made a different Ireland', according to the marketing.[6] Premiered by Barabbas Theatre Company in July 2003 at the Galway Arts Festival, where it played to mixed reviews, it was reworked for a Dublin Theatre Festival production in October of the same year. The central idea in the play is that a group of asylum seekers, refugees, immigrants, and Irish people of varying ethnicities come together in a small town in rural Ireland to form a hurling team. Hurling is of course a sport played almost exclusively in Ireland, where it is immensely popular, with competitions between local clubs, and teams from each of Ireland's thirty-two counties, attracting huge support. As such, it is an example of how local rivalry and identification with place may be used positively within Irish culture. The choice of this sport is interesting in other ways too. Hurling is a traditional Irish sport and, since the mid-1990s, it has successfully transformed itself from being a traditional, rural-based activity to becoming a highly professionalized and commodified element of postmodern Irish life. Many other aspects of Irish tradition made a similar transition from rural to postmodern during the same period: Irish dancing transformed into *Riverdance*, and traditional Irish music into popular 'Celtic' albums from Enya and The Corrs. Gaelic sport is exceptional however, in being the only aspect of Irish culture that has made this transition without any form of endorsement from abroad: it is an exclusively Irish success story that is an intrinsic part of Irish life, and it's more or less unknown outside of the country. Given that Irish culture generally is so globalized, the choice of hurling as the vehicle for a play about multiculturalism is therefore an imaginative gesture.

No attempt is made to pander to an Irish audience with this choice: in the play, the team states that they wish to play hurling *not* so that they can prove themselves worthy of inclusion in Irish society by their ability to use an emblem of Irishness (as with the 'meself'/'myself' symbol in *Done Up Like a Kipper*), but because it is a good game that will relieve boredom for those team-members who, as asylum seekers, are not permitted to work.

The narrative is not particularly original, presenting a conventional plot about a sports team winning against the odds (another example of an Irish play about multiculturalism taking inspiration from popular American film – in this case, the baseball movie). Yet its treatment of racism and prejudice will surprise many members of the audience. The play shows that the issue of multiculturalism cannot be treated simplistically, presenting characters notable for their variety rather than their deviation from Irish notions of 'normality'. Some members of the hurling team are asylum seekers, others are refugees, others are Irish-born children of immigrants, and the audience meets characters from Africa, Eastern Europe, Latin America – and Ireland too. *Hurl* thus makes clear that no single narrative can encompass the experiences of immigrants in Irish society.

Similarly, the mode of performance utilized by Barabbas emphasizes versatility.[7] The playing area is empty, with only a goalpost at the rear of the stage, so the actors use boxes to create sets, as required. The cast switch easily through characters and accents, men playing women, black and Asian actors playing white characters. This enacts the idea that identity does not have to be fixed. The style of narrative shifts from storytelling to the use of miniature sets, tableaux, puppetry, and dance, showing the audience that there are many ways of presenting the same story. This supports the play's theme very well.

Perhaps surprisingly, the problems with the play arise in its portrayal of Irish characters. This is illustrated by the following exchange between a Chinese man and another sports fan:

> **Chinese man.** Lovely day for the game.
> **Man 2**. Begod it is. The finesht.
> *Pause.*
> **Man 2**. Chinese?
> **Chinese man**. Well...yyyes. ...
> **Man 2**. D'you mind me ashkin...are you one of
> them...refugees?

Chinese man. No I am not. I'm a teacher.
Man 2. A teacher no less. What do you teach?
Chinese man. Irish (*Sequence 9*)

It is likely that the audience will, like 'Man 2', assume that the Chinese man is a refugee or recent immigrant to Ireland; that he is a teacher will disrupt their expectations, since they will realize that he therefore contributes economically to Irish society. That he teaches Irish will come as a further surprise. By having their own surprise made objective through the presentation of the exchange between (as the script tellingly puts it) the 'Man' and the 'Chinese Man', the audience's potential discomfort at its own assumptions may be displaced. This displacement will be facilitated by the fact that, unlike the Chinese Man, the Irish man is marked as different as a result of his speech patterns. 'Begod it is. The finesht' he says, marking the character as being from a poor, rural background, with the slang word 'begod', his ungrammatical syntax, and his pronunciation of the sibilant s as 'sh' all examples of a form of Hiberno-English that is becoming increasingly rare throughout Ireland.

This negative mode of presentation is used for numerous *Irish* characters. Sophisticated characterization is not needed for this kind of drama, so it is not necessarily a problem that the play includes a melodramatic villain, and a team-coach whose gruff exterior belies a heart of gold. There is however apparent authorial confusion between narrative type – which is acceptable – and social stereotype, which is not. Sylvie, a character from Fatima Mansions, an area of inner city Dublin then infamous for gangsterism and drug abuse, is presented as inarticulate and prone to violence, in keeping with stereotypical representations of Irish working class males. The play includes unoriginal jokes about the Christian Brothers' 'skill' with sticks, a joke designed to appeal to the urbanized, and recently secularized, middle class audiences' outrage at clerical child abuse (creating an interesting contrast with the Abbey's visiting production of *Festen* a few months later). In the Galway production, the audience is asked to laugh at the pretentiousness of Dublin TV presenters; but in the Dublin production, those TV presenters are from rural Ireland, and are characterized as inept and inarticulate.

The representation of the rural in this play is often very negative. Many rural characters are described as 'ignorant' and 'muck savage', and all use a version of stage Irish speech straight out of Boucicault, but unlikely to be heard in any modern Irish town or village. The worst example of this is the characterization of the play's villain, Rusty Cox, whose speech patterns and physical appearance are firmly in the tradition of the caricatured Irishman identified by critics like Curtis and Foster.[8] Barely articulate, self-serving, and presented as simian, Rusty is the cause of the deportation of the play's hero to Sierra Leone, which concludes the piece. The effect of this characterization is to displace racism onto the so-called 'arsehole of rural Ireland', which is also called the 'third world but with more clothes on' (Sequence 1). At no stage is the audience asked to consider the racism of Ireland's businesses, government and media, or, for that matter, themselves.

There is a further problem: all of the immigrants in the play are characterized as victims of one kind or another. The Chinese schoolteacher is a victim of 'Man's' ignorance. And we also see this in the presentation of a scene in which two Bosnian schoolfriends meet by chance after a ten-year gap in a Dublin lapdancing club, as narrated by Miroslav, the male:

> I am Bosnian, come to this country. In 1994 I live in west. I work – for cash – very dangerous – on building sites. Two boys I work with, they bring me to see All-Ireland final in Croke Park when county wins...Team win first time in many, many years. My friends go crazy. I go crazy too. I drink 20 pints. Peuhh! I have never go to a lap dancing club. But we go. Mad, you know. I couldn't believe. There I see Katerina, dancing. She is from my school in Kumanovo in Bosnia. Peuhh! Crazy. I not see her in 10 years. We talk for few minutes. But Katerina and me – is embarrassed you know. Very soon nothing to say. All we say is life is crazy. Us in Dublin. Me in furry hurling hat. Her in furry g-string. She doesn't offer number – and I don't give mine – to meet again. Difficult. The lads are pissed off – they want her number of course. (*Sequence 3*)

Presumably, the audience is supposed to believe that Miroslav arrived in Ireland as a refugee from the Yugoslav civil wars of the early 1990s; Katerina may also have done so, but she is typical of the large number of young women who migrate from Eastern and

Central Europe to Western Europe to work in the sex trade. The awkwardness of their exchange exposes one of the fundamental truths about Irish immigration. Ireland is for many a refuge from war and poverty, but it has also disgracefully exploited many immigrants.

It is likely that the characterization of the rural Irish other in *Hurl* will mean that the audience relates most to the play's non-Irish characters, whose speech generally is represented in standard form, and whose concerns and attitudes will generally be easier for the audience to relate to (with some exceptions, such as the presentation of Miroslav, above). This kind of intersubjectivity powerfully undermines Irish attitudes to race. Regrettably, the play continues to promote an 'us against them' dynamic in its representation of *Irishness* as other.

A further problem with *Hurl* is that it was produced as part of two arts festivals, in Galway and Dublin. The composition of *Hurl's* audience was therefore strongly predetermined by its appearance within a festivalized framework. Ireland's theatre festivals exist to combine theatre with corporate sponsorship and tourism; the price of tickets to shows in Festivals generally are among the most expensive in Ireland (and they certainly exceed the weekly allowance of an asylum seeker living in Ireland, which, in 2003, was 19 euro). The inclusion of a play that presents positive messages about multiculturalism within such a framework will inevitably predispose the audience to respond in particular ways. It is worth considering who is being addressed in such a situation, and on whose behalf the message is being presented. It could be argued that the existence of such plays as *Hurl* arises not from an attempt to reflect life in Ireland accurately, but rather to use the positive messages conveyed by the play to service the needs of corporate sponsorship and tourism: the message conveyed by *Hurl* is that racism is a bad thing, that immigrants should be accepted if they adopt Irish practices, and that the only people in Ireland who are racist are ignorant farmers from rural areas. The fact that the play aims to challenge certain stereotypes is problematic: in putting characters from central and Eastern Europe, and from other countries, onstage, writers like Charlie O'Neill appear to have assumed that people from those countries will not actually be present in the audience.

This is by no means a new problem. The apparent insularity of Irish theatre has been shown in attitudes towards plays that are translated for Irish audiences – when greater emphasis will be always placed upon the identity of the Irish translator than the original author, as shown below. Brian Friel's name is given greater prominence in the marketing for the 1998 Gate Theatre production of *Uncle Vanya* and Tom Murphy is given exclusive credit for the 2004 *Cherry Orchard* by his publisher (Figure 2). Many such adaptations also Hibernicize the plays – not only putting them into an Irish idiom, but occasionally relocating them entirely to the country itself. There have been some attempts to preserve the foreignness of such works, but producers appear nervous about audiences' reactions to such an approach, and there is a tendency to highlight the familiar at the expense of the new.

Programme and Poster for Brian Friel's *Uncle Vanya*, Gate Theatre, October 1998

Tom Murphy's *The Cherry Orchard*, published in the Abbey Playscripts series, 2004

Histories of the modern Irish stage are dominated by considerations of Irish playwriting, which is frequently represented as a linear narrative that stretches from Synge to Friel, and on to Marina Carr and others. The emphasis on dramatic writing overshadows the importance of many other aspects of Irish theatre.[9] One important issue that has received insufficient consideration is that many Irish theatre companies were established *not* to produce new Irish work, but to challenge a perceived Irish insularity by producing work from abroad, or by importing other cultures' ideas about theatre to Irish settings. For example, the defining moment of the early Irish dramatic movement – *The Playboy* controversy of 1907 – occurred at much the same time as productions on the Abbey stage of Molière's *The Doctor in Spite of Himself* (1906), Maeterlinck's *Interior* (1907), Suderman's *Teja* and Molière's *The Miser* (1908). Goldoni's *Mirandolina* (1910), Hauptmann's *Hannele* and Strindberg's *There are Crimes and Crimes* and *The Stronger* (1913).[10] From 1918 to 1928, the Abbey stage and resources were frequently given over to the Dublin Drama League, which produced plays that, with only two exceptions, were written by contemporary authors from abroad, such as Eugene O'Neill, Jean Cocteau, Pirandello, and d'Annuzio.[11] As Christopher Fitz-Simon points out, 'the fact that these authors attracted good attendances proves that there was a desire in Dublin – if not any other part of the country – to experience the breeze blowing across the seas from America and from the European mainland'.[12] A desire to experience the 'breeze blowing' from America and Europe motivated the Dublin Drama League, and led ultimately to the foundation in 1928 of the Gate Theatre, which was to provide Ireland with 'a kaleidoscopic cross-section of modern European and American drama, at a time when Ireland floated in cultural isolation in mid-Atlantic'.[13] A similar impetus was evident in the 1950s, not only with the establishment of the Dublin Theatre Festival, which has always included Irish and international work in its programme, but also with the opening of the Pike Theatre, the small company that premiered work by Brendan Behan and Samuel Beckett. Alan Simpson describes the establishment of the Pike in 1953 as an attempt to provide an alternative to the work that was then dominating the Irish stage. 'We wanted our theatre to be a revolutionary force of small means which, by its ingenuity, would stir up the theatrical lethargy of post-war Ireland', he writes, explaining that the purpose of the Pike was to present plays that 'for one reason or another, would not otherwise be seen in Dublin'.[14]

Contemporary Irish interest in work from abroad follows the tradition established by the Gate and Pike. Its roots are in the late 1960s and early 1970s, with the foundation of the Focus Theatre and its adjoining Stanislavsky Studio in Dublin, and the establishment of Druid Theatre in Galway. The Focus was one of the first theatres in Ireland to introduce ideas about performance from abroad, while also being at the vanguard of the movement to professionalize the Irish theatre by emphasizing the importance of training. The work of Focus came to fruition in the collaborations between Patrick Mason, Tom Mac Intyre, and the Stanislavsky-trained Tom Hickey at the Abbey in the 1980s. Druid, founded in 1975, is now known principally for its commitment to the development of new work by such writers as Martin McDonagh, Tom Murphy, and others. But its history shows how Irish theatre companies benefit from producing work from abroad, particularly in their early years. The majority of Druid's earliest productions were by writers who were not Irish. During its first year in existence, it presented Fernando Arrabal's *Orison* and Williams's *The Glass Menagerie*; subsequent years saw productions of Edward Albee, Alan Ayckbourn, Tom Stoppard, and many other international playwrights. Almost half of Druid's earliest productions were of work from abroad; this figure fell during the 1980s as the company's interest in new writing grew, until in the 1990s it ceased altogether, the 1992 production of Polish dramatist Teresa Lubkiewicz's *Werewolves* being its last production of an international play. The company's evolution into a producer of new Irish writing seems therefore to be based in its work on foreign writers during its early years. This establishes a model of a company spending its formative years producing work from different cultures before turning to new writing. Druid's Artistic Director Garry Hynes suggests as much, telling Eileen Battersby that the company's commitment to new Irish drama wasn't always the most important part of its activities. 'We did Ionesco and Edward Albee,' she states, adding that it took a while for Druid to 'grow up and look at Irish writing'.[15]

Such a model of 'growing up' to look at Irish work is evident in the development of many other Irish companies. The most prominent of these is Rough Magic, founded in 1984 with a remit of producing new work from abroad. During the first five years of the company's life, it produced fourteen international plays, eleven of which were Irish premieres. Rough Magic's Artistic Director Lynne Parker outlines the importance of international work to the company's development. 'Irish theatre, when we started off, was quite inward looking', she says. 'There was the posh stuff being done at the Gate, and there were the Irish classics being done at the Abbey ... We felt very strongly that we were of a generation whose main influences were British and American television and American film as well, and that we were definitely being influenced by other cultures'.[16] Rough Magic can thus be seen as another company established as a result of its founders' perception that Irish theatre needed to connect with the global influences on Irish life. Like Druid, Rough Magic moved quickly from producing foreign plays to commissioning new Irish writing, so that after their Irish premiere of Timberlake Wertenbaker's *Our Country's Good* in 1989, it produced no further international work until 2000, when it brought Richard Greenberg's *Three Days of Rain* to the Project Arts Centre. In the intervening eleven years, the company had nurtured several young Irish writers, including Gina Moxley, Pom Boyd, Arthur Riordan, Declan Hughes, and Morna Regan.[17] There is again a link between Rough Magic's production of international work in its early years, and its later development as a producer of new Irish writing.

Indeed, throughout the Irish theatre sector, both at present and in the past, the evidence suggests that the production of international work acts as a stimulus for the development of Irish writing and practice. The importance of an international perspective both to young and more established Irish writers may be illustrated by contrasting two essays published in *Theatre Stuff*. The first is by Thomas Kilroy (born in 1934) and the second by Declan Hughes (born in 1963). Kilroy, whose first play premiered in 1969, describes himself as of the earlier generation of writers, whose work he defines as 'a mixture of traditional material and formal inventiveness'.[18] The emergence of a younger generation of writers has caused Kilroy to feel an 'eerie sensation of watching some of the work of one's contemporaries and, worse still, of one's own, becoming historical while one is still alive' (2). As a writer and a founder member of Rough Magic, Declan Hughes has been one of the dominant voices of that younger generation. Asking why contemporary Irish literature continues to ignore contemporary Ireland, Hughes complains that Irish writers 'persist in defining ourselves by the ethnic, the pastoral (and that qualified form, the tragic pastoral). Even if we do it in an iconoclastic way, the iconography remains powerfully the same: half door, pint bottle, sacred heart'.[19] Kilroy's interest in tradition is sincere, but makes him feel 'historical' while he is still alive, yet Hughes considers tradition to be 'habit in fancy dress' (11) and is impatient with it. There is however a great deal in common between the two writers. Kilroy notes with approval that, when Tom Murphy decided in 1959 to write his first play, he declared that 'one thing is fucking sure, it's not going to be set in a kitchen' (5). Forty years later, Hughes, in similarly iconoclastic mood, also writes with distaste for 'the country kitchen' (11), and in doing so carries on a tradition of Irish dramatists being motivated by the desire to undermine received notions of Irish identity and culture.

The most evident shared feature of both articles is a frustration with received forms of Irishness. Irish dramatists are motivated by the desire to undermine received notions of Irish identity and culture, frequently by looking abroad. The role of foreign work in facilitating such iconoclasm is very important, as is the persistence of the iconography against which these writers rebel. The assertion that Irish theatre is insular appears actually to have *driven* the development of theatre companies and writers in Ireland for much of the last century. This demonstrates that insularity is a feature of Irish culture, yet it also reveals a history of writers and theatrical practitioners engaging with international work throughout the twentieth century, often in very positive ways. The production of foreign work in the twentieth century in Ireland has happened in a haphazard way, driven by individuals and groups on an *ad hoc* basis. This shows that there has been a high level of production of foreign work in Ireland, but the uncoordinated – and generally unrecorded – nature of these developments has led to their disappearance from Ireland's cultural memory. Perhaps this is because so much international work in Ireland has been positioned as coming from the periphery of Irish society and theatre, presented as a means of challenging a dominant ideology or practice. Although they were not necessarily perceived as 'marginal' by their audiences, many of the most important producers of international work began their careers on the fringes of Irish society: Edwards and MacLíammóir as gay men in Catholic Ireland, Druid as a regional company headed by a woman, Rough Magic as an urbanized, cosmopolitan company headed by a woman from Northern Ireland. Another problem is the apparent perception that international work is something a company explores in its infancy: Garry Hynes's suggestion that one must eventually 'grow up' and look at Irish work is telling in this regard. Nevertheless, these cases reveal the importance within Ireland of international work: it has motivated and inspired the development of a great deal of Irish drama. The peripheral and iconoclastic status of that work is also important, but it is also clear that Irish theatre has not ignored international work. When writers or theatre companies have turned to writing from abroad, they have done so as a means of challenging mainstream Irish culture, which is perceived to be moribund, conservative. Yet the individuals who use foreign work in this way almost always end up returning to the mainstream. Tom Murphy used Lorca as a route to Synge. Druid Theatre arrived at the country kitchens of Martin McDonagh's Leenane via the plays of Edward Albee and Fernando Arrabel. And many other examples may be cited.

Theatre from Eastern and Central Europe has certainly influenced Irish theatre. The visits to Dublin of the Moscow Art Theatre in 1968 and 1975 had a huge impact on Irish performance and writing; it seems no coincidence that the visits of that company with *Three Sisters* and *Uncle Vanya* were followed within four years by the production of Chekhovian plays like Friel's *Aristocrats*. In 1980 and 1981, the Wrocław Contemporary Theatre visited Dublin and, again, had a huge impact, their approach to movement directly influencing works such as Tom Mac Intyre's *The Great Hunger*, and the original production of Frank McGuinness's *Observe the Sons of Ulster Marching Towards the Somme*.

Yet we must move beyond this model of influence – with international work the cause and new directions in Irish writing an effect – to view the international as a fully integrated part of Irish theatre. There is evidence of the development of such an attitude. Fabulous Beast's *Giselle* appeared in 2003 and is, arguably, one of the most significant new Irish productions of the decade thus far. A relocation of the Giselle myth to the Irish midlands, the play reveals the consequences of the arrival to a small Irish town of a Slovakian dance instructor, who teaches the locals how to blend traditional Irish dancing with Slovakian line-dancing. The Hungarian director László Marton has also had a strong influence on Irish theatre in recent years, notably in his 2003 production of *The Wild Duck*, which was adapted by Frank McGuinness. Finally, we see that performers from Europe are taking their place on the Irish stage in greater numbers. A particularly striking example of this is the appearance of the Slovakian dancer Vladislav Benito in Fabulous Beast's *The Bull*, a 2005 adaptation of *The Tain*, in which he played Cuchulain.

There is also a fascinating history of theatre travelling to Ireland from Russia and Poland and Slovenia, and countless other countries from that part of Europe – and those shows have had a lasting and important influence on the development of Irish theatre – and Irish society too. Also of importance is that people from Europe are taking the stage in Ireland. Impact Theatre Company in Limerick has begun to stage plays in Polish, and the 2007 Dublin Fringe Festival also features productions by Polish people living in Ireland. Perhaps most significantly, people from that part of Europe have begun to write plays about Ireland – and those plays are themselves being produced in the country. In 2007, the Dublin Theatre Festival hosted the première of a new play called *Kebab*, written by the Romanian playwright Gianina Cărbunariu. It's about a trio of young Romanians who move to Dublin in search of a better life. 'If you work hard and stuff, they really appreciate you over there,' says the play's heroine. '*It's different* over there'.[20] Unfortunately, this young woman is exploited by her boyfriend and another Romanian man, and becomes involved in a murky world of prostitution and pornography. *Kebab* can be compared to plays like *Philadelphia, Here I Come!* or *A Whistle in the Dark* in its treatment of how the emigrant must face a clash between the destination they imagine, and the real place to which they arrive. Interestingly, however, it is not Philadelphia or Coventry that's being considered here, but Dublin. In production at Dublin's Project Arts Centre, *Kebab* took on a further layer of meaning, with the lines being delivered in contemporary English accents. This meant that the audience watched Romanian characters speaking about their life in contemporary Dublin – in strong south London accents. This calls to mind the strategies used by Friel in *Translations*, but it also draws interesting contrasts between Ireland's colonial past and its globalized present, the shifting dynamics of Ireland's status in the world dramatized by the delivery of lines in this production.

As productions like *Kebab* appear with greater frequency, we will indisputably require revised ways of thinking about Irish theatre – and those strategies will also allow us to think about old Irish plays in interesting new ways. Yet it would be a mistake to see those changes as introducing something new: Irish drama has always been international, although this fact has been for too long unacknowledged. It is important that as the demography of Ireland changes, its theatre provides space for the articulation of new voices – and perhaps a first step towards doing so is for scholars to reveal a history that up to now has been unfairly ignored, neglected, and forgotten.

---

[1] The other productions were *Dance in Time* [Össztánc] from Vígszinház, Budapest (17-20 March) and a Slovenian adaptation of *A Midsummer Night's Dream* by Mladinsko Theatre Ljubljana (12-15 May).

[2] *Festen* ran from 28-31 January. My comments are based on attendance of the production on 29 and 31 January. The production was also discussed at length during a debate on 'National Theatre and the Nation', which took place at the theatre on 31 January 2004.

[3] It should be noted that the Gate Theatre produced David Eldridge's translation of *Festen* for the 2006 Dublin Theatre Festival. While that translation was written for a London audience, the cast as directed by Selina Cartmell tended to deliver lines in their own Irish accents.

[4] See for example Helen Meany's review on 30 January 2004 in *The Irish Times*: 12. Writing in *The Sunday Tribune* on 26 December 2004, Rachel Andrews described *Festen* as the 'only sublime experience of the Abbey year' (33).

[5] Ken Harmon, *Done Up Like A Kipper* (London: Nick Hern Books, 2002): 26. Subsequent references are cited in the text.
[6] Dublin Theatre Festival, 'Festival Programme 2003' (Dublin: Dublin Theatre Festival, 2003): 11.
[7] I attended *Hurl* on 14 July 2003 at the Black Box Theatre in Galway, and was permitted to watch a videotaped performance of its Dublin run by Barabbas. Unless otherwise specified, my comments about the play relate to both productions. Quotations are taken from an unpublished version of the script, which is presented in numbered 'sequences' (rather than acts or scenes). References appear parenthetically in the text, followed by the sequence number.
[8] Cf. L.P. Curtis, *Apes and Angels*, Rev. ed. (Washington, D.C.: Smithsonian Institute, 1996) and R.F. Foster, *Paddy and Mr Punch* (Harmondsworth: Penguin, 1993).
[9] The discussion of the international dimensions of Irish drama is developed further in Patrick Lonergan, *Theatre and Globalization* (Palgrave, 2009).
[10] Information adapted from the appendix to Lady Gregory, *Our Irish Theatre* (New York: Capricorn, 1965): 265-66.
[11] Cf. Brenna Katz Clarke and Harold Ferrar, *The Dublin Drama League* (Gerrards Cross: Colin Smythe, 1979).
[12] Christopher Fitz-Simon, *The Irish Theatre* (London: Thames and Hudson, 1983): 184.
[13] ---, *The Boys: A Biography of Micheál MacLíammóir and Hilton Edwards* (London: Nick Hern Books, 1994): 13.
[14] Alan Simpson, *Beckett and Behan and a Theatre in Dublin* (London: Routledge & Keegan Paul, 1962): 1-2.
[15] Eileen Battersby, 'The Image Maker', *The Irish Times* 12 June 1997: 13.
[16] Lilian Chambers, Ger FitzGibbon, and Eamonn Jordan, eds, *Theatre Talk: Voices of Irish Theatre Practitioners* (Dublin: Carysfort Press, 2000): 394
[17] It should be noted that many of the writers developed by Rough Magic had originally been actors. Liz Kuti, Arthur Riordan, Gina Moxley, and Morna Regan are prominent examples of this phenomenon.
[18] Thomas Kilroy, 'A Generation of Playwrights', *Theatre Stuff*, ed. Eamonn Jordan (Dublin: Carsyfort Press, 1999): 3. Subsequent references are cited in the text.
[19] Declan Hughes, 'Who the Hell Do We Still Think We Are? Reflections on Irish Theatre and Irish Identity', *Theatre Stuff*, 12. Subsequent references are cited in the text.

[20] Gianina Cărbunariu, *Kebab*. The quotation is from an unpublished translation which I consulted as editor of the programme notes for the 2007 Dublin Theatre Festival. The emphasis is added. A version by Philip Osment was published by Oberon Books in 2007.

2 | Samuel Beckett Comes to Transylvania: the 'Absurdoid' Plays of Géza Páskándi

Donald E. Morse

> **Estragon**. The absurd is dead. It's not even fashionable any more.[1]

The plays of the Transylvanian-Hungarian playwright, philosopher, and writer Géza Páskándi (1933-1995) have proven typical of Central European Absurd Theatre. Thanks to the exiled Romanian playwright, Eugene Ionesco's popular plays beginning with *La cantatrice chauve* (1949),[2] the western Theatre of the Absurd came quickly to post-war Romania where it was radically modified to fit the existing conditions of a harsh police state. Rather than finding subject matter for plays, as Ionesco living in Paris once said he found his 'in my dreams, in my anxieties, in my obscure desires, in my internal contradictions'.[3] Páskándi found his in the external world of the police state that itself determined dreams, created anxieties, limited desires, and projected contradictions. In his plays, language functions as a distorted mirror of contemporary reality; that is, language becomes 'a weapon to disintegrate personality and to eliminate the individual', exactly as language within the communist police state functioned publicly as 'a means of control and manipulation'.[4] That language, together with brilliant visual images, projects a world absurd in its make-up, absurd in its power over the individual, and above all absurd in the dog-eat-dog nature of human relations that, in turn, raises crucial questions of morality and individual responsibility.

If Ionesco paved a way, far more influential on Páskándi's thinking and writing were the translations and local productions of Samuel Beckett's plays that immediately followed Ionesco's. In his introduction to *Todogar jaur Kvárna* (1991-1993) Páskándi stresses repeatedly the importance of Beckett for his work and time. He parses Beckett's name: *Beck* has several meanings including a rocky stream or brook but it also means 'to give a sign, to beckon, to nod.' The ending of his name, *et* in Latin is a connecting word, 'and'. Also, in some contexts 'beck' may mean 'of or being at someone's disposal'. In other words, waiting for a sign or a nod, a beckoning. Samuel in Hebrew means 'god has listened to' or 'being heard by god' (the Hebrew letter, *el* stands for god). 'Even without consulting a biography, Beckett's name itself becomes a treasure-trove,' he concludes. Similarly, he cites Beckett in one of the play's many sub-titles as 'Beckett is seeking on the road while Gaudi finds his way in the church'.[5]

The long three-act play itself makes Páskándi's debt to Beckett obvious beginning with its title, *They Are Waiting for Godot to Come Again*, which was replaced in the English translation by the odd title, *World's Fair*.[6] The play is dedicated to 'The Memory of Samuel Beckett – on the Infinite Roads and in Memory of Antonio Gaudi – in a Church in the Heart of Barcelona.' The main characters, Estragon and Vladimir continue where they left off in *Waiting for Godot*. This time, however, they must wait on a road between limbo and eternity for those documents necessary to certify them as faithful road citizens.

> **Estragon.** ... a document would serve well ... So we can show them proof of our identity. So they'll know we're identified as comers and goers, loiterers and dawdlers; so they'll know we're unwavering movers ... (*Brief pause.*) And we have no territorial demands! In other words, we need that piece of paper...
> **Vladimir.** ... the document ... the certificate of citizenship ...
> **Estragon.** ... identifying us as natives of the roads.[7]

'Into this abstracted world created by language the tragi-comic motifs of the reality of life in the Carpathian Basin oozes through,' rightly claims Zoltán Bertha.[8] For instance, the territory in question ('we have no territorial demands!') was that seized from Hungary after World War I amounting to two-thirds of historic Hungary and then distributed among the neighbouring countries in accordance with the Trianon Peace Treaty. The sentence itself, 'we have no territorial demands!' would be, if anything, overly familiar to Páskándi's immediate Carpathian Basin audience since it was often repeated in public addresses and speeches as well as in numerous documents by the Russian-installed Prime Minister of Hungary, János Kádár. Under dictatorial communism it was dangerous to be found without one's papers, to be undocumented was to be without an official identity.

Much of Valdimir and Estragon's conversation refers directly and frequently to the plight of the Hungarian ethnic minority in Transylvania that resisted assimilation while attempting to preserve customs, traditions, education, and public discussion in the Hungarian language – the use of which became under almost constant attack. Rather than Estragon's plaintive metaphysical rhetorical question, 'We always find something, eh Didi, to give us the impression we exist?',[9] Páskándi's tramps, discussing the philosophical concepts of the abstract moment as opposed to the still point, focus almost immediately on the threatened disappearance of that which constitutes their existence – their language and nation:

> **Estragon.** We'll be run over by the steamroller that will crush us under the surface of the earth ... or we'll marry into them [those in the World's Fair] and disappear. Don't you understand? We'll dissolve among them through our grandchildren ... We'll forget the language ... We'll talk in a mixed language and then in another language ... for a while there, in a foreign language, will be a few pale traces of the old one but after a while only scattered and less and less frequent goat-droppings will indicate where the herd had passed. But even that only until the rain comes ... the droppings will get soft and dissolve in the earth. There you are. The final still point.[10]

In one of the wittiest exchanges in *Todogar jaur Kvárna* [*They Are Waiting for Godot to Come Again*] Vladimir and Estragon discuss the distinction between the official, state language (Állám) and the dream language (Álom) – a passage omitted in the available English translation.

> **Estragon.** Are you talking in your dream ... Are you shouting?
> **Vladimir.** In my mother tongue ... Yes, that's already a dream language ...
> **Estragon.** What sort of state language, Didi?
> **Vladimir.** The state language is not a dream language. The two are not always the same.[11]

The necessity for preserving the Hungarian language in the face of attempted forced assimilation provides a constant theme for Hungarian-Transylvanian drama, in particular, and Hungarian-Transylvanian literature in general. (See, for example, András Sütő, *The Wedding Feast at Suza.*)

In the original Hungarian, *Todogar jaur Kvárna* [*They Are Waiting for Godot to Come Again*] consists in a huge out-pouring of language reflecting this distorted mirror of contemporary reality in the Carpathian Basin. One of the play's distinguishing features is the way in which 'the abundance of intellectual and linguistic fantasy (which includes multiplication and dissemination of meaning) and the emotional and moral bearing structure are built together'.[12] This combination of the fantastic with linguistic invention, emotional appeal, and clear moral standards holds true also for each Páskándi play under discussion.

Beckett, Ionesco, Heidegger, and Páskándi

'The Man' in Beckett's *Act Without Words I* (1956) who 'is flung backwards on stage from right wing'[13] presents a powerful visual image that resonates as a physical representation of Martin Heidegger's notion of human beings flung onto the stage of life or thrown into the 'facticity' of life.[14] Immediately, the man attempts to exit right only to be flung back and when he then tries to exit left, the same thing happens as he is flung back on stage once again. A mysterious whistle sounds first from offstage right, then offstage left, and finally from above calling the mime's attention to various objects that invite inspection and use. Each appears, however, designed to frustrate any action on his part. At the heart of *Act without Words I* is an old vaudeville and silent films routine, but with Beckett, as John Killinger cogently argues 'it has a poignant significance. It is the symbol of man's failure in the physical universe, of his inability to reach what he sees, of the utterly alien domination of things outside his control'.[15] Faced with the utter futility of his situation, Beckett's mime attempts to use the various sized blocks, the piece of rope, and the dangling tree to sustain life by seizing the carafe of water. Unfortunately, the carafe always dances just out of reach. When that effort fails, he tries to commit suicide, but before he can take any meaningful action, whatever object he needs simply disappears. In his Pavlovian world of stimulus, response, action frustrated, the best he might achieve becomes resignation signified by his final act of curling up in a foetal position facing the audience, while ignoring whistles and objects.[16] In *Act Without Words I* life appears to be 'a battle with objects'.[17] As John Peter argues, 'they are not so much real objects fulfilling their normal functions, as things representing the hostility of the universe'.[18] Beckett's use of such objects differs significantly, however, from Ionesco's in, for example, *The Chairs*, *The Lesson*, *Amedée*, and *The New Tenant* where '[t]he unquestion-able[sic] other-ness of ... objects is what matters, not their function; how man feels among them is the play's concern, not what he does with them'.[19] Objects in Páskándi's plays have yet a third function as in *No Conductor* (1967) where the boots become the agent of domination in addition to representing both the 'hostility of the universe' and an 'unquestionable otherness'.[20]

To Beckett's absurd, hostile world where a character experiences an 'alien domination of things outside his control',[21] Páskándi adds an entrenched bureaucracy actively conspiring with the Secret Police. The result in *No Conductor* is that nothing remains stable because everything is arbitrary; in *The Line* (1968)[22] that nothing is as it is proclaimed to be because simply accepting an invitation to make a complaint may lead to death; and in *The Avenger, the Gatekeeper, or: It is Requested that You Wipe Your Feet* (1971) that everyone preys on everyone else. At the beginning of Act II of *Waiting for Godot*, Vladimir and Estragon argue at length and to little effect about whose boots are on the stage, while Mr and Mrs Smith in *The Bald Soprano* engage in a lengthy comical discussion of the various Bobby Watsons, including both the late Mr Bobby Watson and the alive Mrs Bobby Watson who were married to each other. In contrast, there is nothing absurd in *No Conductor* about the situation of a powerful person forcing other people to testify to what they know to be untrue and ridiculous. The four occupants taken together become a variation on Páskándi's typical protagonist who, according to Eugene Brogyányi, is 'an individual who, rightly or wrongly, believes himself threatened by a powerful entity. Rather than confronting power head on, he attempts to insulate himself from it and, in the process, creates a situation in which he becomes his own prisoner'.[23]

In distinguishing the Western absurd from its Central European cousin, Péter P. Müller argues that the Western absurd focuses on what is 'universal, ontological, and intellectual [whereas] the Central European kind ... is primarily national, historical, and emotional'. P. Müller further contends that

> [w]ithin ... post-Stalinist plays, in place of a constant condition there is ... a decisive turning-point. The structure of the Western absurd is mostly either circular ... or post-climatic ... the latter term means that the play takes place after human life and after the history of mankind. The structure of the Central European absurd is often climatic, and the plot is determined by a crucial change ... [24]

such as the killing of the Director in *The Avenger, the Gatekeeper, or: It is Requested that You Wipe Your Feet*, the seizing of a scapegoat in *The Line*, and the betrayal involved in the second appearance of The Booted Man in *No Conductor*.

In *The Avenger, the Gatekeeper, or: It is Requested that You Wipe Your Feet*, the Director of the comically-named first Feet-Wiping Bureau dominates his environment and subordinates through his use of intimidating language: 'Not a step further! Have you wiped your feet?' he shouts, leaping to his feet, whereupon the offending clerk retreats to perform the necessary feet-wiping rite.[25] Such blatant use of language as a 'means of control and manipulation'[26] as exercised by the pompous Director lends sympathy to the man in a wheelchair who, in his turn, exercises power over the Director also through his use of intimidating language but language reinforced by brandishing a gun. In the play's opening scene, the man confined to a wheelchair, Dani Szakáll, a veteran of

World War I confronts and kills this powerful Director of the first Feet-Wiping Bureau in retribution for the time during the war when the Director as a Lieutenant in the Hungarian army ordered him to stand guard in the depths of winter.[27] When the order to retreat arrived, the Lieutenant neglected to relieve Szakáll from guard duty thus leaving him behind, wounded, lying frozen in the midst of a huge snowstorm. As a result of the Lieutenant's neglect, Szakáll's legs had to be amputated at the thigh. Thus, although he would now very much like to obey the Director, his former Lieutenant's peremptory order: 'Go wipe your feet immediately,' he cannot, simply because he has no feet.[28]

The visual image of a man in a wheelchair comes to dominate *The Avenger, the Gatekeeper, or: It is Requested that You Wipe Your Feet* from curtain-to-curtain and may have been suggested to Páskándi by Samuel Beckett's Hamm who appears in *Endgame* (1957) in 'an armchair on castors'.[29] An even clearer parallel, however, to *The Avenger* in Beckett's *oeuvre* occurs in *Rough for Theatre I* (1979), which Beckett sketched out in French sometime in the late 1950s. This two-handed vignette features a man confined in a wheelchair who moves himself forward and backward with a pole and – like Dani Szakáll in *The Avenger, the Gatekeeper, or: It is Requested that You Wipe Your Feet* – continually torments another equally unfortunate man who, in Beckett's short play, is mobile but blind. Finally, the blind man unwilling or unable to endure the torment any longer seizes the pole, thus rendering the man in the wheelchair helpless – a clear parallel with Páskándi's second act. Although written a few years before *The Avenger, the Gatekeeper, or: It is Requested that You Wipe Your Feet*, *Rough for Theatre I* is unlikely to have influenced Páskándi since Beckett's sketch did not become known until after 1979 when it was produced in Hamburg and later in the next decade in San Francisco – both productions occurring almost a decade after Páskándi's premiered.

While acknowledging Beckett's considerable influence on both Páskándi's thinking and dramaturgy, the profound difference between his plays and those of the Theatre of the Absurd in the West, including *Endgame* and *Rough for Theatre I*, derives from the local circumstances dominated by dictatorial communism. Rather than Beckett's plays, a more likely source for Páskándi's visual image of characters in wheeled chairs in *The Avenger, the Gatekeeper, or*: *It is Requested that You Wipe Your Feet* lies in the ubiquitous disabled Hungarian veterans of World War II confined to their boxes on wheels or their primitive wheelchairs that could be seen daily on the streets of Hungary and Romania. Many such veterans were not equipped with the modern large wheeled chair impelled forward by two hands but were confined to a box on either four or three wheels propelled by a crank turned by the right hand. Because the box will move only when the crank is turned by the right hand, in the fight to the death in Act II – if a production made use of such a box on wheels – the two antagonists initially would have to battle one another using their left arms. The visual image Páskándi invokes in Act II of the shadow thrown on the wall by the men fighting which the Director describes as appearing 'like two Stag Beetles' could benefit from using this common post-war box on wheels, but thus far productions have employed the more conventional wheeled chair.

Whatever the inspiration for, or source of, confining the main character to a wheelchair, the dialogue and action between apparently helpless Szakáll in his wheelchair and the commanding Director of the first Feet-Wiping Bureau appears realistic because rooted in the psychology of character, while the plot looks wholly political calling for the powerless to rally, rise up and destroy the authoritarian oppressor. Szakáll appears, to borrow Maxim Gorky's metaphor, 'as straight and unbending as a sword'.[30] In his moral certainty and his defence of the common soldier against the officer class, he becomes almost the Positive Hero of Socialist Realism – a symbol with which Páskándi would be all too familiar and which the remaining acts of the play confound. The play's apparent political direction reaches a climax with Szakáll's shooting the arrogant Director of the Feet-Wiping Bureau. At the sound of the shots, various clerks and a policeman rush in to investigate, gathering around the dead Director in what looks like an *engagé* tableau. But the policeman's Groucho Marx-like line, 'Do you have a permit for that gun?' destroys any vestige of Socialist Realism or political engagement, bringing the play right back into the Absurdoid Theatre as the somewhat obtuse policeman arrests Szakáll, including his wheelchair.

Policeman. (*taking notes*) I arrest you. You come with me (*pointing at the wheelchair*), you bring that, too. [As if Szakáll could move without it.][31]

With Szakáll off stage, Páskándi relaunches his satiric attack on the arbitrary power of the bureaucracy through the action of the ambitious Deputy Director who loses no time in installing himself as the new Director of the Feet-Wiping Bureau. His first act is to discuss in great detail with his covey of clerks their most pressing problem: Exactly what kind of signage does the bureau now require in light of recent tragic events? After a prolonged discussion, they all agree to keep the wording of the current sign at the entrance to the first Feet-Wiping Bureau but to reverse the colours so that instead of black letters on a white background there will now be white letters on a black background. All of them conspicuously ignore the corpse of the Lieutenant/Director lying conveniently out of sight under the table.

In Part Two of *The Avenger, the Gatekeeper, or: It is Requested that You Wipe Your Feet* after the 'crucial change' the former Assistant Director – now the new Director of the Feet-Wiping Bureau – employs Szakáll as Gate-Keeper. Part Two consists of a long intricate Beckettian monologue familiar from the Trilogy and short stories that emphasizes the contingent nature of his new position – what Beckett might have labelled the 'perhaps,' which he identifies as 'the key word in my plays'.[32] Yet even here the issue eventually becomes not – as in Beckett – a metaphysical puzzle of dark and light[33] but a physical conundrum of power and powerlessness as the new gatekeeper moves from being extraordinarily proud of his new position through a series of doubts about that new position to realizing that he has given up much of his freedom and is now under the thumb of the new Director. Going beyond those concerns associated with the Theatre of the Absurd, Part Three (Act II) becomes truly Absurdoid Theatre in Szakáll's confrontation with András Doma. In this final act, Páskándi examines the notion of complicity in the subjugation of others – those far below such echelons of power as represented by the two Directors. The focus remains riveted on how those who are powerless may still inflict great harm on others equally powerless.

If, as Martin Esslin has famously argued, '[t]he spectators of the Theatre of the Absurd are ... confronted with a grotesquely heightened picture of their own world: a world without faith, meaning, and genuine freedom of will',[34] spectators of Absurdoid Theatre also encounter a world of arbitrary power, purposeful contradictions, and genuine co-optation of will. Like other Central European playwrights, Páskándi was 'preoccupied with the absurdities of the phenomenal world, portraying the dehumanizing mechanism of a totalitarian regime'.[35] It is the latter that leads to questions of morality and issues of integrity as one 'poor soul' preys upon another. Such issues contrast to those present in much Western drama that creates powerful images of dictatorship's arbitrary power at the expense of the individual who becomes reduced to insignificance, as, for example, in Beckett's *Catastrophe* (1982), Harold Pinter's *One for the Road* (1984) or *Mountain Language* (1989). In both Beckett's and Pinter's plays the oppressed, humiliated, ruined individual does not lose moral integrity or superiority unlike in Páskándi's and other Central European Absurdist plays. Of all Beckett's plays, *What Where*? (1983) comes close to the Central European model in dramatizing how individuals may be manipulated into becoming instruments of oppression, yet even in this play the emphasis falls not on the moral responsibility and subsequent disintegration of the individual but on the mechanism of power. The result is a potent but abstract model of the abasement of the individual in the service of power. Páskándi's plays, in contrast, all focus on the individual's complicity and despair rather than on the dictator's power. Like Beckett and Pinter, Páskándi ridicules the excesses and failures of dictatorship, but all the while he foregrounds the annihilation of individuality, personal integrity, and self-reliance together with the concomitant failure of those subjected to despotism to unite in the common fight against those exercising power.

The bizarre, senseless and deadly duel in Part 3 of *The Avenger* between two who should unite against their powerful oppressors, for example, when contrasted with the confrontation in Beckett's *Rough for Theatre I* illustrates once more the distinction between the Western Theatre of the Absurd with its preoccupation with metaphysical and philosophical problems and Páskándi's Absurdoid Theatre that combines such metaphysical questions with political and moral issues. In *Rough for Theatre I* the two characters prey on one another but there is no suggestion of any layer of society or power above them manipulating them in contrast to the Director and Assistant Director of the Feet-Wiping Bureau in *The Avenger*. Similarly, Páskándi's plays, like most of those created by post-World War II Transylvanian-Hungarian playwrights, remain focused on a person's response to the dictates of power.[36] The grotesque figure with the Big Boots intimidates, cajoles, and threatens, but it is the four passengers who grant him power by acceding to his demands. Those in *The Line* attack and kill one of their own because in their eyes he appears – but only appears – to have succeeded where they failed and in so-doing they simply fulfil the plan of the person, the bureaucrat in power. Similarly in *The Avenger, the Gatekeeper, or: It is Requested that You Wipe Your Feet*, Szakáll kills the Director who caused his maiming only in his turn to badger and eventually pick a fight with his fellow legless-veteran and petitioner, András Doma, that results in his own death. Doma's victory over Szakáll, in its turn, proves only a momentary respite from subjection to and humiliation by those in power. The new Director coaxes and cajoles Doma into following him up a long flight of stairs with the promise of a job. 'Come along, come along,' he says, as if Doma might be reluctant to follow or be intimidated by the imposing position of the Director rather than being given an impossible physical task for one confined to a wheelchair: 'Doma makes a huge [unsuccessful] effort [to follow him up the stairs] like a crippled Sisyphus'. As the Director reaches the top of the staircase and disappears, he calls back down:

> (*encouragingly in a fatherly manner*) Come along, Doma. Come along after me don't be afraid. Come along bravely! (*Director moves up the stairs and disappears. Doma stares after him in despair. His face becomes tense. He wheels with insane speed back ... and then charges towards the stairs grunting, sweating and from this huge superhuman effort he manages to climb up the stairs almost to the point where the Director disappeared but then the wheelchair rolls back helplessly gathering speed and when it is half-way between staircase and the opened black gap.*

Quick Curtain[37]

If Beckett's *Act without Words I* epitomizes the Western Theatre of the Absurd that focuses on the metaphysical condition into which humans are thrown, then Páskándi's absurdoid plays build upon that general condition to dramatize the unpredictable prescriptions of the Police State's absolute power as exercised on the large scale of corrupt courts and Secret Police in *No Conductor*, as evidenced in daily life in *The Line*, and, most trenchantly, as seen in the petty scale of prison humiliations in *The Avenger, the Gatekeeper, or: It is Requested that You Wipe Your Feet*. Páskándi began writing *The Avenger, the Gatekeeper, or: It is Requested that You Wipe Your Feet* in 1964 shortly after his release from prison and worked on it between 1964 and 1970 until its highly successful premiere 1971 in Nagyvárad (Oradea), Romania. The play ran for nine performances before the Romanian censor ordered it taken off. That order proved part of a more general one that prohibited the staging or publication of any and all forms of the Theatre of the Absurd whether of the West or of the more home-grown variety, thus ending one of the 'most remarkable' periods of 'Hungarian poetry, drama, prose, fine arts and scientific achievements ... in Transylvania'.[38] With the banning of his plays and the prospect of ever-increasing censorship and harassment, Páskándi determined to go into exile in Hungary from Transylvania, Romania, which he was finally able to do in 1974. He continued to write his Absurdoid plays together with historical dramas, poetry, novels, short stories, and essays until the year of his death. Fortunately, a great deal of his work has been translated into several different languages thus making his unique vision available to much of the world.

All translations unless otherwise noted are by Csilla Bertha and Donald E. Morse.

1 Géza Páskándi, 'World's Fair: A Post-exotic Absurdoid Play in Three Acts', *Moment of Sincerity: Nine Plays*, trans. Eugene Brogyányi (Kolozsvár [Cluj]: Polis, 1999): 184. Subsequent references are cited in the text.

2 Vladimir refers to 'the bald soprano' in *World's Fair*, 196.

3 See Eugene Ionesco, 'L'Impromptu de l'Alma', *Théâtre II* (Paris: 1958).

4 Péter P. Müller, *Central European Playwrights within and without the Absurd* (Pécs, HU: JPTE TK Kiadói Iroda, 1996): 69. The

pre-eminent play on this subject was Václav Havel's grotesque comedy, *The Memorandum* (1980).

5 Géza Páskándi, *Todogar Jaur Kvárna: Filozófiai végjáték* [Philosophical Endgame] (Budapest: Széphalom Könyvműhely, 1995): 14-15. Subsequent references are cited in the text.

6 The original title in Hungarian, *Todogar Jaur Kvárna* is composed of nonsense words made by scrambling the letters of the words in the play's subtitle: *Godot-ra Újra Várnak* [They are Waiting for Godot to Come Again]. Páskándi added a footnote to this scrambled title, '[t]hat is the translation of the previous title [They are Waiting for Godot to Come Again] into post-exotic language and style.' Clearly, he enjoyed and was adept at word games. The two main titles are followed by a series of sub-titles, *Todogar Jaur Kvárna, Godot-ra Újra Várnak vagy Anton és Samuel, Filozófiat végjdt* [Nonsense title, They Are Waiting for Godot to Come Again or Anton and Samuel, A Philosophical Endgame]. Anton refers to Antonio Gaudi and Samuel to Beckett.

7 Ellipsis in *World's Fair*, 200-01. An alternative translation might read: It would be good to have a paper, sir so they'd see how we are identified with those who wander ... We are the stable movers, steadfast Mercurys and as such, we have no demands on our territories. We give them up. So we want a document testifying to our being 'The Aboriginals of the Road' and 'The Patriots of the Road', Páskándi, *Todogar*, 214-15.

8 Zoltán Bertha, 'Páskándi Géza "filozófiai végjátéka"', *Sorstükör* (Miskolc: Felsőmagyarország Kiadó, 2001): 401.

9 Samuel Beckett, *Waiting for Godot* (New York: Grove, 1945): 44b.

10 Ellipses in original *Todogar*, 64. *World's Fair*, the only available English translation omits this and other crucial passages.

11 Ellipses in original, *Todogar*, 163.

12 Bertha, 'Páskándi', 404.

13 Samuel Beckett, 'Act Without Words I,' *Collected Shorter Plays. of Samuel Beckett*, (New York: Grove, 1984): 43.

14 *Act without Words I* encapsulates the major motifs found in the western Theatre of the Absurd. John Killinger in *World in Collapse*: *the Vision of Absurd Drama* (New York: Dell, 1971) claims that 'Simone de Beauvoir coined the word "*facticity*" to describe the soullessness, the obduracy, the choicelessness of the world of things' (75). This may be so, but the term remains a common translation of Heiddeger's *in Sein geworfen* from *Sein und Zeit* [Being and Time] (1931, trans. 1962), Martin Heidegger, *Being and Time* (1931), trans. John Macquarie and Edward Robinson (Oxford: Blackwell, 1962). In Beckett's last play, *What*

Where? a similar situation obtains. Beckett's biographer, James Knowlson, in *Damned to Fame* (New York: Simon & Schuster, 1996) speculates that 'if someone is responsible for an unnamed crime [in *What Where*?], that crime appears likely to be Calderon's 'original sin of being born', which Beckett had evoked at the beginning of his career in his essay, *Proust* (Knowlson, *Damned*, 604), and which becomes embodied in *Act without Words I* – 'make sense who may/I switch off' (see Samuel Beckett, 'What Where?' *The Collected Shorter Plays of Samuel Beckett* [New York: Grove, 1984]: 316 – the last lines Beckett wrote for the stage, Knowlson, *Damned*, 604.

15 Killinger, 79.

16 The mime appears not to follow Beckett's famous formula for the contemporary artist that 'there is nothing to express, nothing with which to express, no power to express, no desire to express, together with the obligation to express', Beckett, *Disjecta*, 139, qtd. in Knowlson, 336. While the mime considers suicide, Beckett does not.

17 John Peter, *Vladimir's Carrot*: *Modern Drama and the Modern Imagination* (Chicago: Chicago University Press, 1987): 271.

18 Peter, 271.

19 Ibid., 272.

20 Ibid., 271, 272.

21 Killinger, 79.

22 Compare András Sütő, 'Advent in the Hargita Mountains' (1980), Csilla Bertha and Donald E. Morse, *Silenced Voices*: *Transylvanian-Hungarian Plays,* Selected and Translated by Csilla Bertha and Donald E. Morse (Dublin: Carysfort, 2008).

23 Eugene Brogyányi, Introduction, *New Hungarian Drama*, ed. Eugene Brogyányi (Budapest: Corvina, 1991): 14.

24 P. Müller, 29, emphasis in original.

25 Géza Páskándi, 'The Avenger, the Gatekeeper, or: It is Requested that You Wipe Your Feet', Bertha and Morse, *Silenced Voices* (Dublin: Carysfort Press, 2008)

26 P. Müller, 69.

27 Until the treaty ending World War I, Transylvania had been part of Hungary for over a thousand years. Because Austria had conquered Hungary for four hundred years until the end of World War I, the Lieutenant and Szakáll would have been part of the Hungarian Army forced to fight on the side of the Habsburg Empire.

28 Páskándi, 'The Avenger, the Gatekeeper', Bertha and Morse, *Silenced Voices* (Dublin: Carsfort Press, 2008)

29 Samuel Beckett, *Endgame* (New York: Grove, 1958): 1.

30 The line occurs in Maxim Gorky's *The Philistines* (1901), which John Peter identifies as '[p]erhaps the earliest appearance of the positive hero', *Vladimir's Carrot*, 350. Peter bases his conjecture on the translation of *The Philistines* by Dusty Hughes to which he had access, 363, n.193.

31 All dialogue from Páskándi, 'The Avenger, the Gatekeeper', Bertha and Morse, *Silenced Voices* (Dublin: Carysfort Press, 2008).

32 Tom Driver, 'Beckett by the Madeleine,' *Columbia University Forum* 4 (1961): 23.

33 Beckett famously remarked to Tom Driver in an early interview that 'If there were only darkness all would be clear. ... But where we have both dark and light we have also the inexplicable. The key word in my plays is "perhaps,"' 'Beckett by the Madeleine,' 23.

34 Martin Esslin, 'The Theatre of the Absurd', *The Tulane Drama Review* (May 1960). Rpt. in *Essays in the Modern Drama*, ed. Morris Freedman (Boston: D.C. Heath, 1964): 323. Esslin's essay in *TDR* became the basis for his seminal study, *The Theatre of the Absurd* (1961) that went through several editions and reprintings and remains in print after almost half a century.

35 Paul I. Trensky, *Czech Drama since World War II* (White Plains, NY: M.E. Sharpe, 1978): 102.

36 For an extensive discussion of this issue, see 'Falling through the Cracks', Bertha and Morse, *Silenced Voices* (Dublin: Carysfort Pess, 2008).

37 All dialogue from Páskándi, 'The Avenger, the Gatekeeper', Bertha and Morse, *Silenced Voices* (Dublin: Carysfort Press, 2008).

38 Ildiko Lipcsey, *Romania and Transylvania in the 20th Century*, trans. Peter Csermely (Buffalo: Corvinus, 2006): 146.

3 | Body Politics in a Fictitious East European Dictatorship: Martin McDonagh's *The Pillowman*

Péter P. Müller

Until the Renaissance European drama excluded brutal actions from the stage. Murder, tortures, fights and physical punishment had only been narrated and referred to, but not performed for the theatre audience in the previous ages. The Elizabethan theatre broke this tradition by staging murder, amputation, and torture, a broad variety of violent actions against the body in plays by such dramatists as Thomas Kyd, John Webster, and William Shakespeare. Seventeenth-century French tragedy, early bourgeois drama, romantic and modern drama all returned to the discreet, bashful forms of dramatic action, preferring wordy and intellectual ways of expression to physicality and bodily representation. Although exceptions can be pointed at – like Shelley's *The Cenci*, the French marionette genre of Grand Guignol etc. – the tendency of European drama demonstrated this prudish tradition.

Nowadays a younger generation of playwrights of the Millennium – including the German Marius von Mayenburg, Dea Loher and Theresia Walser, the British Mark Ravenhill, Sarah Kane and Martin McDonagh – labelled by different terms, as new brutalists, representatives of 'in-yer-face' theatre, etc., have demonstrated significant interest in different cruelties against the body. In their plays brutal actions are not reported but acted out on stage, challenging the theatrical representation in the manner that their forerunner, Edward Bond, provoked theatres and audiences in the 1960s and 1970s with his plays *Saved* (1965) and *Lear* (1971).

Approaching the oeuvre of Martin McDonagh from a Hungarian perspective it has to be clarified that the reception of his plays has taken place in Hungary within the context of the phenomenon called New European Drama. McDonagh's plays are looked at as representatives of New European Drama, which is largely the extension of a trend in recent British drama.[1] McDonagh has been seen as a member of this new generation of playwrights, who appeared in the mid-1990s, and who were immediately acclaimed internationally, primarily in Central Europe. A Polish scholar has written on their influence:

> The first ones to be imported were the British plays of Mark Ravenhill, Sarah Kane and Martin McDonagh. They were soon followed by the works of German authors such as Marius von Mayenburg, Dea Loher and Theresia Walser ... These works inspired a debate on the problems of the (realistic) plausibility of the action and the characters; the extent to which they could be treated as representative of society; and the potentional harm that the contents of these texts pose for society. They tend to be regarded as too explicit in terms of both subject-matter and means of expression to be produced by institutional theatres, financed by taxpayers' money, who usually prefer their 'art' to be somewhat more edifying.[2]

As the above citation states, these new plays have been received in Central Europe as representations of today's society, which view is very much true for McDonagh, whose plays have been considered primarily as representations of Irish reality, and *The Pillowman* as that of a twentieth-century East European dictatorship. One of the first critics to debate the realistic approach towards McDonagh's plays has been Fintan O'Toole, noting on McDonagh's first production ever that '[a]ll the elements that make up the picture are real, but their combined effect is one that questions the very idea of reality.' He continues, declaring that, 'the whole idea of theatrical realism becomes itself the biggest double take of all'.[3]

One basic reason why the representation-centred interpretation of McDonagh's plays can be challenged is the universality and extent of violence as a permanent motif and ingredient in these works. The savagery of the plays has been inspired by the mass media, images of accidents, wars, catastrophes, gangster movies etc. The exaggeration of brutality, the depth of violence, the quantity of bloodshed in McDonagh's plays testify to the influence of or at least an affinity with such films as *Pulp Fiction* (1994), *Desperado* (1995) or *Fargo* (1996). The amount of violence in these films turns them into a parody of their own genre, which happens in the case of the McDonagh plays as well. McDonagh 'draws upon multiple styles and genres without distinguishing between high or popular cultural references in an apparently gratuitous display of manic intertextuality'.[4] In spite of these features, the majority of McDonagh's international theatrical reception — including the Hungarian one — has been characterized by the representational approach to these plays, which can partly be explained by the fact that in spite of certain postmodern features, 'formally they are highly conservative dramas'.[5]

After his *Leenane Trilogy* (*The Beauty Queen of Leenane*, *A Skull in Connemara*, *The Lonesome West*) and Inishmore plays (*The Cripple of Inishmaan*, *The Lieutenant of Inishmore*, *The Banshees of Inisheer*) McDonagh in *The Pillowman* depicts a fictitious East European dictatorship, where different violent actions against people are reported, and where a writer creates short stories based on savage actions against children. The exaggeration of brutality, the depth of violence, the quantity of bloodshed which pervades McDonagh's previous plays here transforms into a bizarre see-saw between telling and doing. Two fictitious spheres, storytelling and political propaganda are intertwined with reports on certain events and actions within the framework of a play. A wide variety of bodies appear in the stories of the protagonist, the writer Katurian K. Katurian, and the detectives, who interrogate and torture him.

For thirty-three years I had lived — as detective Tupolski calls it — 'in a totalitarian fucking dictatorship',[6] until the Hungarian party-state collapsed in 1989. I was never imprisoned and never wrote and published a short story, so I have very few things in common with the play's protagonist, and I have to say that I have experienced a rather different world in this East European dictatorship than the one depicted in McDonagh's *The Pillowman*. Although the play does not get its verification from a comparison to historical, political features and events of particular countries, it does not mean that the world in and of *The Pillowman* cannot be considered to be a valid and an authentic one.

The subject matter of *The Pillowman* can, however, be compared to East- or, rather, Central European plays in which the operation of totalitarian states are depicted. A rather paradoxical and parabolic work regarding this issue is the Polish Slawomir Mrożek's *The Police* (1957), while a more personal and journalistic approach is represented in the Hungarian István Eörsi's *The Interrogation* (1965, first produced and published in 1988). Although both plays take place in a prison of a police-state, they focus on the political, ideological, and emotional mechanisms of totalitarianism, rather than on the physical brutality, body politics exercised in these countries. Manipulations as part of the interrogation as well as forms of psychological oppression are more detailed and analysed than physical brutality and practices of torture.

Mrożek's *The Police* revolves around the question of what would happen if all private opinions identify with the one governmental, official point of view. In the totalitarian system of *The Police*, all private opinions have to be detected and investigated, and loyalty has to be declared. Since the holders of power distrust the people, they maintain an institution to control their declared loyalty. Agent-provocateurs walk the streets provoking people to speak against the political system. One of them, a police sergeant reports to his chief on the people's reaction, saying 'I was trying to shout anti-government slogans — and they beat me up ... I was beaten up by the loyal population'.[7] Though the drama is a parable of the totalitarian society, it is placed neither into a post-war East European country, nor into an abstract nowhere land. In the instruction at the beginning of the play Mrożek states that it has to be acted in nineteenth-century costumes, reminiscent of the Habsburg Empire.[8]

Eörsi's *The Interrogation* takes place in a Hungarian prison on 24 December 1953, Christmas Eve. Four political convicts are in a cell, representing four different political and social types, a worker in his mid-twenties, a religious peasant in his early fifties, an ex-bureaucrat of the same age from the fascist period of the early 1940s, and a communist in his early forties. Four members of the prison staff appear too, the prison-commander (a colonel), his deputy (a major), a sadistic sergeant, and a prison doctor. The play tries to capture the absurdity of how comrades imprison each other and the paradox that the holders of power prefer ex-political enemies to fellow-Communists. It is the conflicts of the prisoners that get more attention in the play: in their cell they fight with each other, but the torture of the prisoners is not performed on stage. Similarly to *The Police*, where the beating of the police sergeant is only told about, not demonstrated.

In Mrożek's play we see an intellectual experiment with the basic ideas, principles of totalitarianism. In this state the Police needs at least one prisoner to prove its own existence. Therefore, when the only ex-conspirator signs the declaration of loyalty in the prison, the professional provocateur (the Sergeant) will be imprisoned. The Police Chief convinces the Sergeant with the following argument,

> What do we need? What we need is one person who we could lock up, whom we could arrest for something which could in some very slight degree be described as anti-government activity. Having several times attempted to find this man, it has become apparent that we shall not find him in the ordinary course of events, or in what we might call a natural manner. We must, so to speak, compose this man ourselves. My choice has fallen on you.[9]

The motif of storytelling, child abuse, which are so crucial in *The Pillowman*, are not present in Mrożek's *The Police*, as they are not part of Eörsi's *The Interrogation* either. This latter one is based more on personal experiences, as the playwright had been imprisoned for several years, though not in the time of his play, but during the second part of the 1950s. For his activities in the 1956 revolution he was sentenced to eight years in prison, of which he spent three and a half years behind the bars. *The Interrogation* is a debate-play studying the slight changes in the political system related to Imre Nagy's reformist policy. Nagy was appointed Prime Minister of the Hungarian government in the summer of 1953. He initiated significant changes in the economy and against dictatorial institutions. In his struggle with the Stalinist members of the communist party he was finally relieved of his position. Eörsi's play models these political fights within the context of the political prison.

So while Eörsi reflects a precise political-historical constellation in a naturalistic, journalistic manner, Mrożek sets up a logical experiment based on an absurd premise. Although both plays have direct or indirect references to the East-Central European political systems, both represent a somewhat different world and a different way of playwriting, compared to each other, and to *The Pillowman*. This play of McDonagh — contrary to his other plays — lacks the identification of time and place in which the story happens, and therefore the setting as 'Eastern Europe' remains somewhat abstract and undefined. 'The only specific geographical reference is to the place-name of "Kamenice" ... a very common place-name in the Slavonic settlement areas of East Central Europe'.[10] In his *Leenane* and *Aran* plays McDonagh always gives a precise description of the setting, and defines the age of most of the characters, but from *The Pillowman* most of these features are missing. Contradictory statements are made, and unrelated things are mixed up regarding the context of the prison cell, and the identity of the characters.

All that spectators and/or readers see as locations in *The Pillowman* are two prison sites, a police interrogation room (Act I scene 1, Act III), and a cell (Act II scene 1), and two imaginary sites where two of Katurian's stories are enacted, a child's room with its double (Act I scene 2) to perform 'The Writer and the Writer's Brother', and an undefined site (identical either with the cell or with the child's room) where 'The Little Jesus' story is performed (Act II scene 2). All the rest of the information about the town and the country is a mixture of East European names and references, as it has been analyzed accurately by Ondřej Pilný in his essay, 'Grotesque Entertainment: *The Pillowman* as Puppet Theatre'.[11] The names of characters and places refer to Czech, Polish, Slovak, Serb, Croatian, Jewish and other names from the region (no Hungarian though), which could never co-exist in such a mixture. As the social context is blurred, the features of dictatorship in this imaginary land appear on the personal, rather than on the institutional level in *The Pillowman*.

The pair of detectives represents the authorities – they appear in institutionalized positions, while the brothers in custody remain civilians. Katurian is not an institutionalized writer, he has only one publication. Socially he is a person working at the Kamenice abattoir, and in his free-time writes short stories. But the play presents him as a writer in custody, and during the interrogation he is considered as a writer, and Tupolski even threatens him that the police like to execute writers. As two stories are acted out, the parents appearing in them can be seen as representing a third level, for they stand both for the family as an institution and for the particular mother and father. In this way the parents mediate between the person and the state, and this is the level in which the functioning of a dictatorship can really be experienced.

Considering time, the length of action seems to be equal with the performed story, taking place on a Monday evening, starting with Katurian's interrogation and ending with his being shot to death about two hours later. This reduced time of the major plot is supplemented by scenes of the past (performed and told), and references to the future, for instance in detective Ariel's story about his future retirement. The historical time of the play remains undefined.

Tupolski uses a box of matches to threaten Katurian by putting his stories on fire. There is electricity by which Ariel often intends to shock Katurian. Katurian is very scared to have his stories burned by the police, which implies that there is just one copy of each of them (except the one published), therefore he must have written them by hand and not on a typewriter. It does not necessarily imply that this is a time before the invention of the typewriter, though. Yet it can be inferred that this is a period with limited access to technical facilities, and as Ondřej Pilný formulates, 'probably some time in the mid-twentieth century'.[12]

The reduced, abstract information given about an undefined police state makes Lisa Fitzpatrick write that '*The Pillowman* draws upon clichéd conceptions of Eastern Europe that have very little to do with the events or histories of actual countries'.[13] The second part of her statement I agree with, but I do not think the play draws upon clichés. Its undefined, unsolved, abstract world is closer to Franz Kafka's parabolic fiction than to the schematic writing once practised by writers and preferred — or rather forced — by the authorities in the socialist countries, a style which was officially called 'socialist realism'. Since in Kafka's fiction, short

short stories, parables cannot be seen as representations of the Austro-Hungarian Monarchy, it is not really profitable to come to the conclusion that *The Pillowman* is modelled on East European socialism or vice versa. I rather agree with Eamonn Jordan who writes that '[i]t is more the spirit of totalitarianism that McDonagh is after, and not the preciseness of the socio/political parameters. ... The totalitarian state has dramaturgical, metaphorical as well as symbolic significances' here.[14]

This cited and created spirit of totalitarianism is represented in the play both by physical actions (either performed or narrated) and by psychological means, though in the practice of East European socialism the intimidation of the majority of the people was based primarily on psychological terror rather than affecting the body. A delicate balance was present between psychological terror and bodily punishment, when the psychological pressure was reduced, corporeal trials became stronger, and the other way round.

It is a permanent question, however, both within the play and in the present essay as well, whether there is a direct way from the world of facts to the world of fiction, from telling to doing, from reality to a work of art and vice versa. It is very difficult to resist the representational approach to the play, as McDonagh himself sets up the trap by using the fourth wall convention, the Chekhovian illusionary dramaturgy as if the things happening on stage were real life events of real life characters. But he himself continuously challenges this approach by the meta-fictional and meta-theatrical features of *The Pillowman*, the way he has done it in his other plays.

Actions of and against the body appear on at least three levels in *The Pillowman*. These three levels are often intertwined and opposed to each other. They are (1) the present time actions on stage which are targeted at the body, (2) the characters' recollections of the traumas they had suffered, and (3) the short short stories of Katurian (and Tupolski) read or told throughout the play in which several horrible things happen to the bodies primarily of children. The two strongest actions on stage against bodies are the two murders, which indicate the two dramaturgical culminations of the play. The first is Katurian suffocating Michal by a pillow just before the interval, and the second is Tupolski shooting Katurian in the head near the end, after which only a short, dreamlike epilogue follows. Both killings aim at the head of the victim, both are mediated by a sort of instrument.

In the first case, there is direct physical contact by means of a soft object, and a several minute-long agony representing the homicide; while in the second case everything is the opposite of the first, there is physical distance between the two people, use of a gun, and immediate death. In the first case the murder is within the family, a man kills his brother, and — as Eamonn Jordan points out — Katurian 'sees his suffocation of his brother as a mercy killing, hoping to avoid for him the pains of torture and the trauma of preparing to die'.[15] When Tupolski shoots Katurian at number four during the countdown, depriving him of completing his final story, it shows the irrational, unlawful arbitrariness of the totalitarian dictatorship, represented by a member of the oppressive political mechanism that neglects the dignity of the individual.

Beside the two onstage killings there is a pair of actions which involve the torturing of the two brothers. The one against Katurian begins on stage when 'Ariel pulls Katurian off his chair by the hair, kneels across him and gouges into his face' (12), and later Act II starts with Katurian's screams off stage after which he enters Michal's cell beaten up. Between these two scenes Michal's torturing seems to happen off stage, when we hear the 'sound of a man screaming hideously a few rooms away' (23). Katurian identifies the sound as his brother's voice, and soon 'Ariel returns, wrapping his bloodied hand in white cloth' (23). The screaming and the blood signify torture, but this interpretation turns out to be false (both for Katurian and the reader/spectator), as Tupolski in a quarrel with Ariel says that the blood on Ariel's hand is 'so obviously fake blood' (29), and later Michal confesses to his brother that he was asked to scream though not harmed at all.

In the example of Michal's pretended torture McDonagh implies the very essence of the play. Here Michal, Ariel and Tupolski play 'theatre' for Katurian to make him believe that something has really happened, and to exercise a strong influence on him. They not only refer to the torture, but use further means to pretend the reality of the action. This is the detectives' short term experiment with Katurian, similar to the one once executed by the parents with him. It is really ironic to speak of fake blood in this situation, because in theatre blood is a prop, and actors are normally not bleeding (save by accident), but they use some technical tricks. Furthermore, in the above examples two pairs of actions can be seen against the body. First, there are the two killings executed from different personal relations, based on different motivations, and carried out for different reasons. The second pair of actions comprises the real and the pretended beatings. Both beatings aim at Katurian, to shock and break him, first physically, then emotionally, and the second is the one that has a stronger influence and consequence both on him and on the plot of the play.

All the four characters talk about traumas they had suffered during their lives. Their traumas had originated from their family and not from the political system, not from the dictatorial functioning of the country. Together with Katurian we are informed by Tupolski, that Ariel as a boy had been sexually abused by his father whom later he suffocated with a pillow. Tupolski has lost his son who drowned in a river, and in this context he mentions that his favourite story by Katurian is 'The Pillowman'.

The two brothers had been subject to their parents' experimentation, which included both physical and emotional violence. Their story appears first in the play in Act I, scene 2, which is basically Katurian's monologue in the third person. Together with the telling of the story it is performed by Katurian, his parents, and a child. In this story Katurian and Michal are objects of an experiment that we see from Katurian's point of view. The experiment has three parts, the first is an idyll guaranteed by the parents, which lasts till Katurian's seventh birthday, up to which time he writes only happy stories. The second part begins when on a nightly basis he hears horrific sounds from the neighbouring, always bolted room for seven years, during which his stories become darker and darker. The third, final part has two versions, in the first version Katurian finds the corpse of his brother, while in the second one his brother appears to be alive but brain-damaged. Regardless of the two versions of his brother's fate, the performed scene and the story end with Katurian suffocating both parents by a pillow. The story reoccurs as part of the brothers' quarrel in Act II, scene 1, when Michal criticizes Katurian's story calling it rubbish and questions Katurian's method and right to change events in the tale, diverging from the real facts. Later, Katurian criticizes himself, saying to Ariel that 'I kind of hate any writing that's even vaguely autobiographical ... however, "The Writer and the Writer's Brother" is, I suppose, the only story of mine that isn't really fiction' (76). This story is combined in the final scene with the title story. The already dead Katurian tells us what story he was to make up during Tupolski's countdown, and this final story is a combination of 'The Pillowman' and 'The Writer and the Writer's Brother', which underlines the significance of both stories within the play. And which suggests that the Pillowman is 'Katurian's fictional alter ego'.[16]

To sum up the traumas of the brothers, Michal as a child had been physically tortured by his parents, while Katurian had gone through an emotional torture by hearing the horrific sounds. Although Katurian has saved his brother, he has to live with a heavy conscience because he had killed his parents. In the story of the two brothers, Michal's screams from the secret nursery room explains why Katurian is so sensitive in the interrogation room hearing his brother's screams and why he believes that the same thing happens at the police station that had happened in the family home.

There are altogether seven short stories written by Katurian which are read during the play, and an eighth one made up by detective Tupolski. Katurian's seven stories are — in the order of appearance — 'The Little Apple Men', 'The Three Gibbet Crossroads', 'The Tale of the Town on the River', 'The Writer and the Writer's Brother', 'The Little Green Pig', 'The Pillowman', and 'The Little Jesus'. Tupolski's story is 'The Story of the Little Deaf Boy on the Big Long Railroad Tracks. In China'. There are two further short stories mentioned by Michal by their title, written by Katurian, 'The Face Basement', and 'The Shakespeare Room'.

Most of the stories are about the torture, mutilation, abuse, and stigmatization of people, mainly children. This is the case in the story of the brothers, in little Jesus, the apple men, the rat catcher, and the green pig. The worlds of these stories are even less detailed than the world of the play. We hear/read about horrific, perverse actions performed by and against characters without individual features. What becomes specified is the kind of physical atrocity, and not those people who do them; neither the family, nor the community, nor the society. This leads us further away from being able to identify a clear historical, political context for the play.

Another reason for the abstract, undetermined features represented by the stories is that they are connected to diverse traditions. The basis of 'The Little Jesus' and its influence is our knowledge of the Bible, the original story. Besides, this short story has parallels with 'The Gospel According to Mark' (1970), a short story by Jorge Luis Borges.[17] 'The Tale of the Town on the River' refers to 'The Pied Piper of Hamelin', which is a thirteenth-century legend of an unusual disaster, documented by the Brothers Grimm under the title 'The Ratcatcher of Hamelin'. It is rather ironic that Katurian refers to it as the best of his stories. (19) The story of 'The Three Gibbet Crossroads' refers to an executioner's equipment which was outlawed in the mid-nineteenth century. 'The Little Apple Men' is based on an urban legend connected to Halloween. Jack Santino writes in his *Halloween and Other Festivals of Death and Life*, that 'beginning in 1967 the focus of the legend shifted dramatically from poison to razors and sharp objects in apples'.[18] The legend spread rapidly in North America, and two folklorists published a research study in 1985 on the metamorphosis of the legend under the title, 'The Razor Blade in the Apple: the Social Construction of an Urban Legend'.[19] The pig story can be traced back to fairy tales. The title story with its paradoxical time structure can be connected to 'mythical narratives of primitive societies',[20] and with the timelessness of such comics of popular culture as Batman and Spiderman. Besides, Pillowboy is a Halloween costume, often used by children. The hybrid nature of the stories is concealed by the unity of time and space in the play, the context of interrogation, and by some repeated motifs.

A major motif of the stories is the radical use of bodies. Bodies are opened up, changed or transformed. The solid boundaries of the body are transgressed, and by this the individuals' integration is challenged and ignored. What can really be considered as a statement about totalitarianism in *The Pillowman* is this arrogant, brutal oppression of the individual. Here it is symbolized by the way bodies are treated. The terms 'soft' and 'hard' used to describe – beside other things – East European dictatorships, originate from bodily sensations, tactile experiences. The examples of soft bodies or soft treatment of the body appear in the case of the pillow and the green pig, while the rest of the tales give example of hard bodypolitics. However, there is no essential difference between the soft and hard bodies, as the soft bodies suffer similar brutal aggressions to the hard ones, like the burning of the Pillowboy, and the way ordinary pigs make the little green pig's life a misery and the farmers force him to be painted pink. This is similar to the fact that there had been no essential difference between the hard and soft dictatorships of twentieth-century Eastern Europe.

Performers of these brutal actions against the body in the stories are parents, strangers, criminals, whose situations are described with rather abstract political-historical details, if any. Some of these details come not from Katurian's stories but from the situation of the interrogation. Tupolski speaks about executions, and the way Katurian is shot without a trial refers to the dictatorial nature of the world around the cell. But the relationship between the inside and the outside is full of twists. It cannot be determined precisely how Katurian's stories are related to his fate, and whether the worlds of his stories are representations of the world outside the cell.

Diverging from the regular representational convention McDonagh structures *The Pillowman* in a way that two opposing approaches are present continuously. One of them suggests the regular representational point of view which takes life, reality as the basis and the work of art as its object of reflection. The other approach suggests that it was the stories that create and determine a secondary world outside them. The child killings in Kamenice are said to be the realizations of Katurian's tales. Tupolski looks for clues in Katurian's stories in connection with crimes committed in the town. However, these two opposing approaches do not strengthen each other, in fact on the contrary. They create a situation of insecurity in which it is mostly impossible to decide what can be understood as fact and what can be seen as fiction, and how the two relate to each other. Every significant piece of information appears in different versions, like Katurian's stories themselves are variations of other stories – for instance the short stories of Jesus, or the rat catcher – therefore it is impossible to decide about the truth, about what is made up and what is real yet there is a permanent pressure to choose the one and only correct solution, the true one from the variations offered.

The topic of acting out written stories, committing crimes on the bases of fictional works is a frequent motif of commercial films. One major type of this genre is the detective film, while another is the horror or slasher movie. Laura Eldred draws a comparison between this genre and *The Pillowman* in her essay 'Martin McDonagh's Blend of Tradition and Horrific Innovation'.[21] Drawing upon this convention McDonagh moves further away from the political. Accordingly, forming the centre of the play, the tales of Katurian are more related to a tradition spanning over centuries than to a historically and politically determined moment. Crimes committed by the police in *The Pillowman* have been committed in Western democracies as well, and the examples are too many to choose from. The dominance of narrated stories within the play's structure shows that *The Pillowman* is a 'hybridization of epic and dramatic genre conventions'.[22] The rhythm of the told and enacted stories creates a structure of Matryoska, Russian dolls.[23]

So far this paper has focused primarily on the political aspects of the play. But to sum up, or to subvert the above interpretation — and to give a twist to what has been said so far — it should rather be claimed that the most significant level of the play is neither the political, nor the personal, but the parental one. The parental sphere connects the individual to society and vice versa. And this is also the feature which relates the seemingly different world of *The Pillowman* set up in an Eastern European dictatorship to the dominant world of McDonagh's other plays located in an Irish environment.

This parental level and parent-child relationships are crucial for McDonagh's dramatic oeuvre. In *The Beauty Queen of Leenane* the middle-aged Maureen lives together with her mother Mag, they play their manipulative and humiliating parent-child games throughout the plot, which culminates in Maureen brutally murdering her mom. In *The Cripple of Inishmaan* the protagonist, the teenager Cripple Billy is the target of the stigmatization of the parental, adult world. In *The Lieutenant of Inishmore* the political subject matter dominates, but it is not just a coincidence that the psychopathically violent protagonist, Padraic, terrorizes his own father, Donny, first threatening to kill him and then forcing him to dissect three murdered military colleagues of Padraic. The motif of family violence directs us again to the representational approach.

Related to this aspect, let us refer to Polish-born Swiss psychologist, Alice Miller, who has devoted all her life to the study of child abuse and mistreatment. She writes on the opening page of her website under the title, *Child Mistreatment, Child Abuse*, that

> Humiliations, spankings and beatings, slaps in the face, betrayal, sexual exploitation, derision, neglect, etc. are all forms of mistreatment, because they injure the integrity and dignity of a child, even if their consequences are not visible right away. However, as adults, most abused children will suffer, and let others suffer, from these injuries. This dynamic of violence can deform some victims into hangmen who take revenge even on whole nations and become willing executors to dictators as unutterably appalling as Hitler and other cruel leaders. Beaten children very early on assimilate the violence they endured, which they may glorify and apply later as parents, in believing that they deserved the punishment and were beaten out of love. They don't know that the only reason for the punishments they have (or in retrospect, had) to endure is the fact that their parents themselves endured and learned violence without being able to question it. Later, the adults, once abused children, beat their own children and often feel grateful to their parents who mistreated them when they were small and defenseless.[24]

Body politics in *The Pillowman* is of a kind that originates from the parental mistreatment of children and child abuse, which practice is adopted and exercised by the oppressive forces of dictatorial governing. We see this aspect not only in Michal's and Katurian's fate, in the recollections of their childhood, but in the story of detective Ariel too. Ariel himself turns out to be a victim of child abuse. As his colleague, Tupolski, tells Katurian, Ariel was sexually abused by his father. This parental aspect and sphere is completely missing from the two Central European plays mentioned at the beginning of the present essay. Neither Mrożek's *The Police*, nor Eörsi's *The Interrogation* deal with the personal, family originated relevance of brutality, torture, and violence. These two plays focus on abstract mechanisms and logical, ideological premises, rather than on personal motivations. Both plays offer one dominant view of the depicted world, representing the modernist tradition of composition.

Including personal, domestic, social, and political levels *The Pillowman* turns out to be a more complex, multilevel work in comparison with the two other plays mentioned. McDonagh's play continuously reflects upon itself as a work of art, on the parallelism and dichotomy between telling and performing stories, and the paradoxical relationship of theatre and its double. *The Pillowman* represents a postmodern way of composition, giving up the one and only dominant author's view, and opening up relations with several traditions, works of art, texts, images, levels of representtation, etc. Body politics is just one, though a rather significant aspect of the play which includes several further ones worth examining. Eastern European totalitarianism turns out to serve more like a scenery for the issues discussed within the play for which images, use and abuse of the human body give the central trope, relating the play to contemporary tendencies of stage brutalism, a challenging and exciting form of recent European drama.

I owe thanks to Dr Mária Kurdi for her comments on the previous version of this essay.

[1] Sanja Nikčević, *Nova europska drama ili velika obmana* (Croatia: Meandar, 2005). I have used the English translation of this work, entitled 'Stupid, old fashioned or backard, or how *in-yer-face* hteatre, a violent British trend, became "New European Drama"'.

[2] Malgorzata Sugiera, 'Beyond Drama: Writing for Postdramatic Theatre', *Theatre Research International* 29.1 (March 2004): 16-17.

[3] Julia Furay and Redmond O'Hanlon, eds, *Critical Moments. Fintan O'Toole on Modern Irish Theatre* (Dublin: Carysfort Press, 2003): 160-61. Similar views have been expressed, beside others, in Mária Kurdi, *Codes and Masks. Aspects of Identity in Contemporary Irish Plays in an Intercultural Context* (Peter Lang: Frankfurt am Main, 2000): 41-55, and in Ondřej Pilný, 'Martin McDonagh: Parody? Satire? Complacency?', *Irish Studies Review* 12.2 (2004): 225-31.

[4] Clare Wallace, '"Pastiche Soup", Bad Taste, Biting Irony and Martin McDonagh', *Litteraria Pragensia* 15.29 (2005): 12.

[5] Wallace, 37.

[6] Martin McDonagh, *The Pillowman* (London: Faber and Faber, 2003): 23. Subsequent references are cited in the text.

[7] Slawomir Mrożek, *Six Plays*, trans. Nicholas Bethell (New York: Grove Press, 1967): 19.

[8] Ibid., 11.

[9] Ibid., 31.

[10] Werner Huber, 'From Leenane to Kamenice: The De-Hibernicizing of Martin McDonagh?', *Literary Views on Post-Wall Europe,* eds Christoph Houswitschka, Ines Detmers, Anna-Christina Giovanopoulos, Edith Hallberg, and Anette Pankratz (Trier: Wissenschaftlicher Verlag, 2005): 285.

[11] Ondřej Pilný, 'Grotesque Entertainment: *The Pillowman* as Puppet Theatre', *The Theatre of Martin McDonagh. A World of Savage Stories*, eds Lilian Chambers and Eamonn Jordan (Dublin: Carysfort Press, 2006): 214-23.

[12] Ibid., 214.

[13] Lisa Fitzpatrick, 'Language Games: *The Pillowman, A Skull in Connemara*, and Martin McDonagh's Hiberno-English', *The Theatre of Martin McDonagh* (Dublin: Carysfort Press, 2006): 143.

[14] Eamonn Jordan, 'War on Narrative: *The Pillowman*', *The Theatre of Martin McDonagh* (Dublin: Carysfort Press, 2006): 179.

[15] Ibid., 189.

[16] Michael Cadden, 'Violence, Storytelling, and Irish Aesthetics. A Theatregoer's Guide to Martin McDonagh', *Princeton University Library Chronicle* 68 (2006-2007): 681.

[17] The Borgesian connection is mentioned both in Huber, 287, and in Cadden, 682.

[18] Jack Santino, ed., *Halloween and Other Festivals of Death and Life* (Knoxville: The University of Tennessee Press, 1994). Quoted in http://www.snopes.com/horrors/mayhem/needles.asp (Download, 6 September 2007).

[19] Joel Best-Gerald T. Horiuchi, 'The Razor Blade in the Apple: The Social Construction of an Urban Legend', *Social Problems* 32.5 (June 1985): 488-99.

[20] Pilný, 'Grotesque', 217.

[21] Laura Eldred, 'Martin McDonagh's Blend of Tradition and Horrific Innovation', *The Theatre of Martin McDonagh* (Dublin: Carysfort Press, 2006): 198-213.

[22] Huber, 286.

[23] Huber calls it a 'Chinese-box structure', 288.

[24] http://www.alice-miller.com/index_en.php (Download, 6 September 2007).

4 | 'Suitably Relevant': Irish Drama and Theatre in the Czech Republic, 2000-2007

Ondřej Pilný

Modern Irish drama has maintained a steady presence on Czech stages ever since the early twentieth century. Authors who exercised particular influence in the vibrant theatrical culture prior to World War II included, most prominently, George Bernard Shaw, who had over fifteen plays translated and produced by the end of the 1930s and who also interacted with important Czech writers and intellectuals such as Karel Čapek. Apart from Shaw, Czech audiences enjoyed early productions of J.M. Synge, whose translations by Karel Mušek were among the first in Europe. Oscar Wilde's plays appeared in Czech as early as the early 1900s, and started to be regularly performed in the second half of the century. Translations of Wilde's dramas had moreover been preceded by the enthusiastic publication of Wilde's poetry and essays by Czech Decadents. The 1950s saw another wave of productions of Shaw, while in the 1960s it was the work of Samuel Beckett that significantly influenced young absurdist playwrights like Václav Havel, with *Godot* and *Endgame* also having major impact on ideas concerning set design and the use of space in theatre. Besides Beckett, one of the most widely discussed productions of the sixties was Brendan Behan's *The Hostage*. The 1980s and 1990s featured in turn a number of acclaimed productions of Brian Friel's plays, culminating in frequent revivals of *Dancing at Lughnasa*.[1]

My intention, however, is to examine the most recent developments, particularly in the light of the current interest of shown by Irish and international scholars in the reception of Irish drama and theatre abroad and how it has interacted with European theatre. The internationalization of Irish theatre scholarship has been most recently documented by the foundation of the Irish Theatrical Diaspora Project (2004) on the one hand, and the establishment of the Irish Society for Theatre Research (2007) on the other, whose aim it is to 'facilitate research on Irish theatre in its national and *international* contexts in terms of an engagement with the full spectrum of Irish theatre from page to stage'.[2] It may then be worthwhile to offer in this context the results of field work from a country that has avidly embraced the work of Irish playwrights spanning a number of decades.

Looking at the period between 2000 and 2007, there were over sixty new professional productions of Irish plays in the Czech Republic, out of which almost one half were Czech premieres.[3] These numbers place Ireland easily at the very top of the list of similarly sized countries, and make it approximate the number of British or American plays staged within the same period. Nonetheless, the list of plays produced makes an interesting read: the Czechs have had the entire oeuvre of Martin McDonagh on the stage (i.e., the five 'Irish' plays – most in multiple productions – and *The Pillowman*), four plays by Brian Friel,[4] three plays by Enda Walsh, two plays each by Marina Carr, Conor McPherson, J.M. Synge and two Beckett shows, and a play each by Tom Murphy, Edna O'Brien, Brendan Behan, Marie Jones, Mark O'Rowe, Geraldine Aron, Gary Mitchell and a revival of a Sean O'Casey one-act adaptation. The list may be supplemented with three plays by Oscar Wilde, two by G.B. Shaw and one by Richard Brinsley Sheridan, out of which two 'evergreens' of the Czech scene stand out in particular: *The Importance of Being Earnest* and *Pygmalion*, with a stunning record of six and four new productions within eight years respectively. Needless to say, productions of the individual dramas varied in terms of quality, critical attention, length of run, and venue (eight plays were produced at the National Theatre while, on the other hand, several others took place in fairly temporary conditions); despite that, the list certainly is revealing as regards the choices made by Czech theatres.

The eclectic structure of the record reflects very well the ways in which Irish plays reach the Czech stage. The presence of Martin McDonagh, Conor McPherson, and Marina Carr owes much to their success in London, particularly at the Royal Court Theatre, which has brought them to the attention of Czech dramaturges and/or translators. At the same time, however, the influence of the Royal Court should not be overestimated as, for instance, the most successful Czech productions of Martin McDonagh happened due to the individual effort of translators.[5] Translators' preferences seem indeed to play a major role in determining what gets produced, especially when a translator happens to have direct access to theatres looking for new material. For instance, Tom Murphy remained undiscovered by dramaturges up till the late 1990s, and it was only through the proactive approach of translator and long-time champion of Irish drama Julek Neumann that *Bailegangaire* was staged, fourteen years after its Irish premiere, as the first play by Murphy to have ever been translated into Czech. On the other hand, plays by Edna O'Brien and Geraldine Aron – surely no canonical playwrights – have received production, the former's *Virginia* even by the National Theatre; this happened again largely due to the efforts of their translator, Ivana Bozděchová, who otherwise rarely focuses on drama and acted largely on the basis of personal preference.

There are numerous additional influences and factors that affect decisions as to what kind of drama appears on the stage. First, individual directors tend to make choices that are often the result of chance discoveries. Hence, for example, the commissioning of a new translation of *The Well of the Saints* in 2001, a fascinating play but hardly one that promised to become a major hit or create a significant critical debate either. Furthermore, theatres often wish to revive a successful play from the past, especially if there is reasonable hope that it will attract larger audiences. Recent cases in point include not only the all time favourites *Pygmalion* and *The Importance of Being Earnest* mentioned earlier, but also Behan's *The Hostage* and *Bedtime Story* by Sean O'Casey. The unlikely fame of O'Casey's minor one-act has originated in the fact that a successful theatre adaptation, entitled *Penzión pro svobodné pány*, was televised in 1967 with a splendid cast and became an instant popular classic. Significant also are the practical concerns of ensembles, particularly as regards casting: one of the reasons for the numerous revivals of *Dancing at Lughnasa* by regional ensemble theatres, for instance, has been the pressing need for plays with solid multiple female roles. A similar requirement happily contributed to the production of plays by Marina Carr, notably *The Mai*. Moreover, to mention a curious instance of very pragmatic motivation (as these are, indeed, not too rare), a play happened to be produced *and* equipped with a happy ending in order to facilitate the comeback of a famous actress to the theatre: Friel's *The Loves of Cass McGuire* as staged by Divadlo na Vinohradech in Prague, starring Jiřina Bohdalová.

Occasionally, non-English productions inspire Czech practi tioners. Such was the case of *Disco Pigs*, first seen in the Czech Republic as part of a German-language theatre festival in 1999. The play received a largely negative verdict from established theatre critics, whose debate concerning the production was published in the authoritative journal *Svět a divadlo* (*World/Visegrad and Theatre*).[6] The rejection by the critical establishment was, however, swiftly followed by a translation and a marvellous, innovative production of *Disco Pigs* by theatre students, who included in the programme brochure an irreverent, witty collage of the earlier negative comments of their supposed mentors interspersed with reactions by Pig and Runt, characters from the play.[7]

Finally – although this tends to be regrettably rare – new productions happen due to the initiative of a funding body: it was a translation workshop organized by a theatre agency together with the British Council in 2006 that commissioned translations of Northern Irish playwrights Christina Reid, Owen McCafferty, Gary Mitchell, and Daragh Carville. The workshop was concluded by rehearsed readings of the plays to an audience which included dramaturges, directors and critics, followed by a public debate with Reid, Carville, the translators of the plays and their supervisors. As a result, *In a Little World of Our Own* by Gary Mitchell was given production within a few months, and the work of Owen McCafferty came to the attention of a dramaturge who initiated a staging of *Shoot the Crow* (forthcoming from Západočeské divadlo, Cheb in 2008).

The critical reflection of Irish drama productions has been limited largely to reviews in *Divadelní noviny* (a theatre bi-weekly), national dailies and regional press, with only a handful of articles (nine) in specialized periodicals,[8] complemented by two brief overviews of Irish drama past and present.[9] While in all the publications the authors and/or their plays tend to be designated as Irish,[10] the denomination hardly ever prompts general statements about the 'Irishness' of a particular piece, and rarely serves as an explicit marketing tool either. The one exception to the rule may seem to have been the 2004-2005 'Irish Season' inaugurated in December 2004 by four Prague theatres; nonetheless, the project consisted simply of discount offers for tickets to plays which had already been running, and made little attempt to market the plays as a consistent whole, not even by using 'Bord Fáilte' imagery of Ireland to enhance the sales. Accordingly, the 'Irish Season' was never reviewed or reflected upon as a whole.

What is interesting about the little analysis Irish drama has had from Czech critics as a distinct phenomenon is that apart from a few lines emerging in articles on *The Weir*, *Bailegangaire*, *The Mai*, and plays by Synge, almost all attempts at a definition were triggered by the work of Martin McDonagh. As indicated above, McDonagh unmistakably belongs among the most frequently staged non-Czech playwrights of the last decade. Furthermore, productions of *The Lonesome West* and *The Lieutenant of Inishmore* became the recipients of prestigious national theatre awards, reflecting both the critical and the popular success of McDonagh.[11] Scholars and reviewers were then naturally prompted to muse on the reasons for such astonishing success.

The general agreement has been that what was of particular appeal to Czech audiences was the dark humour, conventional theatrics, well-craftedness, and a 'sheer delight in fabulation',[12] manifest in McDonagh's plays, with all these elements combined in a world that may be viewed as a microcosm which bears a universal message regarding postmodern reality.[13] Vladimír Mikulka, author of two extended articles on the playwright, has noted in addition that despite his ostentatious provocations, the amazingly gifted McDonagh has in fact provided a welcome counterbalance to 'in-yer-face theatre' (called 'theatre of coolness' by Czech critics), as his world-view is essentially conservative, the plays are moralities of a kind, and he does not share the 'parlour socialism' of Mark Ravenhill and other 'cool' authors. In Mikulka's words, McDonagh deliberately ignores or ironizes topics which seem to make his generation tick: 'He does not write about drugs, homosexuality, women's emancipation or ethnic minorities, and does not seem to be concerned about the supremacy of the capital, the alienated social machinery or the mendacious media and politicians; his characters get drunk, lie, murder and swear in a traditional, old-fashioned manner.'[14] As a result, Mikulka argues, perhaps with a touch of irony directed at the unadventurous Czech theatre-goer, McDonagh may be acceptable to a wider audience than the politically and theatrically rather alien 'cool' wave.

It is only very recently that overtly negative assessments of McDonagh have emerged, spurred at least in part by the playwright's ubiquity in Czech theatres: in a review of *The Pillowman* titled 'So Young and Already English!' the playwright was accused of gratuitous, violent provocation used merely to highlight his own greatness, with the reviewer concluding: 'A question begins to germinate as to what remains after the steam over fresh blood has cooled down and the favoured spectator has recovered his/her senses...'[15] A later review of *Howie the Rookie* by Mark O'Rowe has added a scathing comment concerning the 'cheap neoruralist idylls' of Martin McDonagh, to which the raw urban tales of O'Rowe are endlessly preferable.[16] Such voices, however, still remain very much in the minority, and McDonagh continues to hold sway with most commentators and audiences alike.

Many features that were found to be typical of McDonagh have besides been designated as characteristic for the success on the Czech stage of Irish drama as a whole. The best summary has perhaps been provided by Milan Lukeš, professor of theatre studies and translator: modern Irish drama abounds in black humour, 'pleases by its traditional treatment of the categories of plot, character, time and space and fascinates the spectator by its solid structure. It seems suitably relevant but at the same time local enough for it to be pushed aside, if the worst came to the worst, as being "far-off after all."'[17] This outline converges rather well with the observations of most Irish and international critics on the nature of canonical Irish drama. According to Lukeš, the Czech audience, moreover, 'savours with a certain degree of nostalgia the provincial and rural framework' in an Irish play due to what has been a tradition of popular success of rural drama in the Czech lands. And last but not least, in a comment that clearly reveals what kind of Irish plays have travelled well in Europe, the politics of Irish drama is seen by Lukeš as especially pertinent to the contemporary reality since, from Synge on, 'the exquisite Irish ... have born a particular animosity against the so-called values of the Irish national character: they surely know well what they are talking about, having experienced the risks and horrors of nationalist and religious zeal and hatred'.[18] Irish playwrights, in other words, are viewed as deliberately engaged in subverting ideologies of collective identity. This observation on the anti-nationalist and anti-sectarian slant of a lot of Irish drama seen on Czech stages is supported by other commentators as well. What has been noted in specific terms are the apparent reformulations of fervent patriotic ideas that have taken place since the times of Brendan Behan,[19] in the sense that Behan's revaluation of Republicanism has been replaced by wild mockery. A specific element of the satirical treatment given to nationalism has moreover been identified as ironizing stereotypical Irish and English political attitudes, particularly by playwrights like Martin McDonagh.[20]

The broad consensus concerning the characteristics and the merits of Irish drama that may be found in the regrettably limited number of critical analyses has been broken by a single voice only. Věra Ptáčková, stage design expert and theatre commentator, was fairly explicit when writing about *Bailegangaire* and *The Weir* as regards her puzzlement by the need to stage Irish authors whose greatest strength lies, according to her, in providing an opportunity for emotional identification with characters who suffer from 'ordinary, invariably repetitive weaknesses' in situations analogous to those experienced by the spectators in their private lives. In Ptáčková's view, Irish drama serves well the current theatre practitioners and audiences who, alike, crave for genuine emotional experience, instead of being involved in the much more laudable enterprise of employing their imagination under the strain of Brechtian alienation effects.[21] This may be quite a revealing comment too, especially given the manifest lack of political drama productions in Czech theatres on the one hand, and the highly competitive environment in which dozens of theatres strive to attract a limited number of spectators on the other. Nonetheless, Ptáčková's argument is bound to be undermined for most readers by the indiscriminate national stereotyping featured in her articles, which has the Czechs cast as 'commonsensical' and the Irish as 'excited and irrational'.[22]

What is of more significance from the perspective of comparative criticism is the fact that up to date, not a single Czech critic has attempted to make the tempting, but at heart quite spurious analogy between the Irish and the Czechs as postcolonial nations trying to cope with the legacy of British and Soviet (or the earlier Austro-Hungarian) oppression respectively. Not even after Czech productions of plays such as Friel's *Translations*, where the only person prone to characterize the play's relevance in a post-colonial sense seemed to be the American director of an English-language staging of *Translations* in Prague (1997), Nancy Bishop.[23] There is nothing surprising really about the lack of relevance felt as regards colonial subjugation on the part of the Czechs: despite the three centuries spent under Habsburg monarchs, the existence of Czech culture and language has never been significantly threatened. Czech had always been widely spoken, notwithstanding that German became the language of the upper classes, and unlike Irish, had never had to face extinction. More recently, the Soviet dominance over communist Czechoslovakia, though indubitable and drastic, had its own characteristics that were again very different from the British rule over Ireland: despite the poisonous modification of the Czech and Slovak cultures through aggressive, all-pervading ideology and censorship, the Soviet rule never deprived the country of its formal independence and languages. All in all, there may be simply just a widely shared feeling by Czechs of affinity with Ireland as a small country adjacent to powerful neighbours. This sentiment, however, hardly ever creates a need to propose any deeper parallels between national histories and cultures. What this means in terms of Irish drama productions and their reception is that although Irish plays get widely performed in the Czech Republic, and occasionally are discussed by critics as a distinct phenomenon, they hardly ever get analysed as the output of a nation. If anything, Irish drama tends to be viewed rather in comparison with its British, Czech and/or European counterparts.

ꕤ

In contrast to Irish plays and playwrights, contact with Irish theatre practice has been virtually nonexistent. Apart from a single guest performance by the Abbey Theatre in Prague in 2001,[24] it was only at the Prague Quadrennial in June 2007 that Czech theatre-goers, practitioners and critics had a real opportunity to learn about how theatre is done in Ireland. The 2007 participation was the first ever for Ireland in the Quadrennial, the world's largest exhibition of stage design and theatre architecture which celebrated its fortieth anniversary this year with a total involvement of sixty countries.[25] Ireland's comprehensive exhibit, initiated by critic and theatre scholar Cathy Leeney and curated by lighting and set designer and director John Comiskey, was conceived very much in accordance with the fact of this being the very first time Irish theatre practice went on display on such scale and in such a broad international context. Its main part was titled 'Firing the Canon: Masterworks Revisited in Modern Ireland' and displayed over forty stagings produced in Ireland in 2003-2006, mainly of canonical works, as reflected by the title.[26] The structure of the exhibition was among the more conservative ones, showing predominantly photographs and costumes, but it also offered a most welcome opportunity to watch clips from numerous performances and listen to a dozen original sound designs for plays. The body of work was complemented by a minimalist section on theatre architecture and an exhibition of students' work.

Although Ireland was not unique in opting to show a broad range of what inevitably had to be snippets of productions, a radically different approach was adopted by many countries. For instance, the immediately adjacent display of Hungary, entitled 'Liliom in Baghdad', featured a performative aspect and was aimed at making the visitors think about the nature and position of theatre in the contemporary world, rather than presenting a record of achievement. In order to see the Hungarian exhibition, the visitor had to obtain a mock-photographic ID, go through a security check and wait in a line, watching seemingly random samples of scenographic work interspersed with other footage on a TV screen. When finally reaching an official counter, positioned at what appeared to be the door to the exhibition proper, his/her ID was stamped with a sign of official rejection, followed by being immediately shown out. Seemingly focused on a canonical balladic play turned famous American musical, the Hungarian section spoke rather about indulgence, and generally the politics of theatre in a globalized world characterized by ubiquitous control and the power of bureaucracy. Admittedly, the chief drawback of this form of presentation was that the visitor learnt very little about the actual theatre practice in Hungary.

Apart from their introductory purpose, the authors of Ireland's exhibition at the Prague Quadrennial hoped to demonstrate that while their country has traditionally been famous for its playwrights, many of whom it has 'exported', and has been living on 'visual and scenographic influences from abroad',[27] many changes have taken place within the last decade. In the words of Helen Meaney, 'The long-celebrated literary tradition has been infused with a new understanding of what it is possible to create in a performance space – and of what constitutes a performance space.'[28] Moreover, the Irish theatrical community has been growing increasingly vibrant and international, prompting John Comiskey to assert that 'we are an island in geography only'.[29] These objectives were well met, judging by the warm reception that Ireland's participation in the Quadrennial has had, as exemplified by a feature article written for a major national daily by Vlasta Gallerová, a respected Czech dramaturge and theatre critic. Gallerová highlighted Ireland's exhibition as a genuine revelation and went on to say that its surprising richness was in fact quite logical as it merely came to reflect the momentous change the society and its theatre had recently gone through.[30]

Notwithstanding that, Comiskey and his team have high expectations still as to how Ireland's international presentation may enhance its practice of theatre: calling the event 'a landmark moment' for Irish theatre,[31] the curator expressed his hope that a debate would commence on 'how best to nourish talent and develop education in th[e] sector' of stage design, as there are still no full-time courses in Ireland.[32] Cathy Leeney has added a more general wish concerning the expected stimulation of Irish theatre practitioners and students by their participation in the Quadrennial exhibition and programme activities.[33] While it naturally is too early to judge the actual practical outcome, and a single event must surely not be overestimated, it is worth point out that the process should work in two ways: the swift developments in Irish theatre that have been happening in an atmosphere of soaring economic development are more than worthy of detailed examination by practitioners elsewhere, and perhaps particularly in Central and Eastern Europe.[34]

---

1 For details of translations, see 'Czech-Irish Relations: A Bibliography of Books and Articles', an online database maintained by the Centre for Irish Studies at Charles University, Prague. <http://ualk.ff.cuni.cz>

2 Cf. the Irish Society for Theatre Research website. <http://www.istr-ctae.org/>. My emphasis.

3 See the appendix to this article for a detailed list.

4 This, however, includes a guest performance at the Prague National Theatre of *Translations* by the Abbey Theatre (14 October 2001).

5 See Clare Wallace, 'Irish Theatre Criticism: De-territorialisation and Integration', *Modern Drama* 47.4 (Winter 2004): 666. The translator and director of acclaimed productions of *The Lonesome West* and *The Pillowman* claims to have been prompted to read Martin McDonagh by an article in *Time* magazine. The present writer, who translated *The Cripple of Inishmaan*, produced in quick succession by four different Czech theatres, obtained an early copy of the play originally due to its parodic treatment of Robert Flaherty's film *Man of Aran*.

6 'Zázrak a magie divadla' [The Miracle and Magic of the Theatre], *Svět a divadlo* 11.1 (2000): 42-44.

7 Lukáš Trpišovský, 'SADOmasoDISCOkoláž', programme brochure for Enda Walsh, *Disco Pigs* produced by DISK – Divadelní studio DAMU, 2002: 25-28.

8 Věra Ptáčková, 'Ti zvláštní Irové' [Them Strange Irish], *Svět a divadlo* 12.2 (2001): 59-64, 'Příběhy z jiného světa?' [Stories of Another World?], *Svět a divadlo* 13.3 (2002): 56-60; Milan Lukeš, 'Irská zabijačka' [The Irish Butchery], *Svět a divadlo* 13.3 (2002): 61-70; Vladimír Mikulka, 'Martin McDonagh: Z Londýna do Prahy (přes Irsko)' [Martin McDonagh: From London to Prague (via Ireland)], *Kritická příloha Revolver Revue* 25 (March 2003): 30-42, 'Tak trochu jiný McDonagh' [McDonagh Slightly Different], *Revolver Revue* 62 (2006): 238-41; Kristina Žantovská, 'Irský Inishmore na Smíchově' [The Irish Inishmore in Smíchov], *Svět a*

divadlo 15.2 (2004): 43-47; Pavel Trenský, 'Nihilistova přitažlivost' [The Attractivity of the Nihilist], *Svět a divadlo* 15.4 (2004): 40-52; Clare Wallace, 'Irish Theatre Criticism: De-territorialisation and Integration', *Modern Drama* 47.4 (Winter 2004): 659-70; Matouš Lázňovský, 'Irská čerň a česká šeď?' [Irish Black and Czech Grey?], *Svět a divadlo* 16.6 (2005): 24-30. Main source: the *Bibliography of the Theatre Institute* (*Divadelní ústav*) *in Prague*, 28 August 2007 <http://www.divadelni-ustav.cz/kpsys_biblio.asp>.

9 Ondřej Pilný, 'Proměny irského dramatu 1950-1999' [Transformations in Irish Drama 1950-1999], Conor McPherson, *Na cestě duchů* [The Weir] (Praha: Národní divadlo, 2000): 4-24. See Milan Lukeš, 'Šíleně šikovní a šikovně šílení Irové' [The Madly Skilful and Skilfully Mad Irish], *Druhý břeh* 1.3 (2003): 17-20.

10 The labelling of *Shoot the Crow* by Owen McCafferty a 'Scottish situational comedy' in an announcement of a forthcoming 2007-2008 premiere by Západočeské divadlo in Cheb represents a unique blunder; 28 August 2007 <http://www.divadlocheb.cz/main.php?sess=pripr>.

11 *The Lonesome West* translated and directed by Ondřej Sokol at Činoherní klub in Prague was awarded an Alfréd Radok Prize for Best Play 2002, the director received both the Alfréd Radok and the Thalia Prizes as 'Talent of the Year', and the production has been running for over 100 nights now. *The Lieutenant of Inishmore*, translated by Milan Lukeš and directed by Daniel Hrbek at Švandovo divadlo na Smíchově, Prague, was awarded an Alfréd Radok Prize for Best Play of 2003.

12 Lukeš, 'Irská zabijačka', 62. All translations from Czech sources are mine.

13 Cf., in particular, Trenský, 41-42.

14 Mikulka, 'Martin McDonagh: Z Londýna do Prahy (přes Irsko)', 34-35.

15 Alexandra Berková, 'Tak mladý a už Angličan!', *Divadelní noviny* 14.14 (6 Sept. 2005): 2.

16 Petr Šourek, 'Plačky nad rozlitými bojovými rybkami' [A Wake over Spilled Fighting Fish], *Nový prostor* 288 (20 August 2007): 26. This is a review of a guest performance of the Slovak theatre Kontra in Prague.

17 Lukeš, 'Irská zabijačka', 62.

18 Ibid.

19 Žantovská, 47.

20 Mikulka, 'Martin McDonagh: Z Londýna do Prahy (přes Irsko)', 38.

21 Ptáčková, 'Ti zvláštní Irové', 59, 63.

22 Ibid., 64, 62.

[23] Nancy Bishop in a conversation with the present author, Spring 1997.

[24] See note 2 above.

[25] For more information, see the Prague Quadrennial website, which features also an archive of all previous events: <www.pq.cz>.

[26] A catalogue with plenty of visual material was edited by Lian Bell, *Ireland PQ07* (Dublin: Ireland PQ07, 2007): 128 pp.

[27] Helen Meaney, 'The Spaces between Words', *Ireland PQ07*, 10.

[28] Meaney, 10.

[29] John Comiskey, 'Welcome to Ireland's First Participation in the Prague Quadrennial', *Ireland PQ07*, 8.

[30] Vlasta Gallerová, 'PQ jako jedno velké divadlo' [PQ as One Big theatre], *Lidové noviny* 21 June 2007.

[31] John Comiskey, quoted in Sara Keating, 'All the World's a Set Design', *The Irish Times* 12 June 2007.

[32] Comiskey, 'Welcome to Ireland's First Participation', *Ireland* PQ07, 9.

[33] Cathy Leeney, 'Connecting and Connected', *Ireland PQ07*, 7.

[34] I would like to express my gratitude to John Comiskey and Ian Devine for providing me with printed materials on the Irish participation at the Quadrennial.

Appendix: List of Irish Plays Produced in the Czech Republic, January 2000 – December 2007[i]

Geraldine Aron	*My Beautiful Divorce* (Můj báječný rozvod)	trans. Ivana Bozděchová	Viola (Praha), 2003*
Samuel Beckett	*Dramaticules*	trans. Josef Kaušitz	Činoherní studio (Ústí nad Labem), 2002*
Samuel Beckett	*Krapp's Last Tape* (Poslední páska), together with Marcel Mihalovici's opera version	trans. František Vrba, Přemysl Charvát	Národní divadlo (Praha), 2003
Brendan Behan	*The Hostage* (Rukojmí)	trans. Michael Žantovský	Pidivadlo (Praha), 2006
Marina Carr	*The Mai* (Maja)	trans. Jan Hančil	Divadlo F.X. Šaldy (Liberec), 2001*; Jihočeské

			divadlo (České Budějovice), 2004; Národní divadlo moravskoslezské (Ostrava), 2003; Východočeské divadlo (Pardubice), 2007
Marina Carr	*By the Bog of Cats* (U kočičí bažiny)	trans. Blanka Křivánková	Moravské divadlo (Olomouc), 2006*
Brian Friel	*Translations*		Abbey Theatre on tour (Národní divadlo, Praha), 2001
Brian Friel	*Dancing at Lughnasa* (Tanec na konci léta)	trans. Ota Ornest	Pidivadlo (Praha), 2002; Slezské divadlo (Opava), 2003; Divadlo na Prádle (Praha), 2003; Městské divadlo Zlín, 2004
Brian Friel	*The Loves of Cass McGuire* (Lásky paní Katty)	trans. Jiří Josek	Divadlo na Vinohradech (Praha), 2004*

Brian Friel	*Afterplay*	trans. Zdena Hadrbolcová	Divadlo Na Zábradlí (Praha), 2004*
Marie Jones	*Stones in His Pockets* (Plný kapsy šutrů)	trans. Jitka Scoffin-Bendová	Divadlo Rokoko (Praha), 2003*
Martin McDonagh	*The Beauty Queen of Leenane* (Kráska z Leenane)	trans. Lenka Kapsová	Středočeské divadlo (Kladno), 2004; A studio Rubín (Praha), 2005; Jihočeské divadlo (České Budějovice), 2006; Divadlo na Vinohradech, 2006
Martin McDonagh	*The Lonesome West* (Osiřelý západ)	trans. Ondřej Sokol	Činoherní klub (Praha), 2002*; Národní divadlo (Brno), 2003; Západočeské divadlo (Cheb), 2007
Martin McDonagh	*The Cripple of Inishmaan* (Mrzák inishmaanský)	trans. Ondřej Pilný	Divadlo v Celetné (Praha), 2002*; Jihočeské divadlo (České Budějovice), 2005; Západočeské divadlo

			(Cheb), 2006; Moravské divadlo (Olomouc), 2006
Martin McDonagh	*The Lieutenant of Inishmore* (Poručík z Inishmoru)	trans. Milan Lukeš	Švandovo divadlo na Smíchově (Praha), 2003*; Divadlo J.K. Tyla (Plzeň), 2005; Aréna (Ostrava), 2007
Martin McDonagh	*The Pillowman* (Pan Polštář/ Pán polštářů)	trans. Ondřej Sokol	Činoherní klub (Praha), 2005*; Národní divadlo moravskoslezské (Ostrava), 2005
Martin McDonagh	*A Skull in Connemara* (Lebka z Connemary)	trans. Julek Neumann	Švandovo divadlo na Smíchově (Praha), 2007*
Conor McPherson	*The Weir* (Na cestě duchů)	trans. Jan Hančil	Národní divadlo (Praha), 2000*
Conor McPherson	*This Lime Tree Bower* (Slaná voda)	trans. František Maxián	Divadlo Letí (Praha), 2006*

Gary Mitchell	*In a Little World of Our Own* (Náš malý svět)	trans. Lucie Kolouchová	Divadlo Letí (Praha), 2007*
Tom Murphy	*Bailegangaire*	trans. Julek Neumann	Národní divadlo (Praha), 2000*
Edna O'Brien	*Virginia*	trans. Ivana Bozděchová	Národní divadlo (Praha), 2005
Sean O'Casey	*Bedtime Story* (Penzión pro svobodné pány)	adaptation by Jiří Krejčík	Horácké divadlo (Jihlava), 2001; Divadlo A. Dvořáka (Příbram), 2007
Mark O'Rowe	*Made in China* (Made in Čína)	trans. Jiří Popel	Pražské komorní divadlo (Praha), 2002*
G.B. Shaw	*You Can Never Tell* (Člověk nikdy neví)	trans. Milan Lukeš	Východočeské divadlo (Pardubice), 2000
G.B. Shaw	*Pygmalion* (Pygmalión)	trans. Frank Tetauer; trans. Milan Lukeš	Divadlo Příbram, 2000; MDP – Divadlo ABC (Praha), 2002; Národní divadlo (Praha), 2005;

			Studio Ypsilon (Praha), 2006
Richard Brinsley Sheridan	*The School for Scandal* (Škola pomluv)	trans. Jan Hančil	Národní divadlo (Praha), 2004
J.M. Synge	*The Well of the Saints* (Studna světců)	trans. Ondřej Pilný	Švandovo divadlo na Smíchově (Praha), 2003
J.M. Synge	*The Playboy of the Western World* (Hrdina západu)	trans. Karel Mušek; trans. Vladislav Čejchan; trans. Martin Hilský	Studio Marta – JAMU Brno, 2000; Západočeské divadlo (Cheb), 2001; Divadlo v Dlouhé (Praha), 2004; Činoherní klub (Praha), 2007
Enda Walsh	*Disco Pigs*	trans. František Maxián	DISK – DAMU Praha, 2002*
Enda Walsh	*Misterman* (Pančlovíček)	trans. František Maxián	A studio Rubín (Praha), 2004*
Enda Walsh	*Bedbound* (Na posteli)	trans. Ladislav Šenkyřík	A studio Rubín (Praha), 2004*

Oscar Wilde	*The Importance of Being Earnest* (Jak je důležité míti Filipa; Není Filip jako Filip)	trans. J.Z. Novák; trans. Stanislav Rubáš et al.	Horácké divadlo (Jihlava), 2000; MDP – Divadlo ABC (Praha), 2002; Městské divadlo (Zlín), 2002; Městské divadlo (Brno), 2003; Divadlo J.K. Tyla (Plzeň), 2005; Jihočeské divadlo (České Budějovice), 2006
Oscar Wilde	*Salome*	trans. Ivo Fleischmann	Divadlo Čára (Brno), 2004
Oscar Wilde	*An Ideal Husband* (Ideální manžel)	trans. Václav Renč	Divadlo na Vinohradech (Praha), 2007

---

[i] Main source: the database of the Theatre Institute in Prague. Czech premieres are indicated by an asterisk.

5 | Brian Friel Performances in Hungarian Theatres: Problems in Theatrical Adaptation

Csilla Bertha

Adaptation of any kind – whether interlinguistic, intercultural, or intermedial – seems to have risen in estimation lately, sometimes even to overestimation. One fundamental thesis of contemporary adaptation-theory holds that adaptations are not derivative, therefore not secondary to the original, but are rather autonomous works of equal value, 'aesthetic objects in their own right [although] it is only as inherently double- or multilaminated works that they can be theorized *as adaptations*'.[1] The requirement of faithfulness to the original has therefore, become obsolete. But if 'fidelity criticism' is no longer fruitful, then what criteria might we set for a good adaptation – translation, theatre direction, or film adaptation – of literary texts? Accepting the premises that every translation and retranslation is interpretation and that a theatrical performance is a work of art in which the original written dramatic text is only one component among all the other, non-verbal, physical, material-gestural components, I still believe that a translator, a theatre director, dramaturg, stage-/costume-designer has serious responsibilities towards the author whose work s/he uses for whatever form and degree of adaptation. This issue of responsibility obviously raises many questions that I cannot answer here, such as: where are the limits to the freedom with which one can play with the original text in translation and stage direction? Who can or who has the right to judge if the adaptation does disservice to the author by falsifying the spirit, the register, the meaning of the work? How seriously does the adapter take his/her task to create a new work, which does not lower the aesthetic, philosophical, artistic level of the original? In other words, if the name and writing of an author is used as the point of departure for a new creation, what responsibilities do the users have to do justice to the original work?[2] In theoretical writings on translation and adaptation such and similar questions never seem to be asked[3] and in practice it happens far too frequently that masterpieces are turned into mediocre performances due to translators' or directors' aggressive alterations. Moreover, postmodern theatre considers fidelity to the dramatic text senseless, and the theoreticians of new theatricality even believe that it is 'wrong' to attribute an ethical dimension to transcriptions of texts or regard such transcriptions as possibly ruining the original.[4] Due to expelling the 'ethical dimension' and with that, also the value-judgment (the question whether the new transcription is of a lower artistic level than the original), concentrating only on value-free interpretation, the differences might easily disappear between poor direction and respectful but ingenious transformation of a written play into a magical theatrical experience. If a director of Peter Brook's quality 'rearranges plot events, reassigns lines, or cuts characters' – as he frequently and famously does – the resulting radical reinterpretations/-adaptations become valuable 'extended critical and creative engagements' with the text.[5] Such achievements testify to the possibility that after the theatre has freed itself from being the 'handmaiden' of the drama, instead of falling into the opposite extreme and becoming authoritative, it can become an equally important and loving, respectful partner (as the director could be to the author) in the dual existence of dramatic art.

In terms of theatrical adaptation, another issue rarely considered is that different kinds of plays lend themselves to different degrees of alteration and adaptation. Plays loosely written, with hardly any prescriptive, determined ideas about the performance encoded in the text, do allow and invite more additions from the director than highly artistically orchestrated dramatic texts. Brian Friel famously insists on his own ideas about directing his plays which usually arrive with quite precise instructions about stage design, costumes, movements, gestures, and music. His notion of a playscript as an 'orchestral score' is well known: 'I look to the director and actors to interpret that score as it is written. It is not their function to amend, it is not their function to rewrite, or to cut, or to extend. It is their function, their only function – and an enormously difficult one – to interpret what is given them.'[6]

These words of the then young playwright from 1972 sound today very old-fashioned and severe yet, as Patrick Burke argues,

> the ostensible severity of Friel's artistic animus towards directors has in fact long been tempered both in statement and in practice. In statement Friel has expressed admiration for such directors as Konstantin Stanislavsky, Jerzy Grotowski and Peter Brook. Each of them, in Friel's revealingly radical phrase, 'turn[ed] upside down the whole practice of theatrical presentation so that we saw it all anew.' In practice, Friel has worked productively, in a kind of dramaturg capacity, with such directors as Joe Dowling and Patrick Mason.[7]

Burke goes on relating how much Friel cherished what he learned from the director Tyrone Guthrie. All this indicates once again that the problem is not merely directorial intervention *per se* but its quality, and it should be judged on the basis of its aesthetic standard, in other words of its ability or willingness to produce a new work of art that is comparable in artistry to the written play.

The level of Hungarian translations and theatre adaptations of Friel varies greatly. Hungarian audiences were able to witness some high-level renderings of his plays, some honest, good performances and some quite horrendous ones. This paper aims at calling attention to a few problematic examples of Friel's performances in Hungarian theatres that raise serious questions of translation and adaptation beyond their particular cases, without attempting to give any overview of his Hungarian reception, or trying to analyze all the Hungarian productions of his plays.

The performance of a foreign play in the home culture is the result of a two-step adaptation; the first is verbal translation and the second the 'translating' of the written text into the language of the theatre, that is, directing. In the first phase the translator has to decide whether to recreate the world reflected in the play through language or to translocate the play into the home environment. Such decisions help to determine much of what the director in his/her turn will do. The transformation of the text into theatre language includes the choice of setting, props, costumes, gestures, acting style, and all the other facets of stagecraft. As a result of the several subjective filters the original play goes through, the connecting points between the source and target cultures may be either reinforced or neglected whereby familiarity or strangeness may be emphasized. The responsibility of translators and theatre-makers is all the more serious because, as is common knowledge, theatre is a special, potent means of mediation between cultures. Due to the kinship between Irish and Hungarian culture – mostly deriving from historical parallels – this mediation becomes a more sensitive issue since many Hungarian readers and theatre-goers may expect to find echoes of their own lives in Irish plays. As the world-wide respect for Brian Friel's work and the performances of his plays in countless languages bear witness, his plays speak to many small nations, especially those in a postcolonial phase or in the midst of the decolonizing process. Hungary is technically not counted among postcolonial countries, although several theoreticians suggest that it would deserve that consideration as much as Ireland.[8] Psychological, cultural, moral confusion similar to that described in postcolonial societies is certainly experienced in what is known as Hungary today, but the Hungarians' situation is further complicated due to the national tragedy that happened after World War I. In the peace treaties following the war, the new borders drawn by the great powers truncated historical Hungary, giving two thirds of its territory to neighbouring countries. The Hungarians in these territories, who then became ethnic minorities, are going through a decolonizing process after the (partial) abolition of dictatorships as they reclaim their right to use their mother-tongue and re-establish their cultural institutions, which have been under serious attacks by the governing majorities. So it comes as no surprise that many Hungarians on both sides of the present political borders feel a close kinship to the world dramatized in Friel's plays and, therefore, translations and performances of his plays bring more to Hungarian readers and audiences than just valuable pieces of world literature and culture. For the same reason, the choice of which of his plays to perform and the productions themselves are self-reflexive of Hungarian culture and theatre in more than one sense: as much in terms of ideological considerations as of aesthetics. The contradictions involved in the theatrical reception of Friel's plays are closely related to general cultural-ideological contradictions and divisions in Hungarian intellectual life.

Friel has become relatively well-known in Hungary. The first plays published in Hungarian translation appeared in anthologies and journals (*The Loves of Cass Maguire*, 1969, trans. Zoltán Papp; *The Freedom of the City*, 1973, trans. Gábor Mihályi). Three of his plays were published in a 1990 volume: *Philadelphia, Here I Come!* (trans. Béla Nóvé), *Translations* and *The Communication Cord* (trans. Márton Mesterházi). *Dancing at Lughnasa* (trans. László Upor) gave the title of a volume of contemporary Irish plays as *Pogánytánc* – 'Pagan Dance' (2003). A few of his plays were produced as radio dramas from the late 1960s on, and later performed in theatres first sporadically, then in the last decade more frequently. As is common knowledge, the choice of a play for performance depends on a great number of circumstances, reasons, people, sometimes even coincidences still, it would be interesting to speculate on why, out of the three, in the (so far only) 1990 volume of Friel's plays in Hungarian, *Philadelphia* and *The Communication Cord* were the two selected for production in Hungary whereas the third, the world-famous *Translations*, has never been produced by any professional theatre in present-day Hungary (only in Hungarian theatres outside the borders).

Tamás Koltai, the esteemed Hungarian theatre critic, comments somewhat bitterly on the absence of *Translations* from Hungarian theatres saying that because it is a very difficult play to produce, it would raise interest only in places where 'theatre consists not simply in the loud banging of fire-crackers'.[9] While I agree with him that its difficulty might be one reason for *not* producing *Translations*, it seems to me that the choice is more ideological, considering that almost every decision is politicized in present-day Hungary (even more so than in Ireland). The post-communist, post-imperial cultural confusion combined with globalization's anti-national tendencies, the dissolving of traditional communities and quick discarding of traditional values, led to moral and value crises and deep cultural conflicts which seem to divide the population and, even more sharply, divide intellectuals. The dividing line runs between attitudes to traditional national-cultural values, vaguely resembling the Irish revivalist-revisionist duality, with the huge difference that in Hungary those who hold the opinion that corresponds roughly to Irish revisionism, are even more hostile to national (and not only to nationalist) values and maintain a power-position.

Whereas university *students* and ordinary intelligent readers and theatre-goers, coming across Friel's works, and especially *Translations*, usually respond to them with an immediate recognition of familiar experiences, dangers, or concerns, most theatres tend to follow different fashions. A play about issues such as the loss of the mother tongue and with that, layers of an old culture, attitudes to that loss and to colonization in general, dilemmas of resistance to, or necessary compromises with, the foreign power, would be chosen by theatre directors who deem such values important as national identity, cultural heritage, and the survival of a community as a community. Although Hungarian theatres have a strong tradition of being concerned with such values, the majority of the leading contemporary theatres within the borders of present-day Hungary have recently, and often quite militantly, turned away from that tradition. As if to underline this point, *The Communication Cord* received more theatrical attention than *Translations*, although the former, albeit an amusing farce, is a coda or counterpoint (of a slighter weight) to the latter and gains its meaning together with its predecessor – an opinion widely shared among Friel scholars. *The Communication Cord* was produced in 1999 with the Hungarian title 'Vészfék', meaning 'Emergency Cord'. Admittedly, part of the reason for this choice could have been that a comedy is more attractive to bring to the stage than a tragedy or tragicomedy, and the play's point about the failure or lack of communication between intellectuals and the rest of the population was relevant enough to the contemporary Hungarian situation, but some reviewers, typically, used the occasion to sharpen their knives attacking Hungarian intellectuals who do treasure folk culture.[10]

Translations premiered in Hungary – paradoxically, in English – at Debrecen University (1996) in a successful student performance, under the excellent direction of Patrick Burke, guest director from Dublin. The play was well received and student enthusiasm spilled over, leading to the creation of the Debrecen University Drama Festival in English now ten years old.[11] Professional Hungarian theatres outside the borders of present-day Hungary discovered this play in the last decade: the Kolozsvár Hungarian Theatre (the Romanian name of the town is Cluj) produced it in 2000, while the Theatre of Nagyvárad (in Romanian: Oradea) in 2006.

Friel's most frequently performed play in Hungary is *Dancing at Lughnasa*, which, after its world-wide success, opened in Budapest's József Katona Theatre in 1993, then was performed in Kecskemét (1996), Dunaújváros, Sopron (2002), Szolnok (2005), and also by the Újvidék Hungarian Theatre (now in Serbia, named Novi Sad), in 2006. Somewhat surprisingly, *Afterplay* was produced as early as 2003, shortly after its original publication in 2002, under the title 'Húsz év után' [Twenty Years After]. Since Hungarian theatres look back to a long tradition of deep engagement with Chekhov's work, the Budapest studio theatre rendered this overtly Chekhovian Friel play with great sensitivity, beautifully bringing out its poetic and tragicomic qualities.

Philadelphia, Here I Come!

With my first example of a problematic Friel adaptation, the Kaposvár Csiky Gergely Theatre's 2001 production of *Philadelphia, Here I Come!* (1964), I attempt to call attention to the dangers of aggressive transculturation (or rather: trans-subculturation) in translation which then, naturally, has consequences for the stage production. This play has never been performed, to my knowledge, in its first, quite honest – if at times somewhat bookish – translation (trans. Béla Nóvé, 1990) and was retranslated by Kornél Hamvai for this production. The most obvious requirements met by the new translation must have been the practical demand to shorten the play, which Hamvai does, at considerable cost to the play, and to 'update' the dialogue, making the language more contemporary, which led to quite disastrous results.

In his efforts to abbreviate the play, Hamvai accrued a series of significant omissions that obviously resulted in changing the emphases and lightening Gar's serious dilemmas and inner fight. The repeated statements about American life's 'anonymity and facelessness' and the necessity to become 'a hundred percent American' if one emigrates, which are crucial to Gar's hesitation, are simply omitted. Abbreviations of those scenes of central importance to the father-son relationship that lies in the focus of the play, especially the omission of the nervous, hopeful, last attempts of the son to strike a common cord with his father, diminish Gar's suffering and struggle. Shortening the scene when, for the last time, he meets his beloved but now lost girlfriend again takes away the gravity of his losses and deprivations. Such interventions influence the play's character-drawing and meaning-making.

The new translator of *Philadelphia* obviously wanted to produce a fluent, colloquial, playable script but in his attempts to bring the play closer to contemporary young Hungarian audiences, he introduced radical changes in the speaking style, including vocabulary, syntax, and the level of articulacy of the characters. His transculturation seems to target only a certain social stratum, the urban, undereducated, inarticulate youth who might possibly identify with the vulgar, lumpen-style language that dominates the translated play. The protagonist, Gar, thus becomes quite different from Friel's small-town, little-educated, still often eloquent, sensitive young man who can enjoy his own ability to change styles and play language games and who remains far from the vulgarities of his Hungarian counterpart. An even worse translational misjudgement makes Madge, the elderly rural domestic help and mother-substitute, sound rather grotesque when she is given half-articulate sentences typical of uneducated urban youth. Changing the register of the language so aggressively and thereby taking away so much from its richness and flexibility is an especially serious crime in the case of a writer such as Friel, who is so particular, so careful in his use of language. Such crude transformations result in losing variety and layeredness of language as well as the games played with changing styles (since the protagonist's style remains more or less the same throughout the translated play). Hamvai's Gar sometimes resembles more closely a Roddy Doyle or Mark O'Rowe character or some of the translator's characters in his own plays than Friel's. In those plays, all of which focus on the urban lumpen layers of society, such language is, of course, legitimate and often eloquent.

Among the numerous referential problems in the translation, I will mention only two. The Hungarian title, *Philadelphia, nincs más út!* (*Philadelphia, There's No Other Way*!), instead of leaving the dilemma open to unfold in the course of the drama, as the original (and the first translation) does, already suggests the solution. Another misunderstanding had more serious, unintended consequences in the Kaposvár performance. Translating 'black Protestant' into 'black and Protestant' clearly indicates that the translator did not take the trouble to look into Irish culture and see what Catholics and Protestants call each other and how 'black Protestant' simply means the equivalent of a dirty/cursed/bloody Protestant. So, onstage, the good friend of the Irish Catholic couple became a black American, thus shifting the emphasis to racial problems non-existent in the play. Starting from this mis-translation, the director, in his turn, then compounded this gross misreading by bringing onstage an actor in black-face who, in addition, was dressed in a 'zoot suit' of harsh, vivid colours thus evoking – without apparently being aware of it – the racist image of the richly, fashionably but tastelessly dressed black who becomes almost a caricature of himself.

To find the right balance between emphasizing familiarity and otherness usually presents a dilemma in communicating a different culture in translation and on the stage:

> If the conventions of another culture are all preserved ... it might become too alienating ... but if the system of customs and gestures is entirely replaced by those of the home culture, then the otherness, the presentation of a different culture is lost from the work ... Since by emphasizing either otherness or familiarity, we also express our relation to the other, and at the same time, to our own culture and identity, this intercultural problem is worth paying attention to in the process of both translation and theatre direction.[12]

In the Kaposvár production such dilemmas did not seem to be addressed since the young director (András Léner), admittedly, did not find it important that the play was written in and about Ireland, with all the action taking place in an Irish milieu. Instead he concentrated on the process of the young protagonist as an individual growing up, becoming independent and his resulting separation from father and home – in itself, without all the complications of the time and place, not an excitingly new topic. But at least that process was successfully presented on the stage.

The dramatization of Gar's split character – his Private and Public self – worked very well, to a great extent thanks to the excellent acting of the actor playing Private Gar and to the director's inventiveness in mixing realism with surrealism in arranging the appearance and presence of the protagonist's private self. 'The normally clothed Public Gar was paired with a Private Gar always wearing black like a shadow, which interpretation was in place and not overdone, as was the trick of Private first appearing through the wall or standing in the frame of a mirror when Public looked into it.'[13] Thus, in spite of all its limitations, the performance on the whole was still quite enjoyable – a very rich play remains rich even if a lot of it is taken away.

Translations

While *Translations* (1980) is noticeably absent from the theatres in Hungary, Hungarian minority theatres in Romania have presented it in recent years. That is no surprise since Hungarians who live in the parts of historical Hungary that now belong to neighbouring countries, themselves have experienced for decades many of the phenomena and dilemmas that inform Translations.[14] As a result, the familiarity of the situations dramatized in the play sometimes proved traumatic, as, for instance, the actress acting Sarah in the Debrecen student performance in 1996, being from Transylvania 'often broke into tears while rehearsing her role', since 'the forceful changing of old placenames, the erasure of life in ancient settlements were not literature for [her] but living experience'.[15]

Translations, similarly to *Philadelphia*, also has two Hungarian translations, one by Márton Mesterházi, *Helynevek* (1990), meaning 'placenames' – which somewhat narrows the original title and its implications since the play focuses on different sorts of names and naming – and a more recent one by Erika Mihálycsa, *Fordítások* (2000) – bearing the more precise title although the plural of the noun sounds a bit strange in Hungarian. In this case, the new translation was not intended as a criticism of the earlier in any sense since it was commissioned by the Kolozsvár Hungarian Theatre without any knowledge that a Hungarian translation already existed. Mesterházi's translation tends to be very faithful to the original and has especially well-considered solutions for the Greek and Latin quotations but proves weaker in the dialogues using rural dialect, which often have the stamp of an urban speaker's strained effort to imitate villagers. Mihálycsa, on the other hand, has some difficulties in rendering the classical texts but her rural characters speak a beautiful, graphic, flavourful, Transylvanian Hungarian, which is both regional and archaic, preserving the charm of the language of a prelapsarian world, and so sounding natural from the lips of nineteenth-century Irish villagers. This is a kind of transculturation that evokes the original all the more faithfully.

The great dilemma for the translator of this play lies in the names, especially placenames. Famously, the play compresses whole colonial and postcolonial issues, occupations and their consequences, relationships between natives and invaders, tradition and modernity, attitudes towards cultural losses, the workings of personal and cultural memory, into the question of language. Within language, names and naming are foregrounded, particularly in the central metaphor of mapmaking, which involves 'Anglicizing' the Irish placenames. The play's conceit – that on the stage English is spoken although most characters actually speak in Irish – makes it clear for English-speaking audiences which names are Irish and which are English. Yet the decision about how the Irish and English placenames should be used in the Hungarian text is crucial, if complicated. Mesterházi shares some of the translator's particular difficulties in terms of these placenames:

> If I leave those [Gaelic] place names untranslated, the (Hungarian version of the) play will be about nothing. If I translate only the English place names, it is the Irish ones (the very ones outraged in their dignity) from which I estrange Hungarian readers. If I translate only the Irish/Gaelic place names, I leave pieces of English text in the play every (English) sentence of which I have translated into Hungarian. Only desperate audacity seemed to be logical here.[16]

The translator continues with the remark that 'without translating the placenames, Hungarian readers would look with Lancey's indolence at Irish/Gaelic names, and would never notice that the play is about us. About the Hungarian place names chauvinistic régimes around Hungary furiously turned into Romanian, Slovakian, Serbocroat, and so forth after the 1920 Trianon Treaty'.[17]

Mesterházi, with great care, chose beautiful old Hungarian placenames, taken from the nineteenth-century description of Transylvania by Balázs Orbán to stand for the Irish names, and translated them within the play into less graphic Hungarian placenames, which of course stand for their English equivalents. For instance, '"Bun na hAbhann" ... is "Gyöngyöstorka" (with some of the most difficult Hungarian sounds in it) for Owen, mispronounced "Dondos-tarka" by Yolland, and "Forró Föveny" ... for the Name-Book.'[18]

The new translation by Miháycsa, surprisingly, does not change either the personal or the placenames. The programme note of the Northern Irish guest-director, David Grant, informs the audience that he asked the translator to translate all the English placenames into Hungarian so that the whole scale of the process of assimilation should be perceivable, which, as he also understood, is especially poignant in Kolozsvár where it was to be produced. The translator, Mihálycsa, did do so but during rehearsals the actors found that the Hungarian names sounded too poetic and therefore the process of replacement lost some of its violence.[19] Also – and that once again, indicates cultural confusion – translator and actors thought that familiar Hungarian names would narrow the play's meanings since they would direct attention immediately to the relevance of the issue and thus would tend to identify the play too much with the Transylvanian Hungarians' own plight.[20] So, all the placenames remained in the original, which leaves problems unresolved. It certainly is understandable that translating only the English names would cause strange effects because the Irish names would remain untouched, foreign, while the names meant to be foreign in the play would sound familiar. Only if both are translated and related to each other, can the original effect be achieved. In performance, with all the names left in the original, non-English-speaking audiences probably found it hard to distinguish between the Irish and English names, all foreign, none having any meaning, although, judging from the reviews, the meanings of the play transpired clearly enough. Audiences, having lived under oppression, especially under Ceauşescu's tyranny, became well-versed in reading and hearing between the lines. The dynamic production of the Kolozsvár Hungarian Theatre offered a rewarding theatrical experience.

The Nagyvárad *Translations* was, however, the unanimous choice of the local actors precisely on the basis of its relevance to the Hungarian plight. Directed by the Scottish director, Russell Boyce, as the moving performance developed, it became tangible for the audience that the actors deeply identified with the play and were actually enacting much of their own sufferings, dilemmas, and fears. A 'moving performance' – that is, until the very end. This director, with great audacity, changed the ending, and with that destroyed the whole effect of the play. After the rather tragic, resigned closing words of Hugh the schoolmaster, acknowledging helplessness and confusion as the result of cultural dispossession and personal losses, the director gratuitously added a scene that violated the spirit of the play. The heroine, Maire, reappeared on the darkened stage, elevated above stage level in white light like an angel and began to sing in English a shallow, sentimental contemporary pop song, made famous by the Irish pop singer, Sinead O'Connor. This cheap idea left the audience puzzled. The director's aim was – as he explained afterwards – to indicate that after all the changes and losses dramatized in the play, Maire is going to become English and that's what her culture will be like. But, as is obvious, this play in itself conveys such fears of the future but in its own, resonant way (among other means, through having everybody speak in English onstage, thereby acting out the consequences of what happens in the course of the play) and still leaves some ambiguities hovering in the air. The director also wanted to lift the play out of the tragic mood, to give the audience something lighter to end with – another blatant example of condescending and underestimating the audience.[21] This directorial intrusion, employing a theatrical language totally alien to the rest of the performance, ruins the play's aesthetic integrity. Fortunately, several reviews indicated the audiences', or at least the critics', discerning judgement; most of the reviewers, while emphasizing the relevance of the issues dramatized in Friel's play to their own experience and their coming to life thanks to good acting, also condemned the director's misconceived idea of overemphasizing the love theme in that entirely inappropriate additional final scene (the love song), after the play's concluding words conveying the loss of a culture.[22]

Dancing at Lughnasa

Dancing at Lughnasa (1990), in László Upor's excellent translation, premiered in the Budapest József Katona Theatre in 1993. The performance received mixed reviews, some revealing the reviewers' total insensitivity to Friel's art while others, being too much caught up with the Chekhov-parallels, did not see or appreciate enough the particular Friel features. But, going by the opinion of sensitive theatre critics, it must have been expertly directed by Gábor Máté and a successful production with an especially well-choreographed and effective 'pagan dance'. Koltai praises, among other features, the 'organic' structuring of the performance. He may have instinctively touched upon Friel's expectation that the theatre would treat his plays as musical scores when he spoke about the ensemble as if playing a symphony, 'composed in a minor key, in accordance with Friel's basic tone', and he goes on to describe the 'particularity of floating, teasing style on the borderline between reality and surreality, which provides the remembering-poetic framework'.[23]

Other productions posed grave problems, however, and here I single out a recent (2005), outrageously misconceived rendering of the play at Szolnok (a medium-size country town in Hungary) which should be held up as an example to avoid.

This play again could have had many resonances (as all Friel's plays in Hungary), not only as a reminder of Hungarian rural life of the not-too-distant past, but also because of its severe critique of the dominant ideology that condemns the oldest layers of the native culture to be forgotten, hidden, neglected, thus limiting personal and cultural freedom and restricting life in every sense. Instead of either seeking to emphasize cultural similarities or to create an Irish atmosphere, as suggested by the dramatic text, the Szolnok performance abounds in the director's self-serving additions to the play which falsify the original atmosphere, mood, and character-drawing. The use of the theatrical space reflects the director's lack of understanding of the claustrophobic, closed-in world and entrapment of the play's Mundy sisters in their communal isolation. Instead, he positioned them separately, isolated each in one of the studio theatre's four corners with the audience in the centre. Many 'theatrical' moments occur as simple visual gags, adding nothing to the play, only cheapening some of its features as, for instance, a used condom hanging from Rose's neck, instead of the little silver fish-shape pin that she has received from the man she went to see – a crudely outspoken indication of the girl's seduction, the possibility of which was only hinted at in a much more ambiguous and subtle way in the text (an effect similar to the onstage masturbation of Gar in the Kaposvár *Philadelphia* which unnecessarily spells out his adolescent behaviour and desires). Conceiving the figure of Father Jack as an ebullient, huge, strong madman who would laughingly dance around with Kate, his prudish sister thrown over his shoulder while patting her backside, shows poor taste, at least, and ignorance of the text, at worst. The narrator munching a large sandwich on stage as he tinkers with the Marconi before Act II is only superfluous but his cycling onto the stage in the concluding scene to deliver a banal last sentence never written by Friel – announcing that he had bought himself a bicycle – is far more harmful. Friel's famous final monologue brings back the atmosphere of the play's beginning in a cyclical manner, dissolving into memory the bitterness and despair of the tragedies that happened in between. This beautiful, poetic meditation on language, music and dance and their interrelation – an extremely theatrical problem – and on the nature, function, changing quality of memory, all woven together in an undulating rhythm of words and movement, becomes an unforgettable scene in a good performance. In Szolnok, in place of Friel's ending, the audience had to be satisfied with the narrator on his bicycle, until suddenly a céilí band was heard playing Irish dance music first offstage then moving onstage to play jigs and reels joyfully for about ten minutes after the end of the play. The age-old problem struck again: the director (Máté Szabó), while lacking the sophistication to understand the play's subtleties, wanted to be more clever and inventive than the playwright and forced his own poor taste on the underestimated audience.

A counter example, a fine production of *Dancing at Lughnasa*, was given by the Újvidék Hungarian Theatre in 2006. They chose to bring this production to various Hungarian and international theatre festivals. Demonstrating a deep understanding of Friel's play, they conveyed its atmosphere, tragic sense, combination of warmth and despair in a coherent, well-structured, imaginative performance. The whole production managed to strike a good balance between familiarity and the otherness of another culture, without over-emphasizing either. The director's, Sándor László's most noticeable inventive addition to the written text suited the spirit of the play: the narrator Michael often walked around among the characters of his childhood's memory invisible to them – somewhat like Private Gar does in *Philadephia*.

The most recent *Lughnasa* performance in Hungary was a shortened version presented by students from the Institute of Technology in Sligo at the Debrecen University Drama Festival in English, May 2008. Although an English-language performance, it warrants attention here because of its excellent acting and outstanding direction by Ágnes Pallai. This production utilized a seemingly simple, unassuming manner which brought out unexpected depths of sadness and tragedy from such young actors together with the playfulness of many of the work's comic aspects in an emotionally, psychologically, and historically many-layered performance.

Conclusion

Because of the affinities between Irish and Hungarian history and culture it is all the more sad to see how such good opportunities to deepen cultural understanding and appreciate excellent works that abound in qualities familiar to our own culture are sometimes missed or worse, misused. Not deliberately, but usually due to selfishness, arrogance and/or carelessness and ignorance on the part of either or both translators and directors. These few examples are, by far, not enough to draw sweeping conclusions and they certainly are not meant to be representative of all Hungarian theatre life. Yet if such subtle, complex, highly thought-provoking and emotionally challenging plays, written with extremely refined language-sensitivity as Friel's, are sometimes devalued by poor directorial decisions and dragged down to a much less complex, cheaper artistic level, if such careless or aggressive attitudes are tolerated, sometimes even hailed as 'innovative', if audiences' tastes and expectations can be so offensively underestimated, that tends to indicate that the theatrical culture of the country is of a very mixed artistic standard and too often misses the humility with which the greatest artists relate to art itself. Such performances, needless to say, do serious disservice to the playwright and introduce him to Hungarian audiences as a lesser talent than in reality. Which takes us back to the original question of artistic and moral responsibility. And the question remains unanswered: who has any power to stop (aesthetically, artistically) unfair representtations of a writer's oeuvre, or is anything and everything allowed in the name of artistic freedom? Is any – even if poor, cheapening, uninformed – reading of a play manifest in a stage production, acceptable?

While the dilemmas presented by the potential conflict between author's and director's theatre would be too large to consider here, I will only echo Peter Brook's belief that an inventive director is best when using his/her inventiveness in the service of the best staging of a play, not in showing off his/her own ideas, jokes, gags at the expense of the play's integrity.[24] There may be consolation in the knowledge that the plays themselves remain with us, and, hopefully, with theatrical fashions changing yet again, they will find in the future responsible and imaginative directors who will bring them to new life in their real splendour and produce theatrical adaptations that reach standards equal to the written text.

---

[1] Linda Hutcheon, *A Theory of Adaptation* (New York and London: Routledge, 2006): 6. Italics in the original.

[2] Although I am aware that words such as 'falsification', 'intervention', 'doing justice' themselves relapse into seeing adaptations as secondary to the original, I believe that even when we talk about the dialogue between works in different media, that is, dramatic text and theatrical performance, we must not forget that the latter could not

exist without the former for it is to the original that it owes its existence, or, at least, its inspiration.

3 I once asked a young dramaturge if at the Hungarian Academy of Acting and Directing they ever discussed the issue of, or at least ever heard the phrase, 'moral responsibility' towards the author, the work, the aesthetic standard of the written play during their studies. The answer was an unambiguous and definite 'no', never.

4 Árpád Kékesi Kun, *Tükörképek lázadása* [Rebellion of Mirror Images] (Budapest: Kijárat, 1998): 98-99.

5 Hutcheon, 39.

6 Brian Friel, *Essays, Diaries, Interviews: 1964-1999*, ed. Christopher Murray (London: Faber and Faber, 1999): 44-45.

7 Patrick Burke, 'Friel and performance history', *The Cambridge Companion to Brian Friel*, ed. Anthony Roche (Cambridge: Cambridge University Press, 2006): 118.

8 See, for instance Stephen Howe, *Ireland and Empire* (Oxford: OUP, 2000): 236. Having survived four hundred years of Austrian Habsburg imperial rule and more than forty years of Soviet domination, in addition to losing two thirds of historical Hungary's territory (as a result of the Paris Peace Treaties moving the political borders around after World War I) to neighbouring countries, which then exercised different degrees of cultural genocide in treating the new ethnic Hungarian minorities, would, I believe, qualify as a version of colonial experience.

9 Tamás Koltai, 'A Marconi-táncosok' [The Marconi Dancers], *Élet és Irodalom* 14 January 1994: 12.

10 Kövér Tamás, 'Ágendák és derogációk Európából' [Agendas and Derogations from Europe], *Sopron* 2 (1999): 89.

11 A professional production of *Translations* was brought to Hungarian audiences by the Abbey Theatre on their European Tour in 2001 when they gave guest performances in Budapest's Víg Színház. Since only two of their excellent performances took place, and they obviously were in English, they could not, unfortunately, reach a wide audience.

12 Magdolna Balkányi, 'Az irodalmiság és színháziság viszonyáról' [On the Relation of Literariness and Theatricality], *Debreceni Disputa* 5. 1 (2007): 11. My translation.

13 Mária Kurdi in Mária Kurdi and Csilla Bertha, 'Hungarian Perspectives on Brian Friel's Theatre after *Dancing at Lughnasa*', *Druids, Dudes and Beauty Queens*, ed. Dermot Bolger (Dublin: New Island, 2001): 175.

[14] For instance, as recently as the 1970s-1980s it was not allowed to publicly use the old Hungarian place names (incidents related to that issue, unfortunately, still occur in the Romania and Slovakia of the European Union!) or to register a Hungarian name for a new-born baby; sometimes even names on headstones in old Hungarian cemeteries were overwritten by Romanian names; schools were transformed into Romanian, Slovakian or Serbian language ones, collections of Hungarian folk art and church archives were confiscated and disappeared by Romanian authorities or, in some regions, it was forbidden to use Hungarian even in the church as a result of which those Hungarians lost their sacral language. The aim was to assimilate forcibly the Hungarians into Romanian or Slovakian or Serbian culture and society and this way to get rid of any complication or embarrassment caused by the existence of ethnic groups.

[15] Csilla Bertha in Kurdi and Bertha, 'Hungarian Perspectives', *Druids, Dudes and Beauty Queens,* 177.

[16] Márton Mesterházi, 'Translations into Hungarian', *Brian Friel's Dramatic Artistry,* eds Donald E. Morse, Csilla Bertha, and Mária Kurdi (Dublin: Carysfort, 2006): 112.

[17] Ibid.

[18] Ibid.

[19] David Grant, '*Progamme Notes*' to Brian Friel, *Fordítások* [Translations], Kolozsvári Állami Magyar Színház, 2001/2002: 8.

[20] Erika Mihálycsa, oral communication.

[21] It is only frost on the cake that Maire's name was pronounced as Mary so the poor girl was Anglicized (probably unintentionally) from the beginning – a rather annoying discrepancy among all the Irish-named characters.

[22] See, for example, Gálovits, Zoltán. 'Szerelemmel elnyomott ősi város' [Ancient City Oppressed by Love], *Reggeli Újság* 21 Feb. 2006, 3 Jan. 2008. <http://elozo.szigligeti.ro>.

[23] Koltai, 12. My translation.

[24] Peter Brook, Lecture at the Dublin Theatre Festival, 5 October 2007.

6 | Irishness or Otherness: Two Irish Versions of *Uncle Vanya*

Zsuzsa Csikai

Virginia Woolf, one of the earliest critics of Russian writers, when analysing the spirit of Russia and her literature, attempted to account for what she saw as the inability of the English, despite all their enthusiasm, to understand Russian literature, especially Chekhov. She believed that it was due to the difference between the two civilizations, namely, that their civilization bred into the English 'the instinct to enjoy and fight rather than suffer and understand',[1] suffering and understanding used to sum up the features of the Russian psyche. Following her train of thought, one starts to ponder whether the Irish, having to deal with the legacy of colonization, have more in common with the Russian character implied above, which might partly explain the huge popularity of Chekhov among contemporary Irish dramatists, many of whom created new versions of some of his major as well as minor plays or are greatly influenced by them in their own original work. Woolf's idea, though perhaps a summary observation, seems to be justified by Brian Friel, himself an enthusiastic adaptor of classic Russian writers, who explained the attraction Chekhov's figures held for him making the cautious remark that they are not unlike members of his own generation in Ireland, behaving 'as if their old certainties were as sustaining as ever'.[2]

It is not only Friel, sometimes labelled as 'the Irish Chekhov', however, who is attracted to the Russian master. In Ireland, within a wider tradition of rewriting and retranslating European classics, there is a relatively recent trend of reworking Chekhov's plays. A number of the outstanding figures of contemporary Irish play-writing have a Chekhov adaptation or two to their names. Both Brian Friel and Frank McGuinness created versions, or new 'translations', of *Three Sisters* and *Uncle Vanya*; Friel made an adaptation of *The Bear*, a vaudeville, and he also adapted for the stage a short story, *Lady with the Lapdog* under the title *The Yalta Game*, and in his final, most extreme adaptation, *Afterplay*, he used two Chekhov characters from *Three Sisters* and *Uncle Vanya*; Thomas Kilroy's adaptation transposed *The Seagull* into late nineteenth century Ireland; Tom Murphy produced a version of *The Cherry Orchard*. Obviously, a lot more lies behind this fervent retranslating activity than the often mentioned, supposed affinity between the two nations.

Irish history has always positioned the Irish at a crossroads of cultures and languages, which meant that these cultures had to negotiate meaning continuously, making Ireland a translating nation in the widest sense of the word. As Robert Welch puts it:

> for certain cultures, the Irish amongst them, translation is a crucial activity. There are obvious reasons for this, in that before the nineteenth century to speak of Irish culture is to speak of a different language and entirely different ways of seeing. Irish culture, for two hundred years, has in this very obvious sense, been in the business of translating itself to itself and to the outside world'.[3]

One might add that it is also busy translating the outside world to itself and, notably, into its own language, English as it is spoken in Ireland.

When it comes to importing literatures, certain contemporary Irish authors seem to feel an urge to refuse the intermediary role British culture and British Standard English have all too often played in this field. They set out to produce their own Hiberno-English versions of texts with the aim of replacing or updating the already existing and available Standard English translations. The abundance of new translations and rewritings of European classics of literature carried out by contemporary Irish authors and translators during the last two decades, let it be the literatures of Ancient Greece, Scandinavia or Russia, may very well be accounted for by this strong intention to counteract the still felt need to oppose the dominance of Standard English and to define Irish theatre in a European rather than an Anglo-Irish context.

The motivations to produce versions and adaptations, all of them in intersection with the already mentioned cultural-political one, range from a felt affinity with the original author on the translator's side (as it is pronouncedly true in the case of Friel's involvement with Chekhov), or even to ensure a certain kind of authentication for the audience. Thomas Kilroy's thoroughly Hibernicized adaptation of Chekhov's *The Seagull*, for instance, was commissioned by the London Royal Court Theatre with the aim of bringing it closer to its contemporary English audience by, seemingly paradoxically, having it relocated into Ireland. Discussing Irish dramatists' adaptations or translations of Chekhov (originally for English audiences), Michael West claims that, 'Irishness has come to signify authenticity on the stage', and that 'the Irishness makes the Russian more real: this is Chekhov in English, but not an English Chekhov'.[4] It should be noted that English translations and productions of Chekhov's plays have long been generally perceived by literature and translation critics as highly problematic. The way the early translations presented Chekhov first to the British (and consequently to the Irish) audiences had a long lasting effect of distorting the plays as well as Chekhov's image as a writer. The plays' political, historical and cultural contexts were generally ignored, which created an apolitical, sentimental, 'sorrowing evocation of a valuable way of life gone forever',[5] as Vera Gottlieb warns. Not only was Chekhov turned into an honorary Englishman by his translators and producers, but along with the erasure of his Russianness, his comic genius and his use of irony were lost too, to be discovered only recently. It is these features that the Irish versions tend to restore especially successfully.

Although the motives for retranslating/reworking Continental classics, Chekhov among them, are varied, it seems that one of the important contexts for this intense activity of rewriting masters of world literature can be seen as a decidedly political act of resisting standard English influence in the name of the 'decolonization process of the imagination'[6] that Friel and the Field Day Theatre company called for, and of which Friel's *Uncle Vanya* (1998) (his second adaptation of a major Chekhov play, first produced at the Abbey directed by Ben Barnes) is a telling example. However, a completely different emphasis discernible in the retranslation of the same text by a member of a younger generation, Frank McGuinness, suggests that there is a shift away from the agenda of this trend towards a more relaxed intention to embrace internationality in Irish drama.

In the discussions of these Irish versions of Chekhov, as well as other adaptations and reworkings of classics, there is a prevailing terminological uncertainty. No consensus seems to be achieved whether they should be regarded as 'translations', as the authors and critics often label them, and neither is it clear what the terms their authors use to describe them really mean: 'versions', 'after Chekhov', 'a new translation', etc. Some critics find fault with what they see as a certain incorrectness in the application of the term 'translation' to these rewritings. Heinz Kosok, for instance, draws attention to the fact that it 'is not uncommon among Irish critics' that they 'regard the numerous plays by Continental dramatists that have recently been seen on the Irish stage as straightforward renderings of the originals',[7] even though it is well known that the dramatists creating these versions do not speak a word of the source language in question and they work from so called literal translations produced by professional translators.

Most of the time however I also opt for the use of the term 'translation strategies' when discussing Friel's and McGuinness's rewritings of *Uncle Vanya*, although neither of them is translation proper, but rather, adaptation. Referring to them as translations appears to be problematic not only because of the dramatists' lack of any knowledge of Russian, but also due to the considerable distance between the source text and the target text in both cases. My choice of terminology can be justified, however, firstly, by using the terms 'translation' and 'translation strategy' in a wider sense, as obviously, each translation is to some extent an adaptation and vice versa, and the two cannot be conceived as direct opposites since we cannot pinpoint where translation ends and adaptation starts. In contemporary translation studies there is a fading away of the dividing line between translation proper and adaptation, which is implied by Michael Cronin's observation that 'the translation discourse surrounding contemporary work is explicit in its disavowal of literalness'.[8] Secondly, adaptations employ widely used, accepted translation strategies, so when discussing the processes of adaptation it is logical to refer to them as translation strategies. Finally, the fact that the linguistic aspects of translation have been overshadowed in recent decades by its cultural aspects brings adaptation from the periphery closer into the centre of attention within translation discourse. Gideon Toury argues, when giving his broad definition of translation, that 'a translation will be any target language text which is presented or regarded as such within the target system itself, on whatever grounds'[9] and this is exactly the case concerning works by the representatives of the rewriting activity in Ireland.

Although Friel's and McGuinness's versions of *Uncle Vanya* are part of the same tradition of intercultural transfer in Irish theatre whereby foreign classics are retranslated by prominent playwrights, they exhibit great differences in the strategies employed. In fact, they demonstrate two contrasting approaches to translation that dominate much theoretical writing: the foreignizing and the domesticating approaches.

As translation theorists Susan Bassnett and André Lefevere argue, 'translation, like all (re)writings is never innocent: there is always a context in which the translation takes place, always a history from which a text emerges and into which a text is transposed'.[10] Exploring these contexts, or underlying ideological assumptions, and the ways they shaped and informed these two dramatists' versions of the Russian play, might shed some light on certain changes in the way in which Irish theatre culture conceives of itself.

For Friel, the context that both defines and explains his translation strategies is that of intellectual decolonization. His retranslation amounts to a kind of postcolonial resistance to the cultural dominance of Britain when his retranslation challenges the already established Standard English translations, refusing the idea that classics can be heard exclusively in English translations in Ireland. In effect, his aim is to reappropriate a foreign classic for the Irish stage and audience. When making his first version of a Chekhov play, *Three Sisters* (1981), he was explicit about his intention to reclaim Chekhov from a British theatre tradition that anglicized him and to reappropriate Chekhov for an Irish audience in an Irish voice, and thus to establish aesthetic independence in Irish theatre. His version of *Three Sisters* intended to contribute to what he called 'the decolonization process of the imagination', which he saw as 'very important if a new Irish personality is to emerge',[11] and his *Uncle Vanya* seems to have been inspired by this ambition as well. As a result, Friel's first two Hibernicized, domesticated versions of Chekhov have a particular quality: there is a subtle strain of 'cultural imperialism' (not wholly unlike in the case of the thoroughly domesticated, earlier British translation of the plays) or, as Fintan O'Toole prefers to call it, there is an 'attempt at a benign colonization'.[12]

Although McGuinness, a playwright of the younger generation, said he had a similar agenda in his own translation of *Three Sisters* in 1990, his later, 1995 translation of *Uncle Vanya*, which was actually the swan song for the Field Day Theatre Company, demonstrates a difference in approach. Not surprisingly, the play is translated into English as it is spoken in Ireland; however, there are certain elements transferred from the original to the target text that introduce different voices which may very well sound foreign, strange to an Irish audience. It is the work of a playwright who says in connection with his numerous other versions of classics, that he finds it a great liberation to work with a multi-cultural cast outside Ireland, with a mixture of accents and voices. McGuinness has reworked not only Chekhov, but a wide range of European theatre classics from Ibsen to Lorca, and with these retranslations and also by creating intertextual links between them and his own works, he attempts, as Eamonn Jordan observes, 'to introduce different voices and echoes into Irish drama and to give his plays an open European dialectical consciousness'.[13] McGuinness's version of *Uncle Vanya*, which is at points noticeably foreignized, seems to fit into that project.

Whether the strategy of acculturation or that of foreignization is favoured in the process of translation is not a result of arbitrary choices. Behind each word the translator chooses, adds or leaves out, and the way she or he places them, there is, as Roman Alvarez and Carmen-Africa Vidal claim, 'a voluntary act that reveals his history and the socio-political milieu that surrounds him; in other words, his own culture'.[14] Lefevere argues similarly when he says that translation 'can tell us about the self-image of a culture at a given time, and the changes that self-image undergoes'.[15] My point is that Friel's and McGuinness's differing approaches to translation, in their varying emphasis on acculturation, stem from how they perceive the state of theatre in their country and their own role in shaping the Irish cultural landscape.

Although both Friel and McGuinness undeniably created Irish versions, their translations are quite far from each other on the sliding scale of acculturation. At one extreme on that scale there is no attempt whatsoever made 'to acculturate the source text that may result in the text being perceived as "exotic" or "bizarre"' and there is a 'middle stage of negotiation and compromise, and finally ... the opposite pole of complete acculturation'.[16]

Brian Friel's retranslation of *Uncle Vanya* is a product of linguistic acculturation, as it clearly privileges the target language and audience as he produces a Hibernicized and modernized version. He infuses the play with Irishisms, as well as allusions to contemporary Irish reality. As a result, the play becomes Hibernicized and effectively politicized, and thus it is channelled towards new meanings for contemporary Irish audiences. Besides, his assimilation of stylistic aspects of his own plays through numerous additions, cuttings and the altering of linguistic structures, makes it not only a more Irish but a more Frielian play as well. On the whole, he manipulates not just words, but structure and context, and thus the authorship of the translator becomes rather visible.

McGuinness, in contrast, takes quite a few steps into the opposite direction, away from domestication. Instead of a consistent strategy of bringing the original closer to the target audience, he regularly turns towards the source text and source culture, producing a version, which, in line with the Schleiermacher model of translation, respects the strangeness, or otherness of a text, emphasizing the importance of – at least to some extent – preserving the 'foreignness' of the original in the translation. For one thing, McGuinness follows Chekhov's text extremely closely, strictly retaining the structure on all levels. Also, in his rendering of such important elements as idiomatic language and terms of address and endearment, he negotiates a kind of foreignness, oscillating between a sense of the native, the familiar and the foreign. He does not conceal the labour of transference from source to target culture. At points, his Chekhov has a voice that sounds alien, unfamiliar to the receiving language, thus it is not so much the authorship of the translator that becomes visible, but the act and the fact of translation.

The following examples demonstrate how the translation and adaptation strategies applied by the two dramatists bring about these effects. As for the linguistic structure, Friel radically alters it by changing, omitting and adding a great deal. For instance, he changes the typically Chekhovian structure of dialogues when he tends to cut up longer speeches into lively, fast paced conversations, repartees. As well as this, statements are often turned into questions, and a multitude of question tags is introduced, which actually feature rather heavily in Friel's own original plays. The resulting fast-paced, more natural sounding conversations together with the extended lines infuse the play with a sense of Irish verbosity, love of speech. McGuinness, however, follows the original text almost line by line, leaving the structural features of the original intact.

Chekhov

(1)

ELENA. I was told that you love forests very much. Naturally, it must be awfully useful, but doesn't it hinder your real vocation? Since you're a doctor.

ASTROV. Only god knows what our real vocation is.

ELENA. And is it interesting?

ASTROV. Yes, it is interesting (...).

ELENA. You are

McGuinness

ELENA. Yes, I was told you were very keen on forests. I know it's excellent work, but does it not hinder your real vocation? Aren't you a doctor?

ASTROV. God alone knows what's our real vocation.

ELENA. Is it interesting?

ASTROV. The work is interesting (...).

ELENA. You're

Friel

ELENA. Sonya tells me you're passionate about trees.

ASTROV. Am I?

ELENA. But medicine is your real vocations, isn't it?

ASTROV. Is it?

ELENA. It interests you more?

ASTROV. Medicine?

ELENA. Forestry.

ASTROV. Maybe.

(....)

ELENA. It's just that you are a young man—

still a young man, by your look ... well, 36-37 years old, and it must be that it is not as interesting as you say. I think it is dull/monotonous.[17]	still a young man. Thirty-six, thirty-seven, that's what you look. It cannot be as interesting as you say. Forests everywhere — I imagine it must be monotonous. [18]	**ASTROV**. Is thirty seven young? **ELENA**. All right – you're ancient. But I'd have thought that even at your time of day there might be something more exciting in your life than – sitka spruce. A government plantation hasn't exactly the ring of a fun-fair, has it?[19]

Apart from changing the linguistic structure, some other specific alterations that Friel carried out also create intertextual links between this Chekhov version and his earlier translation of *Three Sisters*, as well as some of his own plays. For instance, he adds the theatrical device of the soliloquy of the split self, which was first used in *Philadelphia, Here I Come!* and later re-emerged in almost all his adapted plays. In *Uncle Vanya* both Elena and Vanya have their self-addressing monologues.

> **VANYA.** Why didn't you fall in love with her ... ? I don't know why you didn't, Vanya. I don't understand that. She would be your wife now...you would enfold her in your arms, and you would whisper to her ... (35).

> **ELENA**. ... And listening to you, Elena, I suspect you're not altogether immune yourself. Why are you smiling? Vanya says you have mermaid blood in your veins, doesn't he? ... you're too cowardly and timid. Even though you know in your heart why he comes here every day now, don't you? Oh, yes, you know very well. So really you should be asking Sonya to forgive you, shouldn't you (52)?

McGuinness in his close translation does not carry out any significant additions or omissions. In Friel's version, however, such alterations are a striking feature. Friel's own lines, added to the original, usually enhance the comicality and the irony inherent in the speeches and strengthen character motivation. Also, even more importantly, his numerous added lines often have the power to raise subtle associations with modern Irish history. One instance is the translation of the Russian word '*pustosh*'. It means an uncultivated patch of land, and is rendered by McGuinness in an explanatory translation as 'a field lying empty' (11). Friel however, expands its meaning, and places it in a more politicized context for the Irish audience: he talks about 'that old squabble about the common ground' and a 'discussion document' (20), which, as Cassandra Fusco claims, may serve as allusions 'to the endless, fruitless discussion and procrastination associated with the Northern crisis'.[20]

It is a change of words at the end of the play, however, where Friel most emphatically revitalizes Chekhov's words in the Irish context. In the original, Sonya comforts Vanya with promises of rest, which are, accordingly, translated by McGuinness as 'Rest, we'll rest. Angels, we'll hear them ...' (90). But in Friel's rewriting, instead of rest, Sonya significantly promises peace, and in the added lines she assures the audience that 'all the terrible things we've had to endure ... will be swept away in a great wave of mercy and understanding' (86). She repeatedly pleads: 'Endure. And peace will come to us' (86). This is where the play – in Fusco's words again – culminates in 'a contemporary plea for mercy and peace',[21] which in the context of the relatively recent events of the break-down of the 1994 ceasefire, and the 1998 Good Friday Agreement, amounts to making a 'comment upon the surrounding political malaise' and is 'encouraging individual strength'.[22]

In transposing texts from one culture to another, the treatment of culture-specific elements requires careful consideration. One difficulty posed by Chekhov's texts is that they abound in the typically Russian terms of endearment and terms of address which, in general, would sound rather outlandish if rendered into English, because of their high frequency and the way they are used. McGuinness, however, instead of resorting to omission, renders visible this cultural difference between the source and the target language: he transposes the culture-specific elements into his version, but hardly ever in idiomatic, natural-sounding English phrases. For instance, in his translation, the old servant woman calls her master, the professor, 'little lamb' and 'my loved one';

Elena, a young enchanting city woman, also addresses both Vanya and her stepdaughter, Sonya, as 'my loved one'; Vanya talks about his dead sister as 'my own loved one' and 'sister, loved sister', and in turn, Sonya addresses him as 'my loved, good uncle'. Most of these endearments have either a somewhat laboured tone to them in English, or sound colloquial in an exaggerated way. The phrase of address, 'my loved one', for an Irish audience might evoke its Irish equivalent (a grá, a stór), which, if noticed, can serve as another, hidden indication that translation is taking place. Preserving the multitude of Russian endearments is an act of acceptance and conservation of cultural difference. Indeed, the decision itself to translate, as opposed to simply eliminating such elements of the original, indicates the translator's intention to draw attention to the texture of the language of the original work, to try and convey the flavour of the foreign text, to bring awareness that the process is a translation from another culture. Friel, however, in the spirit of domestication, applies the strategy of omission: he does not even attempt to preserve any of these terms, making sure they do not become a hindrance in the flow of natural sounding conversation.

Similarly, in the case of sayings and idioms, McGuinness's strategy of negotiating between foreignness and familiarity results in a text that seems at points to deliberately jolt the audience out of their experiencing a transparent, natural sounding English. In his version, familiar Hiberno-English phrases alternate with un-idiomatic expressions. Irishisms like 'that's the times that are in it' (4), 'himself, the professor' (4), 'it's yourself, is it?' (28), 'put the heart crossways in us' (78) and 'eejit' (75) are side by side with highly stylized phrases, like: 'It's not willed they live here' or 'will you close your mouth?' (23); or when the two young women drink to their friendship: 'We are as one, you and I?'; or 'she sees her grave with one eye, and the other sees a brave new world' (6). Such unidiomatic expressions come from the mirror translation of Russian sayings, like in yet another instance when McGuinness opts for the literal translation of the Russian phrase 'you're shaking, you'd think the frost bit you' to describe someone shaking with terror. This would hardly be the phrase a native speaker of English would use in a similar situation. This mixing the familiar and foreign seems to be a violation of what Lefevere and Bassnett call 'the textual grids' that a culture makes use of, that is, 'the collection of acceptable ways in which things can be said'.[23] It conveys a sense that the translator is generating a self-consciously odd, estranged, formalized, stylized effect: as if reminding us that it is a work of translation from a foreign tongue and from a hundred years ago.

The different treatment of Russian literary allusions by the two playwrights is also rather telling. McGuinness preserves all the literary references, not only to Gogol's *The Government Inspector* and Turgenev's works, but also to more obscure names, like Batyushkov, Ostrovsky and even translates lines of Russian poems, which, for the Irish, unlike for at least some of a Russian audience, would not carry any associations or meaning; as an effect, they only strengthen the sense of experiencing an exotic, alien culture. Friel, however, in line with his strategies of domestication, completely omits these Russian literary references, whose connotations would be lost on Irish audiences.

As seen in these examples, Friel's domesticated, reappropriated version relocates the alien source material within the cultural experience of the new target audience in terms of not only its language but also its thematic resonances. While updating and Hibernicizing the language, he restores the play to its original, rougher, more immediate and comic mode, and by introducing subtle allusions to the reality of contemporary Ireland, his achievement is that the play has a resonance with its audience similar to the one the original might have had with its own. Thus, while slanting the culture of origin towards the receiving culture, he manages to do what Michael Cronin sees as a task 'to do interpretative and aesthetic justice to the source text'.[24]

McGuinness, with his strategy of making the text oscillate between the familiar and the foreign, creates a language that is not quite transparent, which hints at its being a translated language, which, according to George Steiner, has the status 'of unhousedness, of elucidative strangeness'.[25] By conveying some of the otherness of the original, having his Chekhov speak with a voice that is different, other, McGuinness's version gives one the feeling that in terms of his translations of classics, he has started breaking away from that trend of Irish 'cultural imperialism', or cultural colonization, benign or not, which tends to represent the

Russian experience as a double to the Irish one. Instead, he restores some of the foreignness/otherness of Chekhov's world, which might indicate that the need for reappropriating foreign classics is now felt less urgently by Irish dramatists. It also demonstrates an opening to a larger scale of other voices in Irish theatre. As McGuinness himself explains in an interview with Joseph Long, for him, creating versions 'is the mark of a new confidence in Irish theatre, that we are not frightened to do that. We no longer need to assert that we have a right to do these plays, we take it for granted, of course we do it'.[26]

The ever-changing nature of theatre with its central tradition of continuous reinterpretation, allows it to welcome various idiosyncratic translations and adaptations. These two *Uncle Vanyas* show that each new translation, like each new production, as Carol-Anne Upton argues in her work on theatre translation and adaptation, 'involves a unique set of artistic and pragmatic choices. The result need not claim to be definitive, as long as it finds a voice in which to speak with resonance to its target audience'.[27] Both Friel's version, which shows Russia as Ireland's counterpart, and McGuinness's one, which shows Irish audiences some of the otherness of Russia, have a good chance for this.

---

1 Virginia Woolf, 'Modern Fiction', *The Gender of Modernism: A Critical Anthology,* ed. Bonnie Kime Scott (Bloomington: Indiana UP, 1990): 633.

2 Brian Friel, '*Seven Notes for a Festival Program* (1999)', *Essays, Diaries, Interviews: 1964-1999*, ed. Christopher Murray (London: Faber and Faber, 1999): 179.

3 Robert Welch, *Changing States: Transformations in Modern Irish Writing* (London: Routledge, 1993): ix.

4 Michael West, 'Authentic Fictions', *Irish Theatre Magazine* 4.16 (Autumn 2003): 18.

5 Vera Gottlieb, 'Chekhov in Limbo: British Productions of the Plays of Chekhov, *The Play out of Context*: *Transferring Plays from Culture to Culture,* eds Hanna Scolnicov and Peter Holland (Cambridge: Cambridge University Press, 1989): 164.

6 Quoted in Marilynn J. Richtarik, *Acting Between the Lines*: *The Field Day Theatre Company and Irish Cultural Politics 1980-1984* (Oxford: Clarendon Press, 1994): 120.

7 Heinz Kosok, 'Cracks in the Jug: Recent Translations/Adaptations of Continental Plays by Irish Dramatists', *Drama Translation and*

Theatre Practice, eds Sabine Coelsch-Foisner and Holger Klein (Frankfurt am Main: Peter Lang, 2004): 99.

[8] Michael Cronin, *Translating Ireland*: *Translation, Languages, Cultures* (Cork: Cork University Press, 1996): 182.

[9] Quoted in Maria Tymocko, 'Connecting the Two Infinite Orders: Research Methods in Translation Studies', *Crosscultural Transgressions-Research Models in Translation Studies II*: *Historical and Ideological Issues,* ed. Theo Hermans (Manchester, UK: St. Jerome, 2002): 15.

[10] André Lefevere and Susan Bassnett, 'Introduction: Proust's Grandmother and the Thousand and One Nights: The "Cultural Turn" in Translation Studies', *Translation, History and Culture,* ed. Susan Bassnett (London and New York: Pinter Publishers, 1990): 11.

[11] Richtarik, 120.

[12] Quoted in Eamonn Jordan, *The Feast of Famine*: *The Plays of Frank McGuinness* (Bern: Peter Lang, 1997): 120.

[13] Jordan, 120.

[14] Roman Alvarez and M. Carmen-Africa Vidal, *Translation, Power, Subversion* (Manchester, UK: St. Jerome, 1996): 5.

[15] André Lefevere, 'Translation: Its Genealogy in the West', *Translation, History and Culture,* ed. Susan Bassnett (London and New York: Pinter Publishers, 1990): 27.

[16] Susan Bassnett, 'Still Trapped in the Labyrinth: Further Reflections on Translation and Theatre', *Constructing Cultures*: *Essay on Literary Translation,* eds Susan Bassnett and André Lefevere (Clevedon: Multilingual Matters Ltd. 1998): 93.

[17] Anton Chekhov, *Dramaticeskie proizvedeniâ*, *1889-1904*, vol. 2 (Leningrad: Iskusstvo Leningradskoe Otdelenie, 1985). Translated by author.

[18] Frank McGuinness, *Uncle Vanya*: A version by Frank McGuinness (unpublished manuscript): 12-13.

[19] Brian Friel, *Uncle Vanya*: *A version of the play by Anton Chekhov* (Loughcrew: The Gallery Press, 1998): 21-22.

[20] Cassandra Fusco, '*Uncle Vanya* (1887-1998) "A contemporary Plea for Mercy and Grace"', *Etudes Irlandaises* 26.1 (2001): 43.

[21] Ibid., 33.

[22] Ibid., 50.

[23] André Lefevere and Susan Bassnett, 'Where are we in Translation Studies?', *Constructing Cultures*: *Essay on Literary Translation,* eds Susan Bassnett and André Lefevere (Clevedon: Multilingual Matters, 1998): 5.

[24] Cronin, 185.

[25] Quoted in Jordan, 95.

[26] Joseph Long, 'Frank McGuinness in Conversation with Joseph Long', *Theatre Talk: Voices of Irish Theatre Practitioners,* eds Lillian Chambers, Ger Fitzgibbon, and Eamonn Jordan (Dublin: Carysfort, 2001): 306.

[27] Carole-Anne Upton, *Moving Target: Theatre Translation and Cultural Relocation* (Manchester, UK: St. Jerome, 2000): 9.

7 | Lajos Kossuth and Michael Davitt, Turin, 1885[1]

Carla King

On 24 January 1885, the Irish nationalist, agrarian reformer and journalist, Michael Davitt (1846-1906), paid a visit to the exiled Hungarian leader, Lajos Kossuth (1802-1894), at his apartment on the Via Dei Mille, in Turin. This paper will discuss their meeting and use it as a starting-point from which to compare the men, their politics and their ideas. In terms of their lives – both leaders making their living from public speaking and journalism, and their characters – proud, hard-working, independent-minded men – there are similarities to be drawn. In political terms, too, their nationalism was combined with liberalism and both had links specifically to the Radical wing of British liberalism. However, this paper will also examine their differences, comparing the social and political *milieux* in which they functioned, and asking whether dissimilarities in their approaches to nationalism may also be attributed to developments in European politics between the middle and the final decades of the nineteenth century.

Like so many other European states, Ireland also experienced a revolution in 1848, but while Hungary's war of independence was the longest-lasting and bloodiest of the mid-nineteenth century European revolutions,[2] the Irish rising was a small and almost farcical failure, whatever revolutionary potential there might have been in the country being dissipated by the effects of the Great

Famine.[3] And while Kossuth was leading the Hungarian revolution, Davitt's family, small tenant farmers in Mayo, on the impoverished western seaboard, were struggling with the failure of the potato crop and eventually evicted in 1850, when he was four years old. This formative experience was to remain a motivating force in his lifelong opposition to landlordism. The family emigrated to the town of Haslingden in the industrial north of England, where Davitt, at the age of eleven, lost his right arm in a factory accident. He was sent back to school for two years by a charitable mill owner, following which he worked in a post office-cum printing establishment, spending his evenings reading in the Haslingden Mechanics Institute. It is there that he probably learned of Kossuth from newspapers such as *Reynolds' Political Instructor* or in Holyoake's *Reasoner* or in the *Manchester Guardian*. Kossuth's most enthusiastic reception on his arrival in Britain in 1849 had been in Manchester, the nearest city to Haslingden, (twenty-nine kilometres apart) where half a million people turned out to greet him. The infant Davitt had not yet arrived in England but no doubt in his youth would have met people who had attended the Kossuth events.

Another link was Chartism. The peak of the movement had passed by the time Davitt was of an age to be interested in politics, but the English Chartists, strongest in the north of England, had been prominent in support of Kossuth and were also interested in the Irish Question.[4] The Irish-born Chartist, James Bronterre O'Brien had been part of Kossuth's British network in the 1850s and wrote about him in *Reynolds' Political Instructor* in 1849.[5] Kossuth, in Gregory Claeys's words, 'was a powerful symbol of resistance to oppression and of the right of subject nationalities to survive within empires dominated by other countries, as Hungary was by Austria'.[6] No doubt the young Davitt would have drawn comparisons with Ireland.

At nineteen, Davitt joined the Irish Republican Brotherhood, a secret revolutionary organization dedicated to overthrowing British rule in Ireland, by force of arms if necessary. He became involved in smuggling guns to Ireland and was arrested on the platform of Paddington Station in London in 1870, and sentenced to fifteen years' hard labour, of which he served over seven. Following his release, in 1877, he founded and led the most successful agrarian organization in Irish history – the Irish National Land League, formed in 1879, a body that aimed to resist evictions arising from non-payment of rent. Ireland was experiencing an agricultural depression with farmers unable to pay rent to their landlords. The Land League was innovative in several ways: adopting new tactics, such as mass peaceful mobilization, and was closely linked to a newly assertive Irish representation in the British Parliament, led by Charles Stewart Parnell. The movement rapidly evolved from campaigning for lower rents to demanding the overthrow of landlordism and its replacement by peasant proprietorship. For a while it looked as if the country might become ungovernable and the British government fought back with the imprisonment of over 1,000 Land League leaders, including both Davitt and Parnell. On their release in May 1882, in accordance with an agreement reached with the British Prime Minister, W.E. Gladstone, Parnell moved to end the land movement, putting the emphasis on winning Home Rule for Ireland, rather than pursuing what had been a radicalizing land struggle. Davitt was outraged, later commenting:

> It was the vital turning point in Mr Parnell's career, and he unfortunately turned in the wrong direction. He had hitherto been in everything but name a revolutionary reformer, and had won many triumphs at the head of the most powerful organisation any Irish leader had at his back for a century. He now resolved to surrender the Land League and to enter the new stage of his political fortunes as an opportunist statesman.[7]

While Parnell and his followers moved to the right politically, Davitt's trajectory was leftwards. Shortly after his release from prison he declared himself in favour of land nationalization rather than peasant proprietorship as a solution to the land question and he moved closer to the British labour movement and British Radicals, in an effort to win them to the support of Irish demands. This alienated him from the Irish nationalist leadership and although he remained extremely popular among the Irish population at large, relations with his erstwhile colleagues became strained and unwilling to attack them, he decided to embark on a tour abroad. It was as part of this journey that he met and interviewed Lajos Kossuth.

When Davitt visited him, Kossuth had been based in Turin for two decades and his home had become a place of pilgrimage for Hungarians and other sympathizers. Davitt came to Turin supplied with a letter of introduction from the English Radical, Joseph Cowen MP. Cowen (1829-1900) was a wealthy Newcastle journalist, owner and editor of the *Newcastle Chronicle* and a Liberal MP. He had been a Chartist in his youth and was a supporter of European revolutionaries, whom he assisted both financially and through his paper. Cowen had been an active supporter of Kossuth when he lived in Britain, fundraising and popularizing his cause.[8] Thirty years later he was also an important ally to Davitt when he was in jail in 1881-1882, tabling questions in parliament about his treatment and opposing the introduction of coercive measures in Ireland.[9]

In his notes on the visit, Davitt wrote that he had '[l]ooked forward to this int[erview] with much pleasure as K[ossuth] had been one of my favourite heroes when doing my boyish reading'.[10] Davitt first contacted Kossuth's son, who was chief engineer at SFA Italia, with his office at the railway station in Turin.[11] Cowen's letter evidently had an effect, as although Kossuth, now over eighty,[12] received few visitors, his son referred to Cowen's kindness when his father was an exile in England.[13] He immediately arranged a meeting for that afternoon at his father's apartment at No 22, Via Dei Mille, where Davitt presented himself at 2.30 pm on 24 January. He described the meeting in detailed notes now among the Davitt papers in Trinity College Dublin:

> a house, or rather a block with one common entrance, respectable in appearance & looking out upon a square with some pretensions to a small park, now covered with snow. On inquiring from the concierge which was Louis Kossuth's apartments, she told me the door next the top of first landing. The name "Kossuth" on a well-polished brass plate invited a knock at the door which was opened by a man servant who invited me into an ante-chamber very plainly furnished & hung around with a few pictures & maps. Immediately after sending in my card I was ushered into the adjoining room where seated behind a desk upon which piles of books & newspapers lay I saw the man who in '48 rivetted the attention of all Europe & who for many years after was

> received in Europe & America as an illustrious & incorruptible patriot-exile.[14]

The notes appear to have been written with the intention of publication, although as far as can be ascertained, they do not seem to have been published. Davitt described Kossuth as: 'A man about 5ft 9ins, little bent for his age of 82, hair as white as snow with beard, moderate length same color [sic]; black velvet skul[l] cap, neatly dressed in black; features calm & agreeable with blue or light gray [sic] eyes.'[15] Once again, the effect of Joseph Cowen's name in smoothing the Irishman's way is evident in Kossuth's remarks, the Hungarian leader adding ruefully, however, that by now he had been almost forgotten by the world. Davitt demurred, turning the conversation to current political and social questions in Europe. Kossuth saw the new colonial policy of Germany and Italy as an effort to divert the attention of the working classes from socialist programmes at home. He contended that Britain had managed to avoid socialism by sending its surplus population to the colonies, and that Germany and Italy were trying to follow its example in establishing empires, but that in his opinion they were too late. France he saw as less influential in the 1880s, when actually a republic, than it had been in 1848 and he ridiculed the French expedition to Tonkin, remarking 'How Bismarck must rub his hands with intense glee when seeing French soldiers, ships, treasures sent so far away from the neighbourhood of Alsace & Lorraine.'[16] This was a reference to an undeclared war with China over Tonkin that was eventually to establish for France its new Far Eastern Empire.[17]

Kossuth, very much a European liberal, rather than a socialist, seemed, according to Davitt, unwilling to discuss the purely social question but rather expressed his concern at the spread of socialist and anarchist ideas in Italy and Europe, fearing imminent revolution. 'Here in Italy', he remarked,

> there is little on the surface of political life to indicate what really exists underneath & what will explode before long. Not only socialism, such as you have described it as appearing in England, but anarchism has got a strong hold upon the minds of Italian workingmen. They have their societies in every city & propagandists in every large workshop. They talk openly of the time when the doctrines of communism will be put into

> operation & when the workers will exchange places with capitalists & property-holders in the control of the affairs of state. The same feeling is manifesting itself all over Europe. The manifold crimes that society has committed against the people – the working people – for generations seem to be generating now an epoch of retaliation & I tremble at the consequences. But I am too old to see the next great revolution and I am glad of it for it will be one with which that of 1789 will bear but small comparison in the magnitude of the interests that will go down & the changes which will be effected in European society. I am no socialist and if you were to ask me for a remedy for the evils which generate socialism & out of which the next great revolution will spring, I will tell you I have none. "God only knows the remedy".[18]

He related that King Umberto had once told him that he did not expect his son to succeed him, but that an Italian republic would soon follow. Kossuth looked to Christian doctrines, if implemented, as a solution to social problems. Davitt was a good deal more radical – he was politically on the border between radical liberalism and socialism. He numbered both constitutional and revolutionary socialists among his acquaintances and Kossuth was not to know that only ten days earlier he had met a French socialist in Paris, referred to in his notes only by his alias, 'Moses', to discuss the European socialist movement.[19]

For his part, Davitt related developments in Ireland over the previous four years and described the Land League and its role, at which his host expressed his pleasure. Kossuth recalled that while in exile in London in 1854, he had read a letter in the *Times* which despaired of the Irish problem and asked: 'who under Heaven can suggest a remedy for this ever-occurring Irish trouble?' Kossuth had responded with a letter of his own. He told Davitt:

> I was green enough to believe that this was written in sincerity & sat down to the task of writing a letter in which I described the old land system of Hungary. How, though more of a feudal character than that of Ireland, still it stirred the people to revolt against it. I next detailed the reforms which were effected in this direction through our movement of '48, and then dwelt upon the security & satisfaction which followed to the cultivation of the soil. I then advised, that as human nature was the same everywhere, the application of the same remedy to Ireland which had worked so well in Hungary &

> ventured the opinion that if it were attempted a solution of the Irish difficulty would be found.[20]

What did Kossuth mean in the parallel between his land reforms and those he advocated for Ireland? It would be intriguing to know what he referred to here, as the situations appear to have been very different. Kossuth succeeded in introducing radical and lasting reforms to the land situation in Hungary. Most notably he freed the serfs and abolished various types of feudal payment from them to landlords and the church. However, Ireland had no serfs; tithes to the church had been lifted from tenants in 1838;[21] the problem was not one of feudalism; most of the country had a fully commercialized economy and a landlord-tenant relationship based on contract. It is possible that he was advocating the introduction of peasant proprietorship and the abolition of landlordism, but this would have been more radical than what was undertaken in Hungary. Unfortunately, we may never know because his letter was never published. Having forwarded it to the *Times*, he waited in vain for its publication. His request that his letter be returned was ignored. Similar letters to the *Daily News* and *Morning Post* meeting the same fate, Kossuth had come to the conclusion that the British 'preferred to go on misgoverning the country than to honestly face the simple problem of rendering you simple justice'.[22] Kossuth does not appear to have alluded to Ireland in any of the articles he wrote for newspapers included in Éva Haraszti's collection in *Kossuth as an English Journalist*[23] and elsewhere Haraszti points out that he was cautious about criticizing English domestic policy.[24] Certainly among the forty-two citations of Kossuth in *The Times* for 1854, including several letters to the editor from him and reports of his speeches, his interest appeared to focus predominantly on Hungary, Poland and the Crimean War and in general his journalism seems to have been concerned much more with politics and diplomacy than with social issues.[25] Nevertheless, he certainly knew of Daniel O'Connell and may have had some interest in Irish affairs.[26]

In turning to Kossuth's attitude to Hungary, Davitt elicited the response that although there was no legal objection to his return, he would never now go back.[27] The old man denounced the Hungarian people's acceptance of Austrian rule in the Ausgleich of

1867, commenting: 'That which force takes away time or chance or fortune may restore: but the right which a people voluntarily surrenders is lost forever.'[28] At the end of their conversation the two parted cordially, Davitt recording that 'reverting to his exile and years and to my imprisonment and "ambitious hopes", he [Kossuth] remarked: "no matter what happens, my friend, you and I will do our duty"'. 'Duty,' Davitt remarked, 'seemed to be his highest idea of man's mission in Society.'[29]

In terms of their social background the men were far apart: Kossuth was from a gentry family; Davitt's parents had been poor tenant farmers in the underdeveloped West of the country, and later small traders in Haslingden.[30] However, there were some similarities. Both Kossuth and Davitt had made their way by their own ability,[31] achieving pre-eminence in leading their own people and earning their living from journalism (in which each of them proved innovative) and public speaking. Both men had known imprisonment and poverty – Kossuth had been imprisoned in the Bastion in Buda for three years, suffering harsh conditions and solitary confinement, while Davitt had served seven-and-a-half years of a sentence to hard labour and two further, shorter terms of imprisonment. Moreover, both were fiercely proud, unwilling to accept gifts or testimonials from followers.[32] They were each concerned about poverty and underdevelopment in their societies and were keen to extend educational provisions to the working class. They shared an interest in the economic development of their respective countries, undertaking practical measures to contribute to it: Kossuth founding an unsuccessful industrial syndicate to develop Hungarian industries, while Davitt was a founder of an (also unsuccessful) Irish Woollen Manufacturing and Export Company.

Both men had been prepared to take up arms in defence of their nations but ultimately they favoured the political course. They were liberals, sharing much of the liberal heritage of the French revolution and looking forward to a future nation to be constructed along modern lines, rather than back to any idealized view of the past. Interestingly, each of them defended the Jews in different contexts. When the revolutionary upheaval unleashed mob violence against Hungarian Jews, Kossuth and other leaders of the revolution stood out in defence of their civil rights, although as

István Deák points out, they did hope that the emancipation of European Jewry would induce the Jews to convert and assimilate.[33] Davitt had taken to the platform in London to protest against the persecution of Russian Jews in 1890 and in May 1903 travelled to Russia to investigate the Kishinev pogrom for an American newspaper group,[34] the articles and appeals that resulted attracting international condemnation of the incident and strenuous relief efforts.[35] As a follow-up to his investigations Davitt had written the fifth of his books, *Within the Pale: the True Story of Anti-Semitic Persecutions in Russia* in which he discussed the issue of anti-Semitism and the mistreatment of the Jewish population in Russia.[36] A year later, he denounced as a national disgrace the behaviour of a Catholic priest who stirred up attacks on Jews in Limerick by his anti-Semitic sermons.[37]

Although separated in age by forty-three years, Kossuth and Davitt to some extent shared a network of Radical Liberal associates, such as Joseph Cowen and John Bright who defended the Irish cause, as well as the Hungarian revolution. And both men came under sharp attack by that great defender of conservatism, *The London Times*. In October 1851, the paper came out with a leading article accusing Kossuth of personal aggrandisement and dictatorship and claiming that:

> The revolutionary character of his opinions, the self-seeking and arbitrary spirit of his administration, the enormity of many of his actions, and the extraordinary impostures he practiced with success, on a credulous and enthusiastic people, were the principal causes, not only of the frightful contest which desolated Hungary, but of the intervention of foreign crimes in the war, and of ultimate subversion of the ancient constitution of the land.[38]

The paper went on to accuse him of populism, comparing him to the Irish leader, Daniel O'Connell (a comparison that might not have displeased him).[39] A week later it accused Kossuth of coming to England 'to organize in London a permanent conspiracy against all the power of the Continent, who openly assign for the execution of their desperate project the spring of 1852'.[40] Public response to *The Times* was hostile. At least two pamphlets were issued condemning *The Times*[41] and the paper was publicly burned in demonstrations in front of the Guildhall in London, and in Birmingham.[42]

In Davitt's case, the attack was more serious, though it wasn't directed specifically against him, but against the movement he had helped to create and the leader of the Irish Parliamentary Party, Charles Stewart Parnell. In March 1887, *The Times* published a series of articles under the general heading 'Parnellism and Crime', aiming to establish a link between the Irish national movement and criminal activity.[43] And although the main body of the movement was firmly constitutional, there were incidents of intimidation and violence in the Irish countryside and the Irish-American movement did engage in dynamite campaigns in Britain, which while repudiated by the Irish nationalist leaders, were damaging to the movement. At the centre of the *The Times* allegations were several documents which purported to have been written by Parnell. These were dramatically exposed as forgeries in the course of the Commission's hearings, the forger, Richard Pigott, fleeing to Madrid where he committed suicide. The person who led the Irish movement's defence of its position was Davitt, who gathered witnesses and evidence, questioned witnesses in the hearings and himself gave lengthy evidence.[44]

So there are parallels to be drawn between Davitt and Kossuth, but there were also important differences. Perhaps the most interesting is in their nationalism. In part this may be due to a difference in their times: Kossuth was a mid-century and Davitt a late-century nationalist. Moreover, Magyar nationalism in the mid-nineteenth century was heavily dominated by the landowning gentry, and one of Kossuth's great strengths was his ability in flattering and managing them.[45] On the other hand, by the late nineteenth century Irish nationalism was driven by an upwardly mobile Catholic middle-class and was directed against an old landowning, largely Protestant elite. So the context of their actions was not the same.

Another difference is that while Kossuth had been a reluctant republican, forced into it in the Hungarian context by the intransigent attitude of the Habsburgs,[46] Davitt had been a republican from his earliest political development as a Fenian. Kossuth declared himself a republican in Marseilles in 1849, but on his arrival in Southampton, he paid tribute to 'a most glorious sight to see – your gracious Queen representing on the throne the principle of liberty ... '.[47] Davitt was no fan of the Queen,[48] (nor she of him).[49] More generally, while he was willing to settle for Home Rule – that is, an Irish parliament within a monarchy, his preferred option, of which he made no secret, was for a sovereign republic.[50]

Understandably, given the experience of the Hungarian revolution, Kossuth was far more aware of the issue of conflicting nationalisms than were nationalists in Ireland. Indeed, in the draft constitution for the future government of Hungary he published in November 1851, he pointed out the dangers of nationalism:

> The question of nationalities is the apple of discord which the cabinet of St Petersburg has thrown in the midst of nations in order to draw them under its all-disposing protection. ... In Europe the question of nationality has been thrust into the foreground and liberty will long feel the effects of this mistake. It is disastrous ... .[51]

The issue of conflicting nationalities was not new but it had been sharpened by the rise of nationalism that came to the fore in the revolutions of 1848. Kossuth and his associates, while asserting the right to a sovereign Magyar state, had tended to antagonize other nationalities of the territory: Croats, Slovaks, Ruthene and Transylvanian Romanians, and of course, the Croat army, under Josip Jelačić was to play an important part in the eventual overthrow of the Hungarian revolution. In Ireland the population was far more ethnically homogeneous. The only divisions were over class, religion and political outlook. However, it may be argued that the Irish nationalist movement also crucially underestimated the importance in the late nineteenth and early twentieth centuries, of the Protestant, Unionist opposition to Home Rule centred mostly, though not exclusively, in the industrialized north of the country. Davitt made some efforts to win over farmers in the north, especially in a campaign in 1880-1881.[52] However, they had little impact and in 1886, when the Prime Minister, W.E. Gladstone, declared his support for Home Rule, northern unionists began to voice their opposition to it, bringing forth a movement ultimately strong enough to ensure that the country was partitioned with the granting of Home Rule.[53]

In some parts of Europe, issues of land and nationalism became entwined. The land question in Hungary had been addressed by the revolutionaries partly to stave off an agrarian revolt and partly because Kossuth believed it might be possible to win over the peasants to the revolution. In Ireland in the period 1879-1882, and to a more muted degree in the decades that followed, the land movement became the engine of the national movement, the link between the population mobilized over the land issue and the Irish Parliamentary Party, pressing for Home Rule, was crucial to the relative success of each.[54]

In both countries, the appeal to the rural population brought forth new types of mobilization. Kossuth's great agitation tour in the autumn of 1848, where he called on the newly liberated serfs to fight against the invading Habsburg armies was an example of a new form of political mass mobilization, and as such unusual in the mid-century revolution.[55] Davitt's approach in Ireland, in which he mobilized tenant farmers into mass non-violent opposition to landlords, also represented an innovation in Irish politics. Ireland had, of course, experienced its monster meetings, in the time of Daniel O'Connell, in the 1840s. These were carefully stage-managed rallies in support of the Repeal of the Act of Union.[56] What occurred in the late 1870s and 1880s with the Land League and its successor organizations, was a move toward organized passive resistance. The traditional peasant weapons of what was called ribbonism in Ireland, local initiatives in the form of sending threatening letters, mutilating stock, burning down barns, and occasionally shooting the landlord or his agent was replaced by what sociologists call associational collectivities, a more modern form of action. Such bodies involve nationwide organization; in Ireland it functioned through mass meetings, with speeches reported in the press, organized boycotting of tenants taking farms from which others had been evicted, or boycotting of landlords or their agents, and similar non-violent mass action.[57]

Finally, it might be argued that Kossuth and Davitt came at the beginning and end of a stage in the history of British liberalism. Gregory Claeys has argued that Kossuth and Mazzini were important in deflecting attention away from the mass radicalism represented by the Chartist movement. In his words:

> the popularity of the Continental antisocialist republicanism of Mazzini and Kossuth helped to turn working-class radicalism back towards more traditional concerns… radical interest in the organisation of labor was diverted towards the critique of continental despotism and monarchical absolutism generally … [58]

This meant that the concerns of working class radicalism were less at odds with those of middle-class reformers than might have been the case and the coalition of interests that were represented by the Radical wing of the Liberal Party was able to survive. However, by the time Davitt was active in politics, this coalition was beginning to break down, partly under the pressure of Irish political demands on the British system and partly owing to the more assertive rise of organized labour. A distinct socialist movement began to emerge, first in the form of the Social-Democratic Federation, in which Radicals and Socialists found a voice, and in the 1890s with the emergence of the Independent Labour Party, the precursor of the modern British Labour Party. Davitt was close to both movements, although he did not throw his full support behind the Independent Labour Party until the turn of the century.[59] But practically his last political campaign was in the British elections of 1906 and he was present at the celebration of the winning of the Labour Party's first seats.

If there were important differences in the nationalism of Kossuth and Davitt, the liberal outlook they shared was being replaced in the years that followed their meeting by a decoupling of liberalism and nationalism, as nationalism became linked throughout Europe to more right-wing agendas.[60] In Ireland, this was Irish-Irelandism, which emphasized Irish language and culture, but was also chauvinistic, sectarian and virulently anti-British.[61]

The two actors in this encounter have been remembered in different ways in their respective homelands. István Deák suggests in his biography that Kossuth's legacy continues to divide Hungarians to this day: 'Those who emotionally identify with Hungary's historic nobility often feel that Kossuth betrayed his estate, while those who see the nobility as the bane of the country often feel that he betrayed the people. Radicals believe that he was not sufficiently forceful, and moderates that he was reckless.'[62] In Ireland Davitt is remembered, but only selectively. Thus he is known as a Fenian and 'the Father of the Land League', but his radicalism, his internationalism, his feminism and his close links with the British labour movement, have tended to be overlooked, at least until recently.[63]

---

1 Research for this paper was carried out with the generous assistance of a fellowship from Royal Irish Academy-British Academy Exchange Scheme and the St Patrick's College Research Fund. I should also like to thank the Board of Trinity College Dublin for permission to quote from the Davitt papers.

2 It is estimated that around 50,000 lives were lost on each side in the Austro-Hungarian conflict of 1848-1850. See István Deák, *The Lawful Revolution: Louis Kossuth and the Hungarians, 1848-1849* (New York: Columbia University Press, 1979): 329.

3 Robert Sloan, *William Smith O'Brien and the Young Ireland Rebellion of 1848* (Dublin: Four Courts Press, 2000).

4 Davitt described the Chartist leader, Ernest Jones, as 'the first man after my father whom I ever heard denouncing landlordism, not only in Ireland, but in England,' Michael Davitt, *The 'Times'-Parnell Commission: Speech Delivered by Michael Davitt in Defence of the Land League* (London: Kegan Paul, 1890): 30.

5 James Bronterre O'Brien, 'Kossuth, Mazzini and Ledru-Rollin: their virtues and their calumniators', *Reynolds' Political Instructor,* 15 December 1849; reproduced in Éva H. Haraszti, *Kossuth: Hungarian Patriot in Britain* (London: in association with Corvina Press, Budapest, 1994): 7-12.

6 Gregory Claeys, 'Mazzini, Kossuth and British Radicalism, 1848-1854', *Journal of British Studies* 28. 3 (July 1989): 227.

7 Davitt, *The Fall of Feudalism in Ireland, or The Story of the Land League Revolution* (London and New York: Harper, 1904): 356.

8 J. Holyoake, 'One Thousand Shillings for European Freedom, *The Reasoner* 13 (1852); in Haraszti, *Kossuth: Hungarian Patriot in Britain,* 51.

9 There are seven letters from Cowen to Davitt among the Davitt papers in TCD. Unfortunately, Cowen does not appear to have kept the replies as there are no surviving letters from Davitt among the Cowen papers (Tyne & Wear Archives).

10 TCD MS 9544, notes of interviews, 1885, f. 57.

[11] Kossuth had two sons, Lajos and Ferenc, both engineers. Davitt does not name which one he met.
[12] He was eighty-two. He was born on 19 September 1802.
[13] TCD MS 9544, notes of interviews. 1885, f. 57.
[14] TCD MS 9544, notes of interviews, 1885, f. 57.
[15] TCD MS 9544, notes of interviews, 1885, f. 56.
[16] TCD MS 9544, notes of interviews, 1885, f. 55.
[17] J.P.T. Bury, *France, 1814-1940*, 6th ed. (London: Routledge, 2003): 161-63. See also H.L. Wesseling, *The European Colonial Empires, 1815-1919*, trans. Diane Webb (London: Pearson, 2004): 194-95.
[18] TCD MS 9544, notes of interviews, 1885, ff. 54-55.
[19] TCD MS 9544, ff. 58-59.
[20] TCD MS 9544, f.53, notes of interviews, 1885.
[21] Following the 'Tithe War' of 1830-1838, the government passed the Tithe Commutation Act, 1838, which made the sum payable to the Church of Ireland a semi-annual rent charge payable by the head landlord.
[22] Ibid., f. 53.
[23] Éva Haraszti, *Kossuth as an English Journalist* (New York: Colombia University Press, 1990).
[24] Haraszti, *Kossuth: Hungarian Patriot in Britain*, 3-4.
[25] See list of Kossuth's publications in English journals in Eva Haraszti, *Kossuth as an English Journalist*, 7-9.
[26] There was a considerable amount of interest in O'Connell in Hungary in the 1830s and 1840s and 'multiple references' to him in the 1843 issues of Kossuth's *Pesti Hirlap*. See Thomas Kabdebo, *Ireland and Hungary: A Study in Parallels with an Arthur Griffith Bibliography* (Dublin: Four Courts Press, 2001): 21.
[27] In 1890 Kossuth was deprived of his Hungarian citizenship, but he never attempted to return to his native land during his lifetime. On his death in 1894, his body was repatriated and buried in Budapest 'in the presence of millions'. See Deák, 350.
[28] TCD MS 9544, notes of interviews, 1885, f. 52.
[29] Ibid. f. 51.
[30] His parents began in Haslingden as fruit hawkers. By 1870 his father was an agent to a loan society. T.W. Moody, *Davitt and Irish Revolution, 1846-82* (Oxford: Oxford University Press, 1981): 67.
[31] Davitt reported Kossuth as saying that he earned his own living, and he commented: 'His study bore testimony to the truth of this statement. It was the workshop of a literary man.' TCD MS 9544, notes of interviews, 1885, f. 51.
[32] Deák, 113.
[33] Ibid., 114.

34 Carla King, 'Michael Davitt and the Kishinev Pogrom, 1903', *Irish Slavonic Studies* 17 (1996): 19-43.

35 Meetings were held in cities across Europe, in Melbourne and throughout the United States. See Cyrus Adler, ed., *Voice of America on Kishinev* (New York: Jewish Publications Society, 1904) and Isidore Singer, ed., *Russia at the bar of the American People* (New York: Funk & Wagnalls, 1904).

36 Michael Davitt, *Within the Pale: The True Story of Anti-Semitic Persecutions in Russia* (London: Hurst and Blackett; New York: Barnes & Co., 1903).

37 Davitt, letter to the editor of the *Freeman's Journal* 18 January 1904: 6.

38 *The Times* 9 October 1851. See also, Charles Frederick Henningsen and [anon.], *Kossuth and "The Times" by the Author of "The Revelations of Russia"* (London: Charles Gilpin, 1851): 8.

39 'He scrupled as little as Mr O'Connell to affirm whatever suited his purpose and he obtained the same undoubted results from popular credulity.' *The Times* 9 October 1851; qtd. Henningsen, 11.

40 *The Times* 17 October 1851; qtd. Henningsen, 22.

41 Henningsen and [anon.], *Kossuth and "The Times" by the Author of "The Revelations of Russia"* (London: Charles Gilpin, 1851).

42 Claeys, 247.

43 *The Times* 7, 10, and 14 March 1887.

44 Published by Davitt as *The 'Times'-Parnell Commission Speech Delivered by Michael Davitt in Defence of the Land League* (London: Kegan Paul, Trench, Trubner & Co., 1890). See also, *Report of the Special Commission on Parnellism and Crime, Special Commission Act. Reprint of the Shorthand Notes of the Speeches, Proceedings, and Evidence taken before the Commissioners Appointed Under the above-named Act* [C 5891], Parliamentary Papers (1890), xxvii, 447-640, vols 10 and 11.

45 Deák, 62.

46 Otto Zarek, *Kossuth*, trans. Lynton Hudson (London: Selwyn & Blount, 1937): 114.

47 *Kossuth: His Speeches in England* (London: Charles Gilpin, 1852): 9.

48 He nicknamed her 'Evictoria' during celebrations of the Queen's Jubilee in 1887, in reference to the British government's protection of evicting landlords.

49 Queen Victoria bitterly opposed Davitt's release from prison in 1882. See George Earle Buckle, ed., *Letters of Queen Victoria, 1879-1885*, vol. 3 (London: John Murray, 1928). Victoria to

Gladstone, 4 May 1882: 281; Gladstone to Victoria, 5 May 1882: 281; Victoria to Earl Granville, 7 May 1882: 285.

50 See, for example, Davitt, 'A future racial programme', *The Fall of Feudalism*, 717-24.

51 *Daily News*, 26 November 1851; qtd. in Haraszti, *Kossuth: Hungarian Patriot in Britain*, 134-35.

52 James Loughlin, *Gladstone, Home Rule and the Ulster Question, 1882-93* (Dublin: Gill & Macmillan, 1986): 123.

53 Michael Laffan, *The Partition of Ireland, 1911-25* (Dundalk: Dundalgan, 1983); Pauric Travers, *Settlements and Divisions: Ireland, 1870-1922* (Dublin: Helicon, 1988).

54 Paul Bew, *Land and the National Question in Ireland, 1858-82* (Dublin: Gill & Macmillan, 1978); Philip Bull, *Land, Politics and Nationalism: A Study of the Irish Land Question* (Dublin: Gill & Macmillan, 1996).

55 Jonathan Sperber, *The European Revolution, 1848-1851* (Cambridge: Cambridge University Press, 1994): 156-57.

56 Maura Cronin, '"Of One Mind"? O'Connellite Crowds in the 1830s and 1840s', *Irish Crowds 1750-1920*, eds Peter Jupp and Eoin Magennis (Hampshire: Macmillan Press, 2000): 139-72.

57 Samuel Clark, *Social Origins of the Irish Land War* (Princeton, NJ: Princeton University Press, 1979).

58 Claeys, 225-61.

59 Moody, 'Michael Davitt and the British Labour Movement, 1882-1906', *Transactions of the Royal Historical Society*, 5th ser., iii (1953): 53-76.

60 E.J. Hobsbawm, *Nations and Nationalism since 1780: Programme, Myth, Reality* (Cambridge: Cambridge University Press, 1990): 101-30.

61 Patrick Maume, *The Long Gestation: Irish Nationalist Life, 1891-1918* (Dublin: Gill & Macmillan, 1999); Tom Garvin, *The Evolution of Irish Nationalist Politics* (Dublin: Gill & Macmillan, 1981).

62 Deák, xiv-xv.

63 See recent reassessments by Laurence Marley, *Michael Davitt: Freelance Radical and Frondeur* (Dublin: Four Courts Press, 2007), Andrew Newby, *Ireland, Radicalism and the Scottish Highlands, c. 1870-1912* (Edinburgh: Edinburgh University Press, 2007), Carla King, *Michael Davitt* (Dundalk: Dundalgan, 1999).

8 | A Congenial Race: Irish Literature and National Character in the Hungarian Literary Journal *Nyugat*[1]

Gabriella Vöő

A short sketch by Antal Szerb entitled 'Századvég' [Fin-de-siècle], published in 1934, features four young literati doing the pub circuit in end-of-the-century London. Three of them, Lionel Johnson, Ernest Dowson, and John Davidson are real-life figures, members of the Rhymers' Club, but the last one, laconically referred to as Tyrconnel, is a thinly veiled disguise for Yeats. Szerb captured the atmosphere of the place and the time: rambling interests, refined taste and witty literary small talk, iconic artists like Wilde and George Russell making their brief appearance to crack aphorisms or drop Cabbalistic cards. The characters' portrayal is parodic but appealing, each of them impersonating artists' attitudes characteristic of early modernism – infatuation with art, spleen, indefinite yearning – as well as popular national stereotypes. Davidson is a snobbish symbolist and a calculating Scotsman, Johnson a highly cultivated, but ascetic English Catholic, and Dowson a reserved Englishman who keeps his artist's vocation secret and keeps up the appearance of being in the flax and hemp business. The character of Tyrconnel is the roundest and the most fondly drawn: he is restless, extravagant and meddlesome, his 'Irish soul eager and desirous to make trouble'; an 'ambitious dreamer'; a poet who wrote a symbolist poem about Manannán the sea deity; is lovelorn, dejected, and has not the remotest idea that he would once be awarded the Nobel Prize.[2] Szerb's sketch captures the two major notes of Hungarian reflections on Irish literature and culture in interwar Hungary: vivid interest in literary Modernism, and a certain kind of positive national stereotyping. The security with which he treated his readers to this 'short story à clef' points to a general familiarity with literary trends and authors in Britain during the previous decades, and a sympathetic attitude to what many Hungarian authors saw as Irish distinctness. Also, the allusions to Tyrconnel's extravagant mysticism and to his favourite themes, 'the swan, the apple tree and the lighthouse',[3] suggest that it was the early phase of Yeats's career that had the firmest grip on Szerb and his readers' imagination.

Interest in Ireland and the Irish had been preceded by a long tradition of Hungarian consideration for English culture, politics and economy. The 'anglomania' of the liberal intelligentsia reaches back to the late eighteenth century. The awakening of Hungarian interest in England depended, according to Sándor Fest, on the tightening of political and cultural ties between London and Vienna during the 1780s, the reigns of Maria Theresa and Joseph II.[4] Due to the semi-colonial situation of Hungary within the Habsburg Empire as well as to the resulting political oppression and economic underdevelopment, England was regarded as an epitome of political freedom and economic prosperity. In addition to this, Hungarian intellectuals in this period developed a fondness for English literature and culture, which served as a counter-balance to the German cultural influence dominant at the time. András Csorba in his pioneering work on Hungarian-Irish connections, published in 1944, traces the first relevant signs of Hungarian interest in Ireland back to the 1830s when several Hungarian periodicals informed readers about the poverty and oppression of the Irish and called attention to the similar situation of the Hungarian peasantry.[5] Csorba points out that '[a] certain similarity could be discovered between the history of our country and Ireland's, which was one of the strongest ties binding our nations together'.[6] During the nineteenth century there were many references to poverty and misery in Ireland by Hungarian authors, the major historical novelist József Eötvös among them, who published a pamphlet entitled 'Szegénység Irlandban' [Poverty in Ireland] in 1840.[7] The Irish author who had the strongest impact in

Hungary during the nineteenth century was Thomas Moore. His influence was considerable during the movement of national awakening that preceded the revolution and war of independence of 1848-1849. *Travels of an Irish Gentleman in Search of Religion* was published in Hungarian translation as early as 1836[8] and a couple of his poems were translated by the major Romantic poets Mihály Vörösmarty, Sándor Petőfi and János Arany.[9] During the two decades that followed the defeat of the 1848-1849 revolution Károly Szász translated and published more than fifty poems by Moore.[10]

Early in the twentieth century Hungarian interest in English literature was part of a more general aspiration of intellectuals to absorb and draw inspiration from the culture of Western Europe, especially from English and continental modernism. In January 1908 critics and editors Miksa Fenyő, Ernő Osvát, and Hugó Ignotus launched a semi-monthly literary periodical which became a leading forum of literary Modernism in pre- and interwar Hungary. The name of the journal was *Nyugat*, 'The West', which signalled the commitment of its editors and authors to join the aesthetic and intellectual ferment of Western Europe. It was also the editors' intention to compensate for the peripheral position of Hungary in respect to Europe, both geographically and culturally. From the outset, the majority of the authors publishing in the journal were inspired by such turn-of-the-century European literary trends and movements like symbolism, aestheticism and impressionism. Among the Hungarian literary journals of the time *Nyugat* represented the liberal, cosmopolitan orientation along with a restrained, balanced nationalism.

The normative, canonizing influence of the periodical was highest in the years before and during the First World War when the editors' high critical standards, together with a progressive political and social agenda, allowed the prestigious periodical to represent a wide variety of the period's literary and critical aspirations. However, the turmoil during and after the war brought radical changes in Hungarian politics, society and culture. The bourgeois revolution of October 1918 was followed by a communist coup, and by the installation of the short-lived Communist and Social Democratic coalition government in 1919, which collapsed later in the same year. After the Trianon peace accord Hungary lost two-thirds of its former territory, and the monarchy was nominally restored with the regency of Miklós Horthy. The ensuing conservative rule meant a serious setback for social reforms and also a narrowing of the cultural spectrum in interwar Hungary. In this period *Nyugat* retained its role as the promoter of high modernist principles in both writing and critical thought. However, from the early 1920s until its cessation in 1941 the periodical upheld its high standards of literary quality but lost its central place as a cultural platform. Its orientation was now characterized by a certain elitism paired with an apolitical stance, due to the increasing political and cultural isolation of the liberal intelligentsia in Horthy's conservative régime. *Nyugat* regularly published translations from European literature along with book reviews, art criticism and theatre reviews, and owing to the editors' efforts Hungary, for the first time in its intellectual history, came close to overcoming its cultural belatedness. The journal's lifespan practically coincided with the presence of the leading Irish modernist writers on the European literary scene. Thus, it had an important role in raising awareness that these Irish authors, even though they wrote in English, had a national and cultural background that made their work distinctive.

The present essay proceeds to give an outline of the Irish literary canon as promoted by three generations of Hungarian writers and literary critics associated with *Nyugat* during the first two decades of the twentieth century and between the wars. It will also give a general outline of the Irish literary canon in Hungary during this period, with special attention to the evaluation of Irish writers according to the standards set by the editors and contributors of this high quality, albeit low circulation, literary journal. There were, in this period, tendencies among Hungarian writers and critics to explain the divergence of Irish culture and literary expression from the English by attibuting a distinct 'national' or 'racial' character to Irish culture, the terms being used interchangeably. Such views were, on the one hand, late flourishings of Herderian national characterology and, on the other hand, developed under the influence of Oswald Spengler's philosophy of history which was in vogue among the Hungarian modernist authors of the interwar period. Also, there was at the time an inclination to discover some kind of common spiritual disposition in the Irish and the Hungarians. Beginning with the mid-1930s, however, the term 'racial character' underwent considerable change due to the rising influence in Eastern Europe of the cultural politics of fascist Germany, which prompted the leading authors and literary critics to eliminate the term 'race' from their vocabulary. With this, notions about the distinctness of Irish culture from the English one lost momentum and remained in oblivion until as late as the 1970s, resulting in a considerable impoverishment in the reception of, for instance, Joyce's *Ulysses*.

Dandies and Dreamers: Meeting Points Between Irish and Hungarian Literary Modernism

The editors of *Nyugat* were guardians of a certain standard of quality, not of uniformity of opinion. Critical reflections on foreign literature were alternatively promotional and polemical. By reflecting on the work of their foreign contemporaries writers could articulate their critical views, define their commitments and creative methods in the wider context of contemporary European literature. No other literary journal published so extensively about, and so many translations from literature in English as *Nyugat*, the dissemination of the work of leading West European writers' work pertaining to its western orientation. The influence of the high modernist writers and critics grouped around *Nyugat* reached beyond the pages of the journal through their volumes of essays, criticism and literary histories that were published in this period, and the literary histories by two prominent authors associated with the journal, Mihály Babits and Antal Szerb, are still in print.[11]

The editorial policies of *Nyugat* were in consonance with the cultural modernization that began in Hungary at the turn of the century. The process of urbanization in the decades after the Compromise of 1867 had brought radical changes in the culture of cities nationwide, especially in Budapest which emerged as a regional metropolis within the Austro-Hungarian Monarchy. However, as a result of political dependence and the arrested development of capitalism in Hungary this change also meant economic and social uncertainty which was reflected in the culture of the time. In a retrospective essay published in *Nyugat* in 1937 Gábor Tolnai gives an accurate description about the general atmosphere of indefiniteness and lack of orientation, and evokes the new generation's restless search for new social attitudes and forms of self-expression: '[t]hey are rough and superficial, like their end-of-the-century predecessors. But their superficiality takes inspiration from European models, which alone distinguishes them from the dandy of the 1890s. Instead of their fathers' worn-out compliments they learn wit from the books of Oscar Wilde'.[12] The literary culture of the fin-de-siècle meant a gradual distancing from the culture of the landed gentry which before had served as the social basis for intellectual life in Hungary. The urbanized members of this same class and the emerging bourgeois intelligentsia had difficulties in adapting to the new social and economic circumstances, and compensated for the lack with mannerisms adopted from English and French models. As a critic noted in 1908, Oscar Wilde's antics and paradoxes, along with the eccentricities of Charles Baudelaire, Théophile Gauthier or Barbey d'Aurévilly gained almost cultic status.[13]

In the years before the war Wilde surpassed in popularity any other European author mainly on account of aesthetic views, but his witticisms, provocative behaviour, his trial and imprisonment had profound and divisive effects on both the artists and the cultivated reading public. Wilde's name became a by-word in literary journalism, appearing frequently on the pages of *Nyugat* with a casualty signalling common cultural property. Readers could be relied on to understand the epithet 'Wilde-like', or to envisage his 'dazzle and fresh lyricism' and 'haughty hedonism'.[14] There was only one essayist, Zoltán Szász, who repeatedly expressed in the journal disdain for his 'bizarre way of life and shocking apparel', his 'morbid desire to attract attention, sensation- and curiosity-hunting taken to extremes', and grumbled about 'the epidemic fashion of the Wilde cult'.[15] Such righteous hostility, however, failed to recognize why the Irish author had such a grip on the imagination of authors and readers alike, all of them participants in a paradigm shift that prompted an entire generation of intellectuals in turn-of-the-century Hungary to define themselves as urban, metropolitan, and modern. The extensive admiration of, and familiarity with Wilde was part of the process of rebellion against the conservative, nationalistic trends in literary criticism that saw the historical legacy of rural Hungary as the fountainhead of national culture. The new generation embraced, instead, a creative relationship to the national past and envisioned for themselves a social and cultural ambiance that was modern, and compatible with west-European social and cultural models. The cult of beauty and artistic play, excess in expression, and an attitude of extreme individualism were those characteristics of fin-de-siècle aestheticism that were eagerly adopted by emergent young authors in Hungary.

The new trend and style also brought the rise of the 'dandy' as the accompanying social and literary role model. Wilde was generally credited with refreshing and updating this pattern of behaviour. 'The pedigree of ... literary dandies goes far back, and they have not died out. ... Perhaps Oscar Wilde himself was oblivious of the social relevance of the type created by him', Géza Laczkó claims in a review article about the French symbolist writer Barbey D'Aurévilly.[16] In pre- and interwar Hungary the author most frequently associated with and compared to Wilde was Gyula Szini, essayist and prose writer, the first Hungarian translator of *Salome*,[17] and the embodiment of the 'dandy' in the literary circles of Budapest. Evaluating Szini's work after his death in 1932, Gábor Thurzó points out his likeness to the famous predecessor and literary model: 'The reigning prince of the fin-de-siècle is Oscar Wilde, and Gyula Szini was such a belated dandy'.[18] An enthusiastic advocate of new experiments in literature and criticism, Szini made his début in the 1890s in the journal *Magyar Géniusz* [Hungarian Genius], one of the predecessors of *Nyugat*, with essays about French symbolism, impressionism and the principle of l'art pour l'art in literature. His own work, consisting of short stories and three novels, was consistent with these trends. Szini's chiselled, lyrical prose was impressionistic, characterized by a certain dreaminess, featuring isolated characters lost in fantasy worlds, secretly suffering or longing after imaginary realities that completely engulfed them. His essay 'A mese alkonya' [The Twilight of Fable] published in the first issue of *Nyugat* in January 1908 laments the decline of literary realism into flat recordings of the trite, and calls for the return of our capacity for enchantment by pure art. To argue his point he cites Wilde as an authority on the ontological difference between the real world and the world of art, the latter being 'the one which has to be talked about because it would not exist otherwise'.[19] Like Wilde, Szini was the quintessential artist both in his work and his life which ended, like Wilde's, in tragic oblivion and poverty. His last piece of writing published in *Nyugat* was a commemoration of the thirtieth anniversary of Wilde's death and a fond account of the three bunches of violets that mysteriously appeared on his tomb in the Père Lachaise Cemetery each year on this particular day.[20]

Wilde was also the most extensively translated Irish author in the first decades of the century. For the first generation of authors grouped around *Nyugat*, rendering his poetry in Hungarian was not only a technical tour de force, part of their formative experience as poets, but also an opportunity to put their own poetic experimentations into an international context. The literati who would later become his major translators, Mihály Babits and Dezső Kosztolányi, were poets, prose writers and critics who started their career under the influence of aestheticism, and shared an enthusiasm for Wilde's works. Babits translated several of his poems which were published in a separate volume, *Wilde Oszkár verseiből* [From the Poetry of Oscar Wilde], in 1922. Kosztolányi rendered 'The Ballad of Reading Gaol,' *The Picture of Dorian Gray* and the plays *The Duchess of Padua* and *Salome*.[21] *Nyugat* often published poems in translation in more than one version,[22] and poet-translators frequently discussed and evaluated each other's achievements in order to point out the distinctive marks of their respective individual styles. Reviews about Hungarian versions of, for example, 'The Ballad of Reading Gaol' and 'Charmides', written by outstanding poets, were ingenious pieces of interpretation by close reading.[23] Repeated publications of poetry in translation sustained the readers' interest in international poetry and offered opportunities for exchange of views about the technical problems of translation.

Babits, the major poet, novelist and a leading authority in the literary life of the interwar period was editor of *Nyugat* from 1917 to 1941 and, as an enthusiastic promoter of English literature in Hungary, did the most in his generation to introduce English authors to Hungarian readers. His column of book reviews 'Könyvről könyvre' [Book by Book] regularly informed about new developments in European literature, placing special emphasis on English authors and works. Donne, Keats, Shelley, Tennyson,

Browning, Swinburne, Wilde, and Eliot were the major inspira-ations for his own poetry,[24] and later in his career he also recognized and appreciated the relevance of Yeats.

Wilde had special importance for Babits, whose early poetic development included influences from the neo-romanticism of l'École parnassienne, through the psychology of William James, to late symbolism and impressionism.[25] The poems in his first two volumes, *Levelek Irisz koszorújából* [Leaves from Iris' Wreath] and *Herceg, hátha megjön a tél is?* [But Prince, What if Winter Comes*?*],[26] published in 1909 and 1911, show thematic, stylistic and technical similarities with Wilde's poetry.[27] In addition to artistically wrought settings and decorative imagery, several poems give evidence of the fascination with the Hellenic world that Babits shared with Wilde. In his formative years Babits translated many of Wilde's poems, the first one being 'Charmides' on which he worked at length during the winter of 1906-1907. The translation was published in *Nyugat* in 1911, and anthologized three times during the Hungarian poet's lifetime. Working on 'Charmides' must have meant for the young Babits an initiation into the vertiginous use of poetic imagery that would characterize his poetry throughout his career. In his 1916 volume of translations *Wilde Oszkár verseiből* [*from the Poetry of Oscar Wilde*] he added an explanatory note to this particular poem: 'The translator very well perceives how much of his own imagination, his own poetry has infiltrated *Charmides*. ... He dreamt the poems of Wilde *into these particular forms*, and he admits having diverged from the text just because he liked it better so'.[28] In a later anthology, *Oedipus király és egyéb műfordítások* [*Oedipus Rex and Other Translations*] he made another apologetic remark about the poem which he considered to be more of a rewriting than a translation:

> Charmides in its Hungarian version is somehow of illegitimate birth; I call it, so to speak, translation because I dare not refer to it as an original piece. The young translator handled the English poem quite freely, the way he would not have dared to treat Sophocles or Shakespeare: like an irresponsible freebooter who plunders and alters to his own liking. Faithfulness has its degrees, and the degrees are value judgements.[29]

As his final, rather slant remark reveals, in his mature years Babits turned away from Wilde's influence. Aestheticism had meant for him an introduction, a début into a way of writing the importance of which he later sought to diminish. Thus, translating Wilde meant for Babits an initiation into technical excellence that went only so far as the creative appropriation of certain themes and aspects of style. His further poetic development and mature literary expression has more affinities with the late poetry of Yeats, but he did not acknowledge any direct influence.

Although a Nobel Prize winner, Yeats as a poet and playwright was less popular in interwar Hungary than Wilde. Only one poem, 'He Wishes His Beloved Were Dead' was published in *Nyugat* in the translation of Mihály Babits.[30] Nevertheless, Babits cited Yeats as a major English poet along with Thomas Hardy and John Masefield,[31] and the Macmillan edition of *The Collected Works in Verse and Prose of William Butler Yeats* was favourably reviewed by him shortly after its publication in 1935. Babits was particularly impressed by Yeats's rewritings of his early works and, discerning the important paradigm shifts in the course of the Irish poet's career, remarked that his 'typically nineteenth-century poems were reborn as twentieth-century innovative poetry'.[32] Writers, he held, should address the problems of their time, but transcend the immediate particularities of their condition.[33] Babits's conception of great literature made it possible that Yeats's poetry and drama, instead of being simply shelved with the Celtic Twilight movement or fin-de-siècle decadent poetry, could receive a more accurate evaluation, one that he readily provided in 1935:

> When in the 1890s Yeats's dramas were becoming widely known on the continent they struck us like the strange amalgamation of modern decadence and ancient Celtic myth. ... But for the poet decadence served as a means and prerequisite to make the poems more poetic and thus more exalted and heroic, to give the obsolete myths modern suggestiveness. The main pursuit of Yeats the dramatist is to reconstruct the character of antique drama. He applies the myths of the Irish as Greek tragedians apply those of Homer, and hides among his original plays translations from Sophocles. He is heroic, revolutionary and Irish even when he chooses a modern theme. ... The form of Yeats's drama is poetry fused with poetic prose.[34]

Himself a translator of Sophocles' *Oedipus Rex*, *Oedipus in Colonus* as well as ancient Greek poetry, Babits valued the breadth of relevance Yeats gave to myth. He reinforced this acknowledgement in *Az európai irodalom története* [*The History of European Literature*] published in 1934 and 1935, claiming that '[i]n his old days, Yeats unexpectedly renewed his skills and became modern'.[35] And although a fuller scale of Yeats's evaluation had to wait until the 1970s,[36] the criticism of Babits gave the note to his reception in interwar Hungary.

Owing to the efforts of outstanding writers in the circle attached to the periodical *Nyugat*, especially those of Mihály Babits and Dezső Kosztolányi, Wilde's poetry and drama became accessible to Hungarian readers. Kosztolányi was also the first translator of John Millington Synge.[37] Yeats's critical reception, especially by Mihály Babits, was moderate but accurate, however, he was not widely translated and his poetry failed to have an impact on Hungarian poetry of the interwar period. Outstanding modernist poets regarded the poetry of Wilde as a source of inspiration as well as a challenge for their own technical skills. On the other hand, Hungarian authors' and critics' investment in the modernization of literary culture to match the high standards of West-European literary Modernism produced a critical discourse focussed on the technicalities of writing and formal experimentation in contemporary English and continental literature. Hungarian poet-translators' commentaries on foreign poetry were necessarily formalist, directed towards their own and their fellow-translators' achievements, and putting less emphasis on the historical and cultural contextualization of the work of Irish authors. As a result, major writers like Wilde and Yeats were discussed as belonging to the canon of English literature on the grounds that they wrote in English.

Jesters and Mystics: The National Character of Irish Literature

There was, however, a parallel practice, partly by the same authors and critics, of exploring the national background of Irish authors in order to establish and explain their distinctness from English cultural and literary traditions. The grounds for such differentiation were the rather vaguely defined categories of temperament and national character that, according to critics publishing in *Nyugat*, set Irish authors apart from their English contemporaries. The Irish character was considered to be entirely different from, and antagonistic to, the English. Moreover, their detachment from what was regarded as the mainstream of English culture granted Irish authors a position of moral and intellectual superiority. Anglo-Irish authors of the past and present were regarded by some Hungarian essayists of the pre- and interwar period as relentless satirists of English hypocrisy and philistinism. In an open letter to H.G. Wells, for instance, the writer and humorist Frigyes Karinthy refers to 'the prudery of the English, mocked by the Irish and the Scots.'[38] Swift, Sterne, Wilde, and Shaw were frequently discussed together as major satirists. Gyula Szini's appreciative essay on Shaw clearly points out some tokens of English national identity and character as targets for ridicule:

> [Shaw] is a jester. He gets free hand in everything. He is allowed to mock the 'Union Jack', the Fleet, the aristocracy's code of honour, even the Anglo-Saxon inclination to prudishness which ruined Lord Byron's peerage and Oscar Wilde's life. He is a bit like the 'Sentimental Yorick', the English parson who wrote 'Tristram Shandy' and 'A Sentimental Journey,' and who is said to have lived an immoral life. Yet Lawrence [sic] Sterne's only immorality was his fondness of travelling and cracking cruel jokes on account of the English.[39]

A certain kind of satirical bent, together with an inclination to make masterly use of paradox, was also noticed in G.K. Chesterton whose brilliant epigrammatic style ranked him with Oscar Wilde. Mihály Földi discusses him as pertaining to a long tradition of witty Irish satirists: 'Chesterton is an Irishman, an Irish poet and thinker. He belongs to the spiritual milieu that gave Swift and Sheridan to the world, and of which Wilde and Shaw were born. The Irish spirit seems to provide writers with the sharp weapon of wit and satire when they set out on their voyage to foggy England ...'.[40]

In most cases, contrasting the Irish character with the English one was based on long established notions about national character. Sometimes such national stereotyping did not go beyond evoking the reified image of the stage Irishman. Zoltán Szász, the only unfavourable reviewer of Wilde in *Nyugat*, for example, engages in othering when he directs his attack against both the artist and the man: '[Wilde] was of Irish descent: the English accuse this ancient Celtic race of an inclination to show off, lack of restraint, voluptuousness and frivolousness'.[41] But in most cases these national dichotomies were not cited in order to pass value judgments. Rather, in contrasting the Irish with the English, Hungarian critics stressed the cultural and temperamental differences between the two nations. In his essay entitled 'Faj és művészet' [Racial Character and the Arts] Hugó Ignotus, for example, defines the essence of the Irish national character as an inherent set of mental and psychological markers. He finds the justification for the uniqueness of Irish writers in their 'Irish blood', which accounts for their perennial rebellious conflict with the English. 'It is almost impossible to grasp the enormous difference,' Ignotus contends, 'resting, beyond doubt, in the racial character, between Tennyson, the racially pure Englishman, the Scottish Burns and the Irish Moore, or Swift, or Wilde, or Shaw ...'.[42] The argument of Ignotus is in consonance with the frequently voiced opinion in the Hungarian criticism of the period that the English have an inclination to hypocrisy and philistinism, but the Irish spirit is more honest. In her essay on Jonathan Swift, Laura Lengyel takes this assumption one step further when she attributes the most significant manifestations of Irish creativity to a materialist strain in the culture:

> The Irish race, which has been struggling in England's hands of steel for centuries, which is sharply distinct from the British race in religion, customs, morals, world view, has provided England with figures of great talent. ... [L]et us but refer, apart from Jonathan Swift, to Oscar Wilde and Bernard Shaw. Neither Swift, nor Wilde, nor Shaw can be regarded as nationalists. However, some kind of racial nationalism is present in all three authors.[43]

Both Ignotus and Lengyel use the terms 'race' and 'racial' in the sense of 'nation' and 'national', without reference to any kind of biological determinism. Such explorations of national character and temperament had a long tradition in Hungary, reaching back to the early nineteenth century. The idea of the nation as an organic entity, and of culture as the expression of the national genius (*Volksgeist*, or, innate popular consciousness) introduced by Johann Gottfried Herder had a strong impact in a time when the Habsburg occupation forced the country into semi-colonial dependence, hindering the development of national culture as well. Herder's prediction, made in *Ideen zur Philosophie der Geschichte der Menschheit* [Outlines of a Philosophy of the History of Man] (1784-1791), about the likelihood of the small nations' extinction caused serious concern among Hungarian intellectuals of the period, and gave impetus to three generations of Romantic authors to embrace their folk traditions parallel with the modernization of Hungarian language and culture.[44] After the Compromise of 1867 there was, in Hungarian cultural discourse, a continuing pre-occupation with national identity and destiny that continued unbroken for decades. At the turn of the century, in his influential lectures on the theory of literary history at the University of Budapest, Zsolt Beöthy regarded the full expression of the national spirit as the defining criterion of national literature.[45] In the first decades of the twentieth century already existing notions about an inherent national character were reinforced by Wilhelm Wundt's ten-volume *Völkerpsychologie* [Ethnic Psychology] (1900-1920), which was read and reviewed in Hungary during the 1920s.[46] Salvador de Madariaga's succinct characterizations of nations in *Englishmen, Frenchmen, Spaniards* (1928), was also reviewed and discussed in *Nyugat*.[47]

Notions about the flare of the Irish national character were popular enough to predetermine some authors' perception. Kosztolányi, for example, after his short study trip to the University of Grenoble describes his international experience applying vivid national stereotypes, and gives an enthusiastic account of "[t]he Irish with their red hair [and beard], their ties and souls ablaze.[48] The impressions Kosztolányi recorded here were consonant with a recurring pattern in Hungarian criticism of Irish literature: the endowment of the oppressed Irish with a primordial spiritual energy that revitalizes the culture of the oppressor. The literary historian, creative writer and regular contributor of *Nyugat*, Antal Szerb, remarks in *Az angol irodalom kis tükre* [A Short History of English Literature] published in 1929 that '[t]he nationalist aspirations and the liberating spirit of the

Irish have brought the element of novelty to English literature'. Whereas, he adds, Shaw and Chesterton do not consider their Irishness relevant, Yeats fashioned a national identity out of the storehouse of Celtic mythology. '[W]ith Yeats,' Szerb continues, 'day-dreaming becomes a national act; for him, the life of the imagination, immersion in myth, visions are the best expressions of the Irish national character, these are most suitable for the Irish spirit'.[49]

When writing about Irish authors, Szerb tended to ascribe the distinctness of their work to the overlaying influence of myth. In *A világirodalom története* [A History of World Literature], published in 1941, Szerb dedicates a long discussion to the Celtic origins of Irish mythology. He then makes a suggestion about the persisting influence of this mythology on the Irish mind, remarking that '[u]p to this day, the Irish have little sense of reality, and much imagination'. A well-informed researcher of English literature, Szerb relies, first of all, on Matthew Arnold's *On the Study of Celtic Literature* (1867) when he remarks that '[t]he characteristics of Celtic legends are unbridled, rambling imagination, hyperbole and exaggeration'.[50] An indirect influence, however, of the study by Lajos Prohászka, *A vándor és a bujdosó* [The Wanderer and the Exile], first published between 1932-35,[51] is also discernible in Szerb's hypothesis about the residual Celtic character of the Irish. Prohászka, following the approach of the history of ideas, set out to grasp the essence of national character in the collective historical experience, and the influence of such accumulated experience on the collective spirit and cultural memory of a nation. After setting up a typology of some European nations' psychological and spiritual attributes he outlines the basic attributes of the Hungarian character, his point of departure being their early history, and he traces the pattern throughout the modern history of the nation. Let a small detail illustrate the general note of the argument:

> The French, the Italian or even the English strive to regulate their affectivity, to anchor it in tradition, or put it into the service of his sense of mission. The affectivity of the Hungarian, on the other hand, is unbound and rambling, its intentionality wavering and diffuse, moreover, fantastic. ... In

> this unorganized affectivity ... lies the perennial childishness of the Hungarian spirit.[52]

Szerb must have received as much encouragement from Prohászka's approach as from Arnold's when he claimed that 'it is the living Celtic folk spirit that enriches [Irish] literature', the Celtic Twilight movement being nurtured 'not so much by the traditions of the Celtic past, but by the means of the living Celtic national spirit'.[53] Continuing his discussion of turn-of-the-century Irish literature with the early work of Yeats, he points out that in his poetry inspired by Celtic mythology 'he revives not only the object but also the spirit that created these myths. ... For the Irish, or at least for Yeats, the transcendental is immanent, the other world is present in this earthly one, if only one has eyes to see, if only one knows entrancement, intuition'.[54]

Prohászka's study of national characterology was a typical product of a period of historical crisis. It made an attempt to rationalize, with the theoretical apparatus of the history of ideas, the situation of Hungary in the interwar period: emerging from the war among the losers, going through two revolutions, and a severe loss of territory and population as a result of the Trianon Treaty, all these events regarded as historical and national tragedies. Szerb, on the other hand, was more interested in how it was possible to reconstruct, from the residues of myth and by the means of poetry, a nation's inherent, essential spiritual heritage. When addressing this issue, referring either to the Irish or to the Hungarians, he uses a similar argument and register. It is a particular affinity to the mythical, the presence of the preternatural in the colloquial experience that Szerb regards as the essential quality of both nations' spirit and character. For a reconstruction of his like-minded regard of Hungarians we can find clues in an earlier essay, 'A magyarság mitikus arca' [The Mythic Face of Hungarians], published in 1926. Here Szerb suggested that there must have been a more enigmatic and glorious picture, the 'mythic vision of Hungarians' persisting in the early Medieval European imagination. He argues by bringing up the example of a certain Klingsohr von Ungerlant, a minor character in Novalis's *Heinrich von Ofterdingen*. There is in the novel a recounting of the Wartburg contest of singers where the adversary of Wolfram von Eschenbach is Klingsohr, a Hungarian singer with magical talent. His figure is ample evidence for Szerb that Germans and other Europeans looked upon Hungary as 'the land of singers and enchanters',[55] this deeply imprinted pattern surviving relatively intact over centuries, and serving the artistic purposes of an influential pre-romantic like Novalis. Szerb's appealing hypothesis may not be accurate, but was shared by other Hungarian authors as well. A piece of short fiction by the writer István Komor published in a 1931 issue of *Nyugat* also engages in the theme of some people's affinity to the irrational and the fabulous, and suggests that the Hungarian character shares many features with the Celtic. Komor's writing is a playful pastiche set in the seventeenth century, a romance and ghost story combined, involving an Austrian general, a beautiful ghost dame with a falcon, and René Descartes. Touching upon the theme of ghosts, Komor remarks that '[t]he Spaniard feels anxiety on Hungarian soil, and so do the Germans, Walloons, Italians. The Scottish and the Irish, on the contrary, feel at home ..., for their ghosts, spirits are similar to those of the Hungarians. Thus, they are not frightened, moreover, can even engage in conversation with them.'[56]

However, beginning with the rise, in 1933, of National Socialism in Germany, the term 'race' acquired a darker and politically charged note which was sensed early in Hungarian journalism. The relevance of the history of ideas lost momentum in Hungary, not least because of its availability for ideological appropriation. Thus, after the mid-1930s essayists eliminated the word 'race' and 'national character' from their vocabulary. As a result of this, throughout the Second World War and in the ensuing three decades the social, historical and cultural uniqueness of Ireland and Irish literature were not discussed significantly. Instead of explaining the distinctness of Irish authors with their special nature and condition, Hungarian critics restricted their approach to strictly literary criteria, abandoning the cultural ones that were previously thought to give these texts prominence.

The Waning of Irish Distinctness: Concluding Remarks

In interwar Hungary, earlier and modern Irish authors were most often considered within the context of English literature, but their national characteristics were brought into prominence. In this period the opening to major European literatures by translation and critical reception was part of the process of cultural modernization. Undoubtedly, the three generations of modernist authors whose careers were related to the literary periodical *Nyugat* contributed substantially to the presence of Irish authors, both earlier and contemporary, on the Hungarian literary scene. By their translations and criticism the modernist authors of the interwar period were instrumental in establishing a European literary canon that included the most relevant writers with an Irish background. Still, the reception of Irish authors in this period was rather uneven. Of the contemporary authors Oscar Wilde made the most powerful impact on Hungarian authors and critics. He was the most widely translated Irish author in the first decades of the twentieth century, preserving his popularity during the entire interwar period. Whereas Wilde was primarily a source of inspiration and model for the l'art pour l'art strain in Hungarian literature, Yeats was more difficult to integrate. The late Yeats's modernity was acknowledged by the high modernist poet, translator, critic and editor Mihály Babits, but a wider scale of translation of his poetry was undertaken only much later, beginning with the 1970s.

Also, it was in the decade following the First World War that Irish literature was conceived as the expression of a national spirit in opposition to the English. The Irish were labelled as relentless satirists who criticized English orderliness and philistinism. This tradition was traced back to Swift, Sterne, and Sheridan, and thought to be kept alive by Shaw and Wilde. In addition to their satirical bent, the Irish were considered to be extremely creative and spiritually energetic. Such an idealized image was, on the one hand, a reversal of Matthew Arnold's rather negatively biased stereotypes of the Irish and, on the other hand, derived from the various discourses of national characterology present on the Hungarian cultural scene. By envisaging a psychological affinity with the 'Celtic race', Hungarian critics could pinpoint their own nation's spiritual and cultural uniqueness. In the discussions about the legacy of national culture and literature one of the key concepts was 'race', a notion that was already present in turn-of-the-century criticism, and taken over, with its meaning of 'nationality', by critics embracing the approach of the history of ideas.

Yet with the discrediting of the term 'race' during the 1930s, awareness of Irish uniqueness waned. A telling example of this blind spot is the case of James Joyce's reception. Miklós Szentkuthy, whose 1974 translation of *Ulysses*,[57] is now the standard Hungarian version of the novel, was instrumental in familiarizing the work of Joyce to Hungarian readers. However, even he approached *Ulysses* without paying much attention to the Irish contexts of the novel. In his critical essay 'James Joyce', dated 1947, Szentkuthy offers an appreciative consideration of *Ulysses*, discussing the novel together with the work of Virginia Woolf and Dorothy Richardson, Joyce's Irish background all but forgotten. He points out as a common feature the three authors' stream of consciousness technique, untouched in its essence by Freudian psychoanalysis. Instead, argues Szentkuthy, all three of them are 'English empiricists who care nothing for theoretical hocus-pocus'. He suggests that their inclination to psychological realism derives from a 'narrow-minded practicality' and a 'humorous, curiosity-hunting, silly hobby-horse' motivation, concluding about the three authors that 'one is more English than the other'.[58] In Szentkuthy's analysis Joyce is contextualized with the medieval *danse macabre*, the paintings of Holbein and Van Eyck, the works of Shakespeare and Webster,[59] without any mention of Joyce's investment in Irish history and culture. Although he makes a brief and rather sketchy remark, close to the conclusion of the essay, that Joyce was 'the most Irish among Irishmen' and his novel 'the logical continuation of the ancient Celtic art', Szentkuthy brings his essay to a close with the surprising conclusion that the realistic representation of the mental process by the novel's stream of consciousness narrative is the work of 'a practical, all too sober Englishman'.[60]

Thus, in the pre- and interwar period, Hungarian critical discourse about Irish literature and culture provided important insights into Irish literature and culture even if there were gaps in the reception of, for instance, the mature Yeats. Due to contributors to the journal *Nyugat*, most of them leading modernist writers and literary critics who provided excellent translations and insightful criticism, Irish authors were conspicuously present on the Hungarian literary scene and gave impetus to literary experimentation and critical thought. Reflections about Irish literature and culture in the given decades were instrumental to introducing Hungarian readers to the European experience of modernity.

---

[1] An earlier version of the paper was published under the title 'Centenary from a Specific Angle: Reflections on Modern Irish Literature and the Irish Spirit in the Hungarian Literary Journal *Nyugat* (1908-1941)', *Focus: Papers in English Literary and Cultural Studies*, issue on Anglophone and Hungarian Literary and Cultural Encounters, ed. Gabriella Hartvig, 2008: 37-54.

[2] *Nyugat* 27.10-11 (16 May – 1 June 1934): 555, 556, 559. Unless otherwise stated, all translations from Hungarian are mine.

[3] Ibid., 557.

[4] *Angol irodalmi hatások hazánkban Széchenyi István fellépéséig* [English Literary Influences in Our Country Until István Széchenyi] *(Budapest*: Magyar Tudományos Akadémia, 1917): 12.

[5] *Magyar-ír kapcsolatok 1867-ig* [Hungarian-Irish Relations to 1867] (Debrecen: Tisza István Tudományegyetem, 1944): 34-37.

[6] Ibid., 4.

[7] *Reform és Hazafiság: Publicisztikai írások* [Reform and Patriotism: Publicistical Articles], eds István Fenyő, et al., vol. 1 (Budapest: Magyar Helikon, 1978): 133-205.

[8] *Egy Irlandus utazása az igaz vallás felkeresése végett* [Travels of an Irish Gentleman in Search of True Religion]. See Csorba, 76.

[9] 'Forget not the Field' was translated by Mihály Vörösmarty in 1847, Sándor Petőfi in 1848, and János Arany in the early 1850s. Petőfi and Arany also translated 'Oh! Blame not the Bard' in 1847 and in the early 1850s, respectively. Arany left us one more translation, of 'The Lake of the Dismal Swamp', dated 1848. For a detailed stylistic analysis of the translations see Csorba, 81-85.

[10] *Moore Tamás költeményeiből* [From the Poetry of Thomas Moore] (Pest: n.p., 1853). *Szász Károly kisebb műfordításai* [Minor Translations by Károly Szász] (Budapest: Ráth Mór, 1872). See Csorba, 85-86.

[11] Mihály Babits, *Az európai irodalom története* [The History of European Literature] (Budapest: Szépirodalmi, 1979) and Antal Szerb, *A világirodalom története* [The History of World Literature] (Budapest: Magvető, 1962).

[12] 'Arisztokratizmus és szecesszió' [Aristocratism and Art Nouveau], *Nyugat* 30.5 (May 1937): 333.

[13] Zoltán Szász, 'Tűnj fel!' [Attract attention!], *Nyugat* 1.24 (16 December 1908): 501.
[14] Lajos Hatvani, 'H. Taine levelei III' [The Letters of H. Taine III], *Nyugat* 1.4 (16 February 1908): 210; Margit Kaffka, Mrs. Fröhlich, 'Papp Mariska. *Rög. Elbeszélések*' [Review of *Clod: Short Stories by Mariska Papp*], *Nyugat* 1.5 (1 March 1908): 291; Frigyes Karinthy, 'Shaw Bernát *Caesarja*' [Bernard Shaw's *Caesar*] *Nyugat* 2.7 (1 April 1909): 393-94.
[15] 'Tűnj fel!', 502; 'Wilde Oszkár' [Oscar Wilde], *Nyugat* 1.12-13 (1 July 1908): 652; 'A "mozi" felé' [Towards the 'Movies'], *Nyugat* 1.21 (1 November 1908): 333.
[16] 'Barbey D'Aurévilly', *Nyugat* 1.22 (16 November 1908): 387.
[17] *Salome*, trans. Gyula Szini (Budapest: Lampel, 1903).
[18] 'Szini Gyula emléke' [In Memory of Gyula Szini], *Nyugat* 33.5 (1 May 1940): 241.
[19] Gyula Szini, 'A mese alkonya', *Nyugat* 1.1 (1 January 1908): 28. Szini refers to André Gide's essay on Wilde published in 1901. See André Gide, *Oscar Wilde: in Memoriam (Reminiscences): De Profundis*, trans. Bernard Frechtman (New York: Philosophical Library, 1949): v.
[20] 'Három ibolyacsokor' [Three Bouquets of Violets], *Nyugat* 24.1 (1 January 1931): 60-61.
[21] 'A readingi fegyház balladája' ['The Ballad of Reading Gaol'], *Nyugat* 19. 10 (16 May 1926): 892-99; *A páduai hercegnő* [*The Duchess of Padua*] (Budapest: Lampel, 1910); *Dorian Gray arcképe* [The Picture of Dorian Gray] (Budapest: Genius, 1922); *Salome* (Budapest: Genius, 1923). Dezső Kosztolányi was not the first to translate either *Dorian Gray* or *Salome*, but being an inspired stylist as well as a great poet and novelist he produced the most accomplished translations to this day. Before Kosztolányi, *Salome* was translated by Gyula Szini (Budapest: Lampel, 1903) and Géza Battkay (Budapest: Révai, 1907); *Dorian Gray arcképe* [The Picture of Dorian Gray] by Aladár Schöpflin (Budapest: Lampel, 1907).
[22] Previously, 'The Ballad of Reading Gaol' had been translated by József Kun, Lóránt Thaly, and Antal Radó. The first translation published in *Nyugat* was the work of Árpád Tóth, *Nyugat* 12.14-15 (June 1919): 954-73. The poem was also published later in the translation of Kosztolányi, *Nyugat* 19.10 (16 May 1926): 892-99.
[23] Lőrinc Szabó dedicated an essay to the discussion of Árpád Tóth's translation of 'Reading Gaol' in 'Tóth Árpád Wilde-fordítása' [Árpád Tóth's Translation of Wilde], *Nyugat* 14.10 (16 May 1921): 790-93. Dezső Kosztolányi's later, 1926 version was commented on

by fellow writer and friend, Frigyes Karinthy, in 'Kosztolányi: "Readingi fegyház"' [Kosztolányi: 'Reading Goal'], *Nyugat* 19.12 (16 June 1926): 1103-04. The translation of 'Charmides' by Mihály Babits, published in *Nyugat* 4.8 (16 April 1911): 705-18, was anthologized in his 1920 volume of translations *Pávatollak* [Peacock Feathers]. The volume was reviewed by Árpád Tóth who, discussing the translation of 'Charmides,' considered it to be, along with that of Tennyson's 'Lotus-Eaters,' the best in the volume. 'Babits műfordításai: *Pávatollak*' [The Translations of Babits: *Peacock Feathers*], *Nyugat* 13.3-4 (February 1920): 212-15. In 1940 a posthumous collection of Babits's translations of poetry, *Babits Mihály kisebb műfordításai* [Minor Translations by Mihály Babits], was reviewed by György Rónay who also praises 'Charmides' as a masterful rendering of Wilde's poem. 'Babits a fordító' [Babits the Translator], *Nyugat* 33.1 (January 1940): 48-51.

24 István Gál, *Babits és az angol irodalom* [Babits and English Literature] (Debrecen: Tisza István Tudományegyetem Angol Szemináriuma, 1942): 21.

25 See György Rába, *Babits Mihály költészete, 1903-1920* [The Poetry of Mihály Babits, 1903-1920] (Budapest: Szépirodalmi, 1981): 49, 54-57, 82-83.

26 The titles of volumes are Lóránt Czigány's translations, *A History of Hungarian Literature from the Earliest Times to the Mid-1970s* (Oxford: Clarendon, 1984).

27 Gál was the first to point out Wildean influences in the work of Babits in his seminal study, *Babits és az angol irodalom*, 44-45. Wildean influences, according to him, appear in artistic settings and scenes, sharp dialogues, decorative images.

28 Quoted in Gál, 35.

29 *Kisebb műfordításai* [*Minor Translations*], ed. György Belia (Budapest: Szépirodalmi, 1981): 419, n.363. Emphasis in the original.

30 'Szerelmesét halottnak kívánja' ['He Wishes His Beloved Were Dead'], *Nyugat* 23.14 (16 July 1930): 140.

31 Mihály Babits (B.M.), '*Angol költők a huszadik században*. Binét Menyhért versfordításai' [English Poets in the Twentieth Century. Translations by Menyhért Binét], *Nyugat* 25 (16 June 1932): 728.

32 Mihály Babits (B.M.), 'Teremtő utánzás' [Creative Imitation], *Nyugat* 31.6 (June 1938): 462. Babits, who was at the time the editor-in-chief of *Nyugat*, probably felt the need to point out the salient qualities of a long poetic career, and implied that authority and freshness were not mutually exclusive.

33 'Új klasszicizmus felé' [Towards a New Classicism], *Nyugat* 18.18 (1 October 1925): 19-20.
34 Mihály Babits (B.M.), 'Költő, forradalom és heroizmus' [Poet, Revolution, and Heroism], *Nyugat* 28.3 (3 May 1935): 260.
35 *Az európai irodalom története,* [The History of European Literature] (Budapest: Szépirodalmi, 1979): 474.
36 Csilla Bertha, 'The Hungarian of the West: Yeats's Reception in Hungary', *The Reception of W.B. Yeats in Europe*, ed. Klaus Peter Jochum (London: Continuum, 2006): 156.
37 Maria Kurdi, 'Transplanting the Work of "that rooted man": The Reception of John Millington Synge's Drama in Hungary', *Comparative Drama* 41 (Summer 2007): 221.
38 'Levél H.G. Wells-hez' [Letter to H.G. Wells], *Nyugat* 18.14-15 (1 August 1925): 142.
39 'Shaw margójára' [Marginalia on the work of Shaw], *Nyugat* 4.3 (1 February 1911): 229.
40 'Chesterton ortodoxiája' [Chesterton's Orthodoxy], *Nyugat* 10.21-22 (November 1918): 709-10.
41 'Wilde Oszkár' [Oscar Wilde], *Nyugat* 1.12-13 (1 July 1908): 651.
42 *Nyugat* 22.11 (1 June 1929): 716.
43 'Swift Jonathán' [Jonathan Swift], *Nyugat* 22.5 (1 March 1929): 328.
44 For a discussion of Herder's impact on conceptions of culture and nationality in Hungary and the neighbouring countries, see T. Iván Berend, *History Derailed: Central and Eastern Europe in the Long Nineteenth Century* (Berkeley: University of California Press, 2003): 46-49.
45 *Az irodalomtörténet elmélete* [The Theory of Literary History] (Budapest: Királyi Magyar Egyetemi Nyomda, 1940): 9. The volume contains his 1901-1902 lectures at the Budapest University.
46 In *Nyugat*, most references to Wundt occur in reviews of Hungarian works. There is one review essay evaluating his work: György Király, 'Wundt', *Nyugat* 13.19-20 (October 1920): 988-89. On the impact of Wundt on Hungarian philosophy in the interwar period see Ferenc Pataki, 'Nemzetkarakterológia?' [National Characterology?], *Magyar Tudomány* (February 1997): 169-79.
47 Olivér Brachfeld, 'Spanyol nagyságok tündöklése és bukása [The Rise and Fall of Spanish Notabilities], *Nyugat* 28.6 (June 1935): 518-19; László Passuth, 'Madariaga', *Nyugat* 19.7 (July 1936): 63-65; Gyula Ortutay, 'Kolumbusz Kristóf. Salvador de Madariaga könyve' [Review of *Christopher Columbus* by Salvador de Madariaga], *Nyugat* 34.2 (1 February 1941): 73-74.

[48] 'Bábel tornya' [The Tower of Babel], *Nyugat* 18.16-17 (1 September 1923): 248.
[49] *Az angol irodalom kis tükre* [A Short History of English Literature], 237.
[50] *A világirodalom története* [The History of World Literature], 169.
[51] Lajos Prohászka's study was published in installments in the periodical *Minerva* between 1932 and 1935, and in book form in 1936 (Budapest: Minerva Könyvtár).
[52] A vándor és a bujdosó [The Wanderer and the Exile], 131.
[53] *A világirodalom története* [The History of World Literature], 785.
[54] Ibid., 785-86.
[55] *Hétköznapok és csodák* [Weekdays and Wonders], ed. Csaba Papp, vol. 3 (Budapest: Magvető, 2002): 57.
[56] 'Magyar ostor, német vasderék' [Hungarian Whip, German Back of Steel], *Nyugat* 24.22 (16 November 1931): 67.
[57] *Ulysses* was translated by Endre Gáspár (Budapest: Nova, 1943) and Miklós Szentkuthy (Budapest: Európa, 1974). For a detailed discussion of the Hungarian reception of Joyce see Márta Goldman, 'Belated Reception: James Joyce's Work in Hungary', *Comparative Critical Studies* 3.3 (2006): 227-48.
[58] 'James Joyce', *A múzsák testamentuma* [The Testament of Muses] (Budapest: Magvető, 1985): 106.
[59] Ibid., 104, 107.
[60] Ibid., 111, 114.

9 | Gulliver's Umpteenth Voyage in Hungary: the Most Recent Sequels

Gabriella Hartvig

Jonathan Swift's heritage in twentieth-century Hungary seems to be more diverse than that of any of his fellow-writers from the eighteenth century, excepting, perhaps, Laurence Sterne. When Frigyes Karinthy's first complete translation of *Gulliver's Travels* came out in 1914,[1] no definitive translations from the works of Daniel Defoe, Henry Fielding, Samuel Richardson or Tobias Smollett had yet been published. By contrast, the Eliza cult of sentimentalism that swept through Europe in the late eighteenth century gave rise to a translation of Sterne's *A Sentimental Journey* in 1798 although the humorous novel of 'the second English Rabelais', *Tristram Shandy*, had to wait until 1956 to come out, following the publication of *Tom Jones* (1950) and *Jonathan Wild* (1954) in Hungarian.[2] Eighteenth-century classics such as *Peregrine Pickle*, *Pamela*, or *Clarissa* still await their translation. Karinthy's rendering of *Gulliver* was preceded by a number of adaptations and rewritings which were meant for the youth. His translation was shortly followed by three other full renderings which went side by side with the early imitations, as many as three among them belonging to Karinthy himself, and an equally, if not more significant, sequel produced by Sándor Szathmári.[3] While these early imitations have been unanimously acknowledged and appreciated, the most recent sequels seem to appear only as sporadic attempts to further deepen the Dean's popularity in Hungary. Today, the best known Gulliveriads are Klára Siklósi Horváth's two sequels, *Gulliver in Joygorod* (1998) together with its Hungarian language version, *Gulliver Bolgorogyban* [Gulliver in Bolgorod, 1999], and *Gulliver legújabb kalandja Pinkwellben* [Gulliver's Latest Adventures in Pinkwell, 2001],[4] Endre Gyárfás's *Gulliver utolsó utazása* [Gulliver's Last Voyage, 2001], Tivadar Papházi's *Új Gulliver* [New Gulliver, 2003], and László Rab's *A magyarok között: Gulliver sokadik utazása* [Among the Hungarians: Gulliver's Umpteenth Voyage, 2005].[5]

Many of the older interpretations exploit the allegory of men and horses found in the fourth book, where Gulliver travels to the land of the Yahoos and Houyhnhnms. Early twentieth-century authorial purpose in the Hungarian tradition of Gulliveriads can best be characterized by the classical 'hard school' of interpretations which usually claims that Swift was a mad misanthrope and Gulliver's character must be taken seriously and that the whole work, rather than being a comic satire which the 'soft school' suggests, is black and pessimistic.[6] Contrary to later Gulliveriads, *Faremidó, Capillária,* and *Kazohinia* are free of direct political references. The first two, by Karinthy, combine science fiction and utopian elements while Szathmári's work gives a strong philosophical character to the Swiftian heritage. *Kazohinia*, introducing the philosophy of the 'kazo', identifies the lunatic world of the Behins with humankind whereas the perfectly organized, overruled, and rational lives of the Hins resemble the way the Huyhnhnms live. The author's view of both worlds is devastating and proves that there is no 'compromise solution',[7] the satirical status of the novel is only a disguise which serves to show human misery: 'We are all Behins, strangers to perfection which remains incomprehensible and horrifying for us. What Swift suspected and Madách uttered, Kazohinia wants to explain.'[8]

After a longer period of comparative neglect, Hungarian Gulliveriads emerged again after the political transition of 1989. It is characteristic of most of the new Swiftian sequels that they are highly politicized and, as literary achievements, because of the too obvious social criticism they demonstrate, perhaps less interesting. Still, they are unique in their handing down of the Swiftian tradition for a new generation of readers and also in blending the well known and characteristic features of Gulliveriads with a variety of borrowed elements of twentieth-century genres such as science fiction and dystopia. Thus the handling of past and future, the unproblematic viewpoint of the narrator, or the rather enigmatic endings link some of these sequels to science fiction whereas the presentation of the totalitarian society found in the new world, or the idealogical nature of the language spoken in those countries are the common traits of dystopia. In what follows, I would like to give an overview of the most recent Hungarian sequels of the Dean's main work.

Orwellian Dystopias: *Gulliver in Joygorod*, and *Gulliver legújabb kalandja Pinkwellben* [Gulliver's Latest Adventure in Pinkwell]

Joygorod and *Pinkwell* open the line of post-transition Gulliveriads in Hungary although the earlier work had been written long before it was actually published. *Joygorod*, introducing a totalitarian state, is a social satire written against the political dictatorship of the previous socialist regime in Hungary while *Pinkwell*, describing the way in which people live in an all too liberal society, attacks the kind of personal and political freedoms that, in the writer's view, offered as great a challenge after 1989 as earlier political dictatorship. The author of the two sequels to *Gulliver's Travels*, Klára Siklósi Horváth (1939-), began her career as a musician and teacher of music in Pécs. After moving to Budapest in 1971 she became a freelance journalist. Since 1991 she has produced eight novels two of which introduce the further adventures of Swift's protagonist.

In both of her sequels, Siklósi gives a twist to the conventional Swiftian narrative structure where, in the end, Gulliver always returns home, leaving behind everything except his own memories. In the earlier work the Joygorodian dreadful creatures, reminders of the Yahoos, seem to slowly occupy England, following Gulliver back to his homeland, while in the later narrative we cannot know for sure whether Gulliver managed at all to return home. What we have is his memoirs, Gulliver's fate remains uncertain. These obvious deviations from the topoi of the imaginary voyage where the narrator, and he alone, always returns back from the countries that he visited thus embedding his adventures in a strictly ruled narrative framework already familiar to the reader, place Siklósi's novels in the wider and more modern contexts of science fiction and dystopia.

In the preface to *Joygorod* the narrator calls attention to the difficulties of writing and the reason why he earlier decided never to write about his further adventures:

> And anyway, where would I find a publisher who is interested in some voyage to an island that I can't even place anywhere on a map! Isn't it absurd? And what of the plot? Adventure? These things are quite suspicious. Where are the deep psychological analyses, the stylistic backbends, the enchanted word formations? On top of it all, my experiences were so dismal that even if I could set aside my inhibitions concerning writing (which I must admit, is very difficult) I find it hard to deal with my concealed memories (5).

What makes Gulliver's pondering about the possible disinterestedness of the reader in *Joygorod* even more interesting, is the circumstances of the publication of the book: sunk into oblivion, the manuscript of *Joygorod* rested over thirty years in a drawer waiting for publication. After Siklósi prepared it in 1972 she lay it aside believing that she would not find a publisher who would venture to print a social satire in the age of socialist realism. When moving to another place in 1997, a long way after the political transition, she rediscovered the manuscript and took it to the publishing house Littera Nova where the story was favourably received by the general editor, so much so that it was chosen by the house for being sent to Frankfurt where Hungary was Guest of Honour at the Frankfurt Book Fair 1999.[9] This explains why the English language version, *Gulliver in Joygorod*, was published a year before the Hungarian original, *Gulliver Bolgorogyban*. Interestingly enough, *Joygorod* was presented among children's books at the Book Fair. It is subtitled 'The Second First Edition' after the merely virtually existing 'First, "Prohibited" Edition.' Borrowing many elements from the irrationality of the Orwellian world, the story of this new *Gulliver* reflects on the highest period of the socialist regime.

In *Pinkwell*, deviating from the narrative rules of previous Gulliveriads, Gulliver writes his story in Paccservaccs concluding that this was possibly going to be his last voyage from which there was no return. We never find out whether or not Gulliver managed to return to England, which, as the reader can learn, would defy the flow of time: 'But I decided that tonight, if it did not rain, I would once again take a walk to the park ... Perhaps,when I fall asleep, my fate and time will, at last, have mercy upon me and, violating the laws [of time], will fly me home to my sea-smelling country, back to the company of my loved ones' (139).[10] Although *Pinkwell* was published merely three years after *Joygorod* first came out, almost as many decades have elapsed between the writing of the two narratives. In this later Gulliveriad the rapidly growing possibilities and free choices of a postmodern society come under strong criticism where the level of standard lies always in the individual. The truest of all freedoms is 'the unrestrained, undisciplined, senseless, and insane violance which is free of everything' (139).

The eighteenth-century topos of the 'found manuscript' orients the narrative of the novel. Similarly to the circumstances of how Swift's original manuscript of *Gulliver's Travels* was found on the threshold of Benjamin Motte the publisher,[11] the manuscript of *Pinkwell* 'got there [to the floor of the editorial office] in a mysterious, or better to say, in an entirely inexplicable manner the previous night' (5). We can never learn how but Gulliver's voyage to Pinkwell manages to reach the editorial office of Péter Ó, the editor-in-chief of an English journal, who, however, has never heard the name of Jonathan Swift. He angrily throws away the yellow papers of the manuscript, which, in turn, will be found by *Bodza bácsi* [Uncle Bodza], the door-keeper and an admirer of the great writer. He steals the sheets from the editorial desk and reads them overnight. The postscript informs us that the manuscript landed on the table of the editor the following morning with the door-keeper's dearest hope that, despite Péter Ó's insulting ignorance of the eighteenth-century masterpiece, the adventures of this twentieth-century Gulliver would be chosen for publication by him.

Both narratives display the traits common to most dystopias such as the strict and unchangeable stratification of the different groups of society visited by Gulliver, ruling politics in the form of authoritarian oppression or, to take the opposite end, chaos and absolute freedom from social responsibilities. The significance of the use of ideological languages is expressed even in the names of the countries, Joygorod (Bolgorogy in the Hungarian text), and Pinkwell.

In the earlier story Gulliver, in the 1960s, arrives in the land of the most irrational beings that live in a strictly ruled, totalitarian society: the capital, Joygorod, 'is the headquarters of the CHWSO, the Commencement of the Highest Wisest Spiritual Organization, consisting of the council of the most important and most intelligent persons, making decisions in a most prudent and most rational way' (15). He is captured and cast into a cell on the island called Ljugyka (just like Bolgorogy or Joygorod, a word of Russian origin: gorod=city, ljugyi=people) by a commander in a uniform decorated by 'four wide red ribbons' (11). In his prison he then quickly learns the Ljugykian language. After his release he is placed under 'secret surveillance' and learns about the two worlds in Joygorod. The past represents true history which must be blocked from people: 'My dear Gulliver', his companion, Gonor, tells him,

> from your story it is indisputable that the fickle hand of fate dropped you on our shores on the Past side ... Since the Great Pyramid Catastrophe, Ljugyka was spliced into two parts. To the left of Joygorod stands the past while the present flows on the right ... after the catastrophe they modified instantly to make up the NEW-CHWSO and ordered a blockade of the Pyramid: the side of its left was isolated and time was stopped. In this way, they prevented the future from becoming infected. Since that time, only clean and constant present flows on the island of Ljugyka (41).

This denial of the past reminds the reader of the 'reality control' of the Party as well as the pyramidal shapes of the ministries in Oceania. Gulliver, because of his knowledge of the truth, has become an enemy, as Gonor, his companion, explains to him one day. He tells him how dangerous it is to laugh at things that one finds funny, and to 'perceive things in the way they actually occur' (71) and to really think what one says. Gulliver openly speaks about his own ideas, 'which is outright enraging, dangerous, and entirely too extravagant' (72).

Gulliver's crime realized, his 'brain massage programme' begins to alter his way of thinking and to finally see everything, as the Great Sentu wants him to, through pink glasses:

> What happened was that every time I put them on, by some unknown device, two blinkers grew out from either side of my forehead like that of a horse, while the room turned into a dark tunnel with no view either left, right, up or down. The only view the glasses allowed was what I could see at the end of an extremely long and thin tube. It was a fantastically terrible, uneasy feeling ... Suddenly, my brain clouded over, when I realized the absurdity of the tragicomedy I was forced to act in. I started swearing (75-76).

The metaphor of seeing the world pink, to be deluded into believing that one experiences reality when one does not is a central thought in *Joygorod* and *Pinkwell* alike: in both societies the ruling political group makes people believe something that is not true. Gulliver the outsider sees through the delusion and becomes, as in most social satires, the voice of opposition.

In the second novel, *Pinkwell*, Swift's hero finds himself in a society where the inhabitants are called *globkukuccs* or *degreviccs*, the latter meaning something like 'blockheads' (51). Their Parliament is called *Ládzshajusz* ['large house'] where MPs are shown to be guilty of the most outrageous criminal acts such as rape and murder. After his money gets stolen in the Hotel, Gulliver is invited to stay in another, more peaceful, district full of nice *Bildics* ['buildings'] of Pinkwell called *Pacservacccs* where his friend and companion, Glorio, invites him. Here he finds his own rest and begins to write down his latest adventures. His rejection of the social structure and ruling ideology of the Pinkwellian world is similar to the one in Joygorod: in this society people share the most liberal ideas without any moral views. In Pinkwell everyone is free to act in the most selfish way which they call freedom. The canon or standard of all human activities is guided by the 'I' that gains his own authority through force and aggression and is ruled by selfishness. The *degreviccs* resemble the Yahoos in that they show unrestrained passions and are unable to act in a reasonable way. Similarly to Houyhnhnmland, however, here Gulliver also finds a species of noble creatures, the *bugyutacs* [bugyuta = silly in Hungarian] who represent the norm but who, sadly, do not acccept him.

The ending in both novels deviates from the common narrative rules which are so characteristic of creative reception. When

Gulliver returns home in *Joygorod* something unnerving happens to him: after putting the final touches on his adventures, he goes for a walk to the harbour where, suddenly, he seems to recognize the silhouettes of the most dreadful creatures that he met during his journey: 'Despite the partial darkness, I clearly depicted their ugly heads and legs in two directions hanging out from under their grey pants' (99). Thus he becomes restless, feels unsafe even at home and hopes that what he saw was only a delusion – the book ends in a question mark: 'The End?' (101), signalling that further adventures can be expected. In the later sequel, surprisingly, he probably never manages to return to his home country, neither do we learn how his memoirs get to the editorial office of Péter Ó.

Siklósi offers a sharp critique of a historical period in both works in the form of presenting an imaginary social system led by the most irrational and stupid dictators called the Great Sentu in one and *Ládzshajusz* in the other novel. The national hymn of Joygorod expresses the self-deluding ideology of both countries, Joygorod and Pinkwell alike:

> Yes is yes,/and yes is no,/joyful are the joyful,/and the unjoyful are also joyful,/for yes is yes,/but yes is no./And wealthy are the wealthy,/the poor are not poor/and great is the dwarf/and dwarf is the great,/for yes is yes/but yes is no / and the Great Sentu,/as God himself,/is immortal (87).

These Gulliveriads display a variety of the commonest themes found in dystopias, borrowing elements from the best known examples. For instance, the borrowed Russian words with Hungarian inflection in the Ljugykian language resemble Nadsat, the constructed language in *A Clockwork Orange*. Similarly, in *Pinkwell* we can find transliterated words from English such as *lájtszier* ['light seer'] or *loszier* ['law seer'] (52). Further thematic likenesses are the political propaganda or the mental rehabilitation programme that Gulliver goes through in *Joygorod*.

Utilizing the allegorical potential of the Gulliver metaphor, Siklósi offers a reliable spokesman for her satires thus simplifying the role of the narrator who, in Swift's masterpiece, himself becomes one of the targets of the tale. Nándor Gion's critical view on *Joygorod* well expresses how the character of Gulliver here loses the traditional role of the gullible and comic figure and becomes the one-sided story-teller of a social satire: 'The immortal ship surgeon's new journey is an ironic story. The island where he has been cast by the hand of fate is the caricature of real life socialism as well as a description of today's alienated, success-orientated post-industrial world lacking true ideals.'[12]

The Fantastic-Utopistic Tradition: *Új Gulliver* [New Gulliver]

The scientific-fictional tradition in which *Gulliver* lives on in the twenty-first century is indicative of the great attraction that the adventures of the true-born Englishman still have for young readers in Hungary. The story of *Új Gulliver* (2001) is written in third person perspective, which, among other thematic features, places the work in the long tradition of juvenile Gulliveriads. The author of this fantastic-utopistic novel, Tivadar Papházi (1925-2005), is a late follower of Karinthy and Szathmári in that he shows an explicit sign of the engineer's interest in the latest scientific inventions and the most recent developments of social sciences. As a secondary school teacher in Vác, Papházi also published volumes of dramatic plays, poetry, as well as documentary essays on several aspects of the history of his hometown, among them his own reflections on the events of 1956.

Adaptations for the youth in Hungarian reach back to the nineteenth century, longer than translation activities. The first Gulliver story, the translation of a rewriting for children from German, was prepared in 1865 by Imre Battlay[13] and this was shortly followed by a large number of other rewritings. Papházi's *New Gulliver* seems to be a late follower of this early proliferation of children's versions. Similarly to the clearly stated didactic aim of those juvenile works, where the young are cautioned to follow the moral principles that the story provides, Papházi also wrote his *New Gulliver* for pedagogical reasons. The book is subtitled a 'fantastic-utopian novel', which places it in the tradition of futuristic fiction. To employ Gulliver the great traveller as the protagonist of the story seems to serve as a link to activate the Swiftian heritage in the reader's mind.

The protagonist of 'New Gulliver', a 'space-Odysseus', is a late twenty first-century descendant of Lemuel Gulliver who, after a shipwreck, finds himself in the most modern underwater world of Antarctica called 'Esperanza' ['hope' in Spanish], perhaps a direct reference to Szathmári's life-long devotion to the Esperanto language. Upon learning that the Earth was destroyed by an Atomic Explosion, Gulliver, the captain of a spaceship, leads several expeditions into the cosmos, with the aim of finding the best possible place for the growing number of people in Esperanza to live in the future. With his team, to study what other societies might exist in the cosmos, he visits several planets each of which introduces a dystopian setting.

The first stage of Gulliver's space journey is the planet 'Eden' invaded by Kanmu the fascist biologist who arrived from the 'Planet of the Scientists'. From there the ship moves on to the planet of 'Back Wardness' with its three islands, two of which show a strictly ruled society led by the most radically conservative and hypocritical politicians, the third being the opposite, the island of Liberty and freedom. The country called 'Liberty' shows a highly modern world where artists produce the most incredible works of art: one painter, for example, shows Gulliver his 'painting', a blank canvas, entitled 'The Pointlessness and Incomprehensible Infinity of Existence' (135). The country of 'Collectivism' offers another example of a totalitarian society: Gulliver and his companions are received by armed soldiers who believe that the strangers are spying on their country. The political structure of the country resembles the communist regime in Hungary: 'Collectivism' is governed by one party without opposition called the 'Party of Honest People'. Streets are named by slogans such as 'Long live the eternal friendship of peaceful nations' or 'Long live our dearly beloved wise Leader' (139). The final stage of their space travelling leads Gulliver and his companions to the 'Old-World' (Antivilág) which they find to be the best possible place for mankind to occupy in the future. The inhabitants of this planet are well-educated, enlightened people who are not only rational beings but they highly value human emotions as well. In a strictly isolated part of the country called 'Reservation', surrounded by electrified wires, Gulliver meets some of the old inhabitants of the Earth who escaped the atomic explosion: he finds that they are treated as the wildest savages belonging to a very ancient civilization. The depiction of everyday life in the 'Reservation' is another direct critical response of the author to the worst effects of a consumer society: the daily papers are full of scandals, their politicians always point at each other, they keep lamenting about the past rather than build the future (197).

Characteristically, in each country Gulliver receives first-hand information on the educational system: a priest or a teacher always explains the main pedagogical methods of teaching the youth in the given country. With his fantastic-utopian work Papházi seems to reach back to the Karinthian line with such forefathers like Jules Verne, or H.G. Wells. Placing the work in the tradition of post-apocalyptic fiction and employing a modern Gulliver as a space Odysseus, gives a new direction to Hungarian Swiftian sequels.

Political Satires Disguised as Literary Parodies: *Gulliver utolsó utazása* [Gulliver's Last Voyage, 2001] and *A magyarok között: Gulliver sokadik utazása* [Among the Hungarians: Gulliver's Umpteenth Voyage, 2005]

The following imitations introduce two caricatures of the generic conventions of the imaginary voyage while they also provide metafictional reflections and remarks on a number of current political issues. The first offers a rewriting of the Lilliputian story, the second, also reflecting on the act of writing in an ironic way, leads Gulliver to contemporary Hungary to make him experience some of the absurdities occuring in a recently formed democracy. *Gulliver utolsó utazása* is a parodic narrative of the first voyage in which Gulliver accidentally returns to Lilliput only to experience the sadly altered conditions of Lilliputian life. The author of this continuation, Endre Gyárfás (1925-), is a well-known and prolific writer of poetry, novels, and children's books. His *Gulliver* is a literary parody as well as a social satire which, through exploiting a number of recognizable scenes in the original story, offers a humorous response to some of the questions that were left open in the original's first book. The illustration on the cover page, by the humorist Tibor Kaján, sets the tone of the book: Captain Gulliver is sitting in a wheelchair which is equipped with sails to enable it to move forward. Gulliver here arrives back in Lilliput and reflects on his previous travels. His ironic way of telling what happened to the Lilliputian people since his last visit offers perhaps the most entertaining reading among the twenty-first century imitations. The narrative picks up the line where it was left off last time when Gulliver returned from Lilliput: 'I rose and looked around. I found soft grass as high as my nails and palm trees not bigger than a rose-bush' (130). When he finds out that he was cast ashore again on the land of little creatures, he begins to worry: 'So this was Lilliput and not Blefuscu. I felt a bit uneasy because I could not know whether or not the death sentence which was reduced into the loss of my eyes was still in force' (131). Fortunately, the article of impeachment against Gulliver had since been invalidated when the emperor's power ended. Gulliver shortly learns what caused the death of the emperor and empress and how Lilliput became the supplier of Brobdingnag: during the ceremonious signing of the trade agreement between Brobdingnag and Lilliput, the 'ruling family and our government' (154) were being held in the hands of the giant king of Brobdingnag who, out of politeness, forgetting about himself, clapped his hands at the end of the little emperor's speech, accidentally squeezing him, his wife, and the whole 'government' to death:

> His Majesty the Emperor of Lilliput was giving his official speech. He uttered beautiful and touching words about the eternal friendship of the two nations, our common ancestors, the prospects of our cooperation, and about the windmill, which is right behind us, and which, as he was saying, I will never forget, is a pledge – a pledge of peaceful cooperation, and mutual understanding. Oh, God! This was his last word: a pledge! (154-55)

The Lilliputian government then forms a 'Public Charity Coalition' [Közjótékonysági Társulás] (135) where each individual is allowed to create his own one-member party. Gulliver goes for a walk to take a look around the country only to experience the impoverished state of the Lilliputian people and their suppression by Brobdingnag. Being informed about the causes of the economic decline he begins to ponder how he could help the Lilliputian people to be released from the oppression of the giants. However, before he could decide what he should do, he becomes captured. As during his previous visit, his hair, legs and feet are again fastened to the ground. Numb with horror, he realizes what the little creatures aim at: to remove all the hair from his body and sell it to

Brobdingnag. The last words that Gulliver imagines that, could he speak, he would utter, in which he would promise help, are uttered while the little creatures are steadily removing his teeth from his mouth.

Gyárfás's narrative is curiously ironic: when Gulliver understands that he is back in Lilliput and is free to ask all the questions he once imagined he would ask, he suddenly realizes that he has lost interest:

> At home in Albion when I told my stories about Lilliput in the club it occured to me that I cannot answer this or that question and, were I to get back, I would have to find them out. Now, that I was once again here, my curiosity evaporated. If, by the help of the Almighty, I can get home again, I do not mean to write down or tell my adventures to anyone, anyway (141).

The plot also contains remarks on a number of current political issues. For instance, one can hardly miss the possible application of the next passage to the multiplication of parties in the 1990s and the coalition government formed after the 1998 elections in Hungary when Szeniszlar the Second Master of Ceremonies explains the advantages of one-member parties in Lilliput to Gulliver:

> Let us see! According to an older statute the state has to sponsor parties having more than ten members. Thus it does not sponsor any parties. There are no party headquarters, party offices, designers of party image, or electoral canvassers. You do not have to pay membership fees – why should I put the money from one of my pockets into another? There are no faction quarrels, faction meetings, and the humiliating procedure of admission into the party has ceased, we are not vexed at those who withdraw from a party neither at those who turn out to be traitors ... And the main thing is that now noone embezzles the party funds.
>
> I had to admit: to this high level of practicality good old England will not arrive within centuries (137).

With its enigmatic ending and humorous style, *Gulliver utolsó utazása* reflects on some of the absurd features of post-transition Hungary.

László Rab's book, the most recent Hungarian rewriting of the Gulliver story, is another example of self-conscious fiction. Rab is the writer of several novels and is a journalist with the major left-wing political daily *Népszabadság* [People's Freedom]. Similarly to the other most recent satires, *A magyarok között: Gulliver sokadik utazása* [Among the Hungarians: Gulliver's Umpteenth Voyage], expresses the author's disillusionments with the post-transition period in Hungary while it also ironizes the arbitrariness of the Swiftian impact. The text is accompanied by a parodic subtext which mostly appears in the form of footnotes, questioning the authenticity of the narrative. Gulliver asks his friend, John Kovacs, who understands the language and knows Hungarian culture, to read and correct his story. 'Johnny' appears in the role of Richard Sympson although he is more critical of the manuscript: 'Mr. Gulliver has the right to be offended by my added remarks, which he thinks were unnecessary. However, I could not act otherwise since I had decided, as much as it was possible, to adjust the text to the mental capacity of the average Chelsea fan' (13-14). In the manner of Sterne, the author pokes fun at other novelistic conventions, too, such as the name-giving of his hero: this late offspring is called Jonathan (not Lemuel) Gulliver in the novel because of his father's love of Swift. At one point John Kovacs becomes so annoyed with Gulliver's eccentric and inauthentic story-telling that he decides to leave the text to its own fate and to quit his job. In response, a letter by the publishing house is attached in which the editorial board begs him not to quit his editorial work: 'We are kindly asking you, Mr. Kovacs, to re-consider your decision, and not to leave us alone with Mr. Gulliver because that will be our end' (59).

Here, Jonathan Gulliver arrives in twenty-first century Hungary. He is a mathematician and a software engineer delegated by his English boss, Leslie Partridge, to introduce the latest software called 'Superparliament 2010' for counting votes. There are two political parties called 'Kaffogók' ['yapping' politicians] and 'Hümmögők' ['humming' politicians]. Through the eyes of this uninformed English mathematician the reader gains insight into the political battles and the different levels of corruption in the Budapest of the 1990s. Swift's distant offspring spends nine months in the country although after the fourth month it becomes obvious that he can do nothing to improve the morals of politicians and lessen corruption which exists at every level of the society.

In Gulliver's figure Rab offers the viewpoint of the Western-European traveller who is a stranger to the political climate of a country which, although now belonging to the European Union (since 2004), still suffers from the worst effects of post-Socialist tendencies so characteristic of East Central-European societies. After a few months of forced idleness and inactivity Gulliver understands the national character of the Hungarians:

> Hungarians can lay the foundations of new times in the EU by introducing their most ancient national traditions, envy and disagreement. The main characteristic trait of the Hungarians is that they begin to thwart the realization of plans already at the birth of the idea. In their language it is called 'screwing up' [somebody else's efforts: 'keresztbe tevés']. What they win by this is that the inventor of the idea, perceiving the obstacles, will go to even greater pains to carry [his plans] through. I now know it for sure that this is the reason why the Hungarians have given so many Nobel Prize winners to the world (48-49).

Gulliver's Last Voyage and *Gulliver's Umpteenth Voyage* as parodic novels both belong to the group of 'soft' school approaches in that they exploit the gullibility of the protagonist and offer a tragi-comical ending to the story. Gulliver's futile efforts to amend people and to extinguish 'Party and Faction', to 'correct every Vice and Folly to which Yahoos are subject'[14] are shown as impossible utopian schemes. In both cases, he appears as the enlightened and educated Englishman who can only witness but never fully understand the absurdities of the place he visits. In *Gulliver's Umpteenth Voyage* the repeated attempts and ultimate failure of the protagonist to understand the irrationality of political thinking in Hungary is the latest case study to exploit the political potential of the Gulliver metaphor.

Conclusion

Among the works that belong to the creative reception of eighteenth-century English authors, Swiftian rewritings seem to dominate in Hungary in the twentieth century. What makes

Gulliver a seminal reading for a wide range of readers from children to adults up to the present day is its successful integration into the national literature in the form of imitations following the manner of dystopias, science fictional works, literary parodies, or political satires. Although we can find an alteration of the narrative situation only in Papházi's *Új Gulliver*, some of the other imitations show parallels to children's versions, too, which is a sign that *Gulliver*, to an extent, still belongs to juvenile literature in Hungary. With the exception of Gyárfás's continuation, which offers the most direct response to Swift's text, it is fair to say that in each of these contemporary sequels Gulliver's character takes up the role of the rational observer in a social satire. This is the kind of reduction of the protagonist's complex character that we can find in children's versions which usually limit their scope to the first two books of *Gulliver*.[15] What makes the figure of Gulliver so often exploited in the creative European, especially in the German re-writings of Swift's masterpiece, is that, through the eyes of 'Mr. Everyman', it offers a complex anatomy of human nature: 'On the whole, the structure of *Gulliver's Travels* is dichotomous. In Swift's narrative strategy, the rhetorical forces of historical 'experience' combine with those of philosophical 'reason'; they unite the historian's 'example(s)' (Books I-III) with the philosopher's 'precept' (Book IV).'[16] In the most recent Hungarian sequels each author is careful to put some distance between their authorial viewpoint and the society whose corruptions they want to reveal. Leaving out the philosophical insight and the ironic treatment of the narrator on the author's part, they do not attempt to preserve the complexity of Swift's novel. Although these narratives, in large, join the didactic trend of interpretations, the comic versions, through their metafictional reflections, raise the latest Gulliveriads into the group of postmodern novels. The existence and growing number of new sequels prove the capacity of the Swiftian heritage to survive and incite an unambiguous Hungarian interest. Gulliver's most recent encounters in Hungary continue to inspire new interpretations thus enriching the impact of the Dean in the field of creative imitations. Hermann J. Real's words prove that this tendency is part of the larger European context: 'He simply never lets his readers feel at ease. At no time, therefore, did Swift fall prey to cultural amnesia anywhere, nor is it probable that he ever will.'[17]

---

[1] Jonathan Swift, *Gulliver utazása* [Gulliver's Travels], trans. Frigyes Karinthy (Budapest: Révai, 1914).

[2] Laurence Sterne, *Érzékeny útazások Franczia- és Olaszországban* [A Sentimental Journey through France and Italy], trans. Ferenc Kazinczy, *Kazinczy Ferenc Munkái*, vol. 4 (Pest: Trattner, 1815): 87-346. Laurence Sterne, *Tristram Shandy úr élete és gondolatai* [The Life and Opinions of Tristram Shandy, Gentleman], trans. Győző Határ (Budapest: Új Magyar Könyvkiadó, 1956). Henry Fielding, *Tom Jones*, trans. Viktor Julow (Budapest: Franklin, 1950). Henry Fielding, *A néhai nagy Jonathan Wild úr élettörténete* [The Life of the Late Jonathan Wild], trans. Viktor Julow (Budapest: Szépirodalmi, 1954).

[3] Frigyes Karinthy, *Utazás Faremidóba: Gulliver ötödik útja* [Voyage to Faremido: the Fifth Voyage of Gulliver] (Budapest: Athenaeum, 1916), *Capillária: Gulliver hatodik útja* [Capillaria: the Sixth Voyage of Gulliver] (Budapest: Kultúra, 1921). An English translation has also been published, *Voyage to Faremido. Capillaria*, trans. Paul Tabori (Budapest: Corvina Press, 1965). Sándor Szathmári, *Gulliver utazása Kazohiniában* [Gulliver's Travel in Kazohinia] (Budapest: Bolyai Akadémia, 1941). In English, *Kazohinia*, trans. Inez Kemenes (Budapest: Corvina Press, 1975).

[4] See Klára Horváth Siklósi, *Gulliver in Joygorod*, trans. Ildikó Noémi Nagy (Budapest: Littera Nova Publishing, 1998); *Gulliver Bolgorogyban* [Gulliver in Bolgorogy] (Budapest: Littera Nova Kiadó, 1999); *Gulliver legújabb kalandja Pinkwellben* [Gulliver's Latest Adventure in Pinkwell] (Budapest: Orpheus Könyvek, 2001). Subsequent references are cited in the text.

[5] See Endre Gyárfás, *Gulliver utolsó utazása: szatírák, humoreszkek és egy kisregény* [Gulliver's Last Voyage: Satires, Humorous Sketches, and a Short Novel] (Budapest: PolgArt, 2001). Tivadar Papházi, *Új Gulliver: Fantasztikus-utópisztikus regény* [New Gulliver: A Fantastic-Utopian Novel] (Budapest: Accordia kiadó, 2003). László Rab, *A magyarok között: Gulliver sokadik utazása* [Among the Hungarians: Gulliver's Umpteenth Voyage] (Budapest: Népszabadság könyvek, 2005).

[6] See James L. Clifford, 'Gulliver's Fourth Voyage', *Quick Springs of Sense*, ed. Larry S. Champion (Athens: University of Georgia Press, 1974): 33-49.

[7] Clifford, 33.

[8] Sándor Szathmári, 'Mit akartam mondani Kazohiniával?' [What did I mean to say with Kazohinia?], *Magyar Út* (21 August 1941): 3. Imre Madách was a major Hungarian writer of the nineteenth century. His main work, *The Tragedy of Man*, is a Miltonian dramatic poem about Adam and Eve's expulsion from Eden and their travel through the history of mankind.

[9] For these pieces of information I am indebted to Klára Horváth Siklósi.

[10] All translations from Hungarian into English unless otherwise noted are by the author.

[11] Downie quotes from Pope's letter to Swift: 'Motte receiv'd the copy ... he knew not from whence, nor from whom, dropp'd at his house in the dark, from a Hackney-coach ...'. See J. A. Downie, 'The Political Significance of *Gulliver's Travels*', *Gulliver's Travels*. Norton Critical Edition, ed. Albert J. Rivero (New York and London: Norton, 2002): 337.

[12] See Literature/Children's books, 16 June 2008 <http://www.frankfurt.matav.hu/angol/kiadvanyok/eng/5.htm>. See also Siklósi's own website, Siklósi Horváth Klára, 16 June 2008 <http://www.siklosihorvath-knoll.hu>. For a review on Pinkwell, see Tibor Tüskés, '*Gulliver legújabb kalandja Pinkwellben.* Siklósi Horváth Klára regénye' [Gulliver's Latest Adventure in Pinkwell. A novel by Klára Horváth Siklósi], *Polísz* 62 (2001-2002): 90-92.

[13] Imre Battlay, *Gulliver utazásai ismeretlen országokban Swift Jonathántól* [Gulliver's Travels into Unknown Lands by Jonathan Swift] (Pest: Bartalits Imre, 1865).

[14] Rivero, 255.

[15] See Heinz Kosok, 'Gulliver's Children: A Classic Transformed for Young Readers', *Proceedings of The First Münster Symposium on Jonathan Swift*, eds Hermann J. Real and Heinz J.Vienken (München: Wilhelm Fink Verlag, 1985): 135-44.

[16] See Hermann J. Real, 'Gulliver's Travels into Remote Eighteenth-Century Germany', *The Novel in Anglo-German Context. Cultural Cross-Currents and Affinities*, ed. Susanne Stark (Amsterdam: Rodopi, 2000): 18.

[17] Hermann J. Real, Introduction, *The Reception of Jonathan Swift in Europe*, ed. Hermann J. Real (London and New York: Thoemmes Press, 2005): 4.

10 | Venturing onto Licensed Premises. Translating Flann O'Brien's *At Swim-Two-Birds* into Hungarian

Erika Mihálycsa

> I'm thirsty, he said. I have sevenpence. Therefore I buy a pint. I immediately recognized this as an intimation that I should pay for my own porter.
>
> The conclusion of your syllogism, I said lightly, is fallacious, being based on licensed premises.
>
> Flann O'Brien, *At Swim-Two-Birds*

If translation as language transfer is not merely difficult but an impossible project, few books have more right to be labelled impossible to translate than Flann O'Brien's *At Swim-Two-Birds*. Translating Flann O'Brien (Brian O'Nolan/Ó Núalláin, alias Myles na gCopaleen, Brother Barnabas etc.) into any language certainly means to venture on premises where (poetic, linguistic, stylistic) license is the *conditio sine qua non*. The author whom James Joyce, Graham Greene, William Saroyan, Anthony Burgess and others admired is deeply embedded into what is currently described as the Anglo-Irish comic tradition ranging from Swift to Beckett's early English fiction, showing a curious interface with literary postmodernism. It has become much of a critical commonplace to refer to *At Swim-Two-Birds,* alongside Beckett's *Murphy* and Joyce's *Finnegans Wake*, as a work marking the great divide between modernism and postmodernism; accordingly, O'Brien has long been situated in the canon of the great path-openers, as the other 'illstarred punster' to react to Joyce's pervasive formal, linguistic experimentation in strikingly original fictions. Still, O'Brien has received relatively little attention in the Hungarian-speaking area: although his only novel to be written in Gaelic, *An Béal Bocht* (1941, translated into English by Patrick Power as *The Poor Mouth*, 1973) was translated as early as 1982 under the idiomatic title *A fába szorult féreg* (trans. Júlia Veres, Budapest: Európa), followed by the translation of *The Third Policeman* in 2003 (*A harmadik rendőr*, trans. Gábor Török, Budapest: Geopen), the author remains the reading of a small anglophile coterie. Far from the status of cult-author he enjoys, especially in the German-speaking countries with two translations of *At Swim-Two-Birds* available, the second by no less a name than Harry Rowohlt who is also the translator of O'Brien's collected works (published by Kein & Aber, Zürich, 2002-2006) and an Austrian film based on the novel (*In Schwimmen-zwei-Vögel*, 1997, dir. Kurt Palm).

The Hungarian translation of *At Swim-Two-Birds* is the product of a four-handed work-in-progress carried out between 2005-2007 by Gábor Csizmadia, PhD candidate specializing in O'Brien's work, and the author of the present paper, MA in Irish Studies and PhD student researching the fiction of James Joyce, Flann O'Brien and Samuel Beckett. The final, joint and 'corrected' version was preceded by two independent translation texts elaborated by the two translators before learning about each other's versions; these two initial versions were then processed, edited, transformed, *translated*, and rewritten into the 'corrected' version, scheduled to appear in the spring of 2008 at the bilingual Koinónia Publishing House, Kolozsvár/Cluj, Romania.[1] The present paper proposes to explore some of the main translation problems encountered, starting with the issue of dialect, the parodies of style and self-parodies, including Celtic legends that have no stylistic equivalents in the target language. Lastly, it tackles the methodology and problems of creating a seamless text out of the two existing translation versions, of amalgamating the different speech registers and local variants of Hungarian used by the two translators.

The very first issue to be addressed when approaching the translation of any writer of Hiberno-English, Flann O'Brien in particular is, *into what language* to translate. *At Swim-Two-Birds* (1939) displays thirty-odd parodies of style and discourse which are all embedded in the variant, or – in Deleuzian terms – minor language of English called Hiberno-English which, with its playful linguistic energies and unfathomable inventiveness, markedly deviates from Standard English. There is a vast literature on the linguistic politics of Hiberno-English, backed up by the literary tradition perhaps most justified to claim to have made the major language minor; arguably the essential ingredient of this 'hyphenated tongue' is translation – 'transluding from the Otherman' (*Finnegans Wake*).[2] Hiberno-English is a jocose, ex-centric language that abounds in Gaelic inflections, word-for-word translation from the Gaelic, especially concerning the use of prepositional phrases, compound words: e.g., 'The nose *to* his white *wheyface* was a headland *against* white seas with height *to* it, in all, the height of ten warriors man on man and with breadth *to* it the breadth of Erin ... He rose *to* a full *tree-high standing* ... *To* each of the two eyes in his head was there *eye-hair to* the fashion of a young forest.'[3] The unnamed student-narrator's uncle and his company speak a mannered variant of this idiom, while the 'Ringsend cowboys' Shanahan, Lamont, Furriskey, Shorty Andrews and Slug Willard, hired by the fictional author Trellis to act in his moralizing novel, speak the Irish brogue of the 'plain people of Ireland' that is frequently the butt of Myles na gCopaleen's/The Brother's tongue. The latter certainly differs from the 'stage Irish' consecrated by Synge and the Revival: its immediate precursor was, as with many of the style parodies, Joyce, who had an acute ear for the inflections of Dublin speech (see especially 'Cyclops' where one can spot quite a few of the 'originals' of the witticisms and table talk in *At Swim*; many of these phrases, however, could as well be common jokes in Dublin parlance). Every now and then, the reader of *At Swim* stumbles upon literary landmines, Joycean echoes that the translator has to consider, look up: the bombastic hyperbole of the Finn parody, for instance, are patterned on the Citizen's Finn-style portrait in 'Cyclops'; Orlick's work-in-progress with its *tour de force*, the ironic transubstantiation of the three Ringsend cowboys into paragons of their sex harks back to the pedantic, mock-catechistic prose, heavily laden with pseudo-scientific Latinisms, of 'Ithaca' and, partly, 'Eumaeus'. O'Brien, whom the critics' misplaced charge of Joycean epigonism dogged throughout his life, obviously took great pleasure in placing such allusions for the initiates; in these cases the translator, similarly, would have to play upon the (established) version of the *Portrait* or *Ulysses* text in the target language.

Since Hiberno-English works as a dialectal version within English, it can have certainly no equivalent in Hungarian. Firstly, because Hungarian does not have dialects or minor languages with their own extended, well-established literary tradition, but only regional variants of 'Standard' Hungarian, differing in pronunciation mostly. Secondly and more importantly, for the translation of Hiberno-English one would need an idiom equally founded on translation, hybridity, and foreign inflections. Within this idiom, the 'brogue' is at once rural and urban, so the Hungarian translator cannot opt for a rural idiom or modern slang either – not to mention the awkwardness of a, hypothetical, *székely* (the most characteristically colourful Hungarian dialect in Transylvania, present-day Romania) report on Sergeant Craddock's jumping skills, localizing the ironically subverted Irish-English conflict in a geographically and ethnographically narrow, quintessentially rustic Hungarian context. A further problem is, into what slang to translate: since the novel was completed in 1938, one cannot make indiscriminate use of up-to-date slang forms – on the other hand, the use of obsolete, historicizing slang could take the edge off the text. The formula adopted, for instance, to translate 'this is all my bum', Brinsley's replica to the budding postmodernism of the student-narrator's literary manifesto, is a turn-of-phrase with a folkish rather than contemporary urban touch to it ['Nesze semmi fogd meg jól', appr. 'Take this nothing, grab it tight']. As a case in point, Miklós Szentkuthy, translator of the 'authoritative' 1974 Hungarian *Ulysses*, systematically resorted to contemporary slang forms, lowering the speech register of the characters as a rule, in order so to preserve the text's linguistic shock-effect. This solution, however, often leads him not only to awkward anachronisms but also to contextually highly problematic shifts and blurring of speech registers and style, as pointed out by András Kappanyos (1997, 2002). One of the obvious traps of translation is to render the brogue in a merely ungrammatical, low colloquial parlance: this amounts to a value-judgment on the characters' social background, it could therefore never function as a marker of difference – not to mention the danger of levelling the inexhaustible verbal inventiveness and rhetorical flourish of stock phrases and nonsensical statements turned out with an aphoristic gravity ('Oh I'm telling you, Casey was a man in twenty thousand, there's no doubt about that. He knew what he was at, too true he did. If he knew nothing else, he knew how to write a pome. A pint of plain is your only man,' 78; 'The fiddle is an awkward class of a thing to carry ... it's not what you might call a handy shape. They say you get a sort of a crook in the arm ...' (151)). The only conclusion, quoth learned Lamont on the art of playing the fiddle: the ear is the main thing and the aspiring translator can wear the last tatter of skin off his/her knuckles and still won't get as far as his/her own shadow if s/he hasn't got the ear. 'Have the ear and you're half-way there before you start at all' (154).

Since Hungarian contains no such distinct variant that incorporates translation, the translator has to invent it in the target language (TL). The main problem of translation will be that the linguistic forms so invented would not resonate in the TL with the same mark of difference and hybridity as in the source language (SL). The two translators of *At Swim-Two-Birds* tried to invent an eclectic language which follows the original text's deviations from the standard, the original's 'foreignizing' effects; regional, rural forms (mostly Transylvanian – according to the translators' intention, however, not belonging to any *one* of the regional rural dialects found there) are mixed with (low) colloquial and slang elements. The inflections of Transylvanian Hungarian have, for the ears of the average Hungarian speaker, a distinct non-standard ring, owing to a condition of (historical, cultural) marginality. The fact that within the Hungarian-speaking area Transylvanian regional dialects have long been stereotyped as somewhat picturesquely archaic, their speakers being associated with qualities never far removed from folklore, traditions, and ultimately, (social, economic, cultural) backwardness, has led to many tentative parallels with the status of (stage) Irish within the English-speaking world. While such a parallel between two marginal(ized) minor languages may appear as fruitful, playing on stereotyping –

of either the starry-eyed, or the subversively self-ironic variety – is both problematic and fallacious, especially considering the inherent (political, contextual) patronizing gesture in both these attitudes. The use of stereotypically Transylvanian Hungarian turns-of-phrase, collocations, words as markers of difference should not therefore prevail in the translation of any text written in Hiberno-English; instead of such culturally 'eroded' markers or labels, the ones found in the final Hungarian translation text are rather formulae, turns-of-phrase which add a note of rhetorical flourish or verbal over-elaboration, especially in the casual conversations of the Ringsend cowboys. In this respect I consider the novel's Romanian translation, by Adrian Oţoiu (*La Doi Lebădoi*, Piteşti: Paralela 45, 2005) highly interesting: here the 'brogue' is a savoury mixture of turns-of-phrase evoking the language of end-of-nineteenth-century comic playwright Ion Luca Caragiale's characters (half-educated upstarts who speak a corrupted Romanian teeming with French malapropisms), Transylvanian rural dialectal forms, as well as the *mahala* language, typical to the outskirts of contemporary Romanian cities, in vogue not only by virtue of the media but also of the Romanian literary 'New Wave'.

A significant feature of Flann O'Brien's novel is that almost all characters speak an idiom of their own, resulting in a wildly comic heteroglossia. The distinctness of lingos is carefully maintained throughout the novel, one of the main sources of textual comedy being when mutually exclusive styles or registers are juxtaposed, e.g., the cowboys interrupting Finn Mac Cool's recital of Mad King Sweeny's legend with side-splitting anecdotes of their own. Similarly, the verses sung by Sweeny (taken from *Suibhne Geilt*, the early medieval legend comprising some of the finest Irish nature poetry – probably the only textual component of *At Swim* to be relatively untouched by parody, as demonstrated by a comparison with Seamus Heaney's modern English translation) willy-nilly enter a bardic competition with the *pomes* of Jem Casey, the Poet of the Pick, thus throwing an oblique light on the different and mutually relativized ideas of what poetry should be. The translator has to keep these voices scrupulously apart, with the exception of the instances where O'Brien's novel willfully plays at stylistic cross-breeding – namely, in Trellis's Sweeny-style passion written by Orlick, or in Orlick's ironic characterization of his half-educated literary pals Shanahan, Lamont and Furriskey in the catechistic manner of Joyce's 'Ithaca'.

Every single level of fictionality in the novel comes in the form of the parody of some literary style or discourse, having its own related, or embedded, manuscript excerpts that present further parodies and pastiches. This strategy obviously harks back to *Ulysses*, especially to the 'Oxen of the Sun' and 'Cyclops' episodes which take the reader along the history of English and Anglo-Irish prose styles. The road to Flann O'Brien's prose leads through Joyce and through *Ulysses* (however much chagrin the constant parallels to Joyce caused O'Brien); the Hungarian translator can thus draw, where possible, on the linguistic solutions found by Miklós Szentkuthy, one of the 'control texts' of the present translation.[4] Arguably, the greatest translation problem is the rendering of the 'manivaried' parodies of style, some of which have no stylistic 'original', nor any diachronically analogous stylistic 'relatives' in the TL on which to rely. This task necessitates a double invention in the TL: of linguistic-stylistic forms which could function in a manner somewhat analogous to the original's parodies and pastiches that can rely on the reader's recognition of some pre-existing stylistic framework in the SL, and the transfer of O'Brien's parodic effects.

The frame narrative with its pedantic, circumlocutional style and playful self-reflexivity holds up the cracked looking-glass to Joyce's *A Portrait*, ironically mimicking Stephen's aesthetic digressions. Fragmented into manuscript excerpts and quotes from comically eclectic sources, each with a subtitle, with recondite figures of style that come up in casual conversation carefully pointed out, this frame narrative offers itself as a jocose catalogue of rhetorical figures, turning the tables on the aphoristic definition of the (Cartesian) author in *A Portrait*, foregrounding the novel's artificiality:

> I rejoined that if his finances warranted such generosity, I would raise no objection, but that I (for my part) was no Rockefeller, thus utilizing a figure of speech to convey the poverty of my circumstances.

> Nature of figure of speech: Synecdoche (or Autonomasia) (46).

A consistently pedantic style to translate, with much academic clowning, the narrative framework comes closest in style to Joyce's 'Eumaeus', fragments from 'Aeolus' where the text foregrounds its own artificiality and juxtaposes different types of rhetoric, and 'Ithaca'. The translation text has therefore to create a highly mannered, obtuse style whose principal strategy, akin to that of Joyce's 'Eumaeus', draws on linguistic overplay, its mannerisms and (mock-) academic terminology as a rule creating the effect of puzzlement through delayed understanding. The translator is given the green light to play on dead metaphors – clichés – to such an extent and in such concentration as to defamiliarize them, departing thus significantly from, or blatantly defying, linguistic norms of fluency and communicative readability. Such a text seems to invite what, since Lawrence Venuti's seminal study *The Translator's Invisibility*, is termed foreignization in translation:

> Foreignizing translation signifies the difference of the foreign text, yet only by disrupting the cultural codes that prevail in the target language. In its efforts to do right abroad, this translation method must do wrong at home, deviating enough from native norms to stage an alien reading experience – choosing to translate a foreign text excluded by domestic literary canons, for instance, or using a marginal discourse to translate it.[5]

The translator would have to create a specific locus of foreignness within the TL where language use would constantly and consistently frustrate the reader's expectations of readability and domestication to native linguistic and discursive norms, drawing attention to the idiosyncrasies of style.[6] An additional difficulty is that one cannot rely on the stylistic 'original' of the SL parody. In Hungarian literary tradition, understandably, the text of Joyce's *A Portrait* is not embedded and assimilated to an extent comparable with (native) classics; much of the intertextual byplay and plotline parody of the frame narrative is thus, if not lost, at least not readily assumed by the TL audience. For instance, such sentences as the famous definition of the artist-God of creation hidden above, behind his handiwork, paring his fingernails, that lurks behind the playful literary programme expounded by O'Brien's narrator would not be immediately identified. However, the style of the frame narrative is relatively straightforward in comparison with the linguistically more remote parodies of style which in the SL function as double translations – of Gaelic originals and of their English translatorese, none of which have any possible linguistic or stylistic analogy in the TL. One of the most memorable and most explosively comic threads of such parody in the novel is the one centred around the mythological figure of Finn Mac Cool, the Hercules-like hero of an extensive cycle of Old Irish legends, the *Fianna*. Some of these early legends – actually, the ones best preserved in oral tradition – already contain the grain of hyperbolic descriptions and mushrooming catalogues. They were 'recycled' in relatively tame English translations by the Revival, their explosive linguistic energies and wildly comic hyperbole being put to full use, once again, by Joyce's *Ulysses* – namely, in the Finn-style portrait of the Citizen in 'Cyclops'. O'Brien's Finn parody should be compared to both the legend versions circulated by the Revival and to Joyce's 'Cyclops' (for the Hungarian reader, to Szentkuthy's Joyce). Where O'Brien departs from these earlier English renderings of the Finn legendry is, on the one hand, his greater proximity to the Old Irish originals (O'Brien was fully bilingual, being fluent not only in medieval Irish but in Old Irish as well – as a student he was a regular contributor to the *Comhthrom Féinne*, 'Fair Play' magazine, with a satirical column written in Old Irish in order to elude state censorship), and partly in the sweeping, unbuttoned comedy of language.[7]

In rendering the valences of the Finn parody's (Gaelicizing) prose, the translator can resort to archaic variants of the TL. A major problem is the invention of formulae and turns-of-phrase which could create an effect similar to the defamiliarizing phrasing of the original, functioning as a 'translatorese' from Gaelic: 'The mouth *to* his white wheyface was *to* the width of Ulster ...' – here the translator willy-nilly has to resort to, more or less domesticating, archaic ritualistic formulae in the TL. Whereas, for instance, Gaelic-type compound words ('wheyface', 'manivaried') have little or no defamiliarizing effect in Hungarian, the rendering of 'foreign' prepositional phrases is much more problematic: Hungarian, an agglutinating language, has no prepositions but expresses spatial and temporal directions by postpositions attached to the qualified word, and these as a rule have a narrower semantic field than prepositions in English. The solution adopted by the translators in coping with sentences like 'Three fifties of fosterlings could engage with handball against the wideness of his backside, which was wide enough to halt the march of warriors through a mountain-pass' (15) was that of stylizing in excess, departing, where possible, from the (contemporary, or archaic) linguistic norm – with Fritz Senn's term, of 'provecting' language effects (alliteration, rhythm, imagery). An additional 'provecting' effect was to introduce some intertextual byplay into the invented comic-archaic language of the Finn passages. In the Hungarian description of Finn's eyeballs echoes from *Toldi* (nineteenth-century Hungarian national verse epic by János Arany) surface, heightening the effect of bombast – all the more so, since the (historical) hero of the Hungarian epic who very nearly acquired the status of a national hero triumphs due to his legendary strength. Similarly, in the macabre table talk that takes place at the Furriskeys, Mrs Furriskey candidly expresses her wish to die in bed – a sentence which, in the Hungarian version, reverts the opening line of one of the programmatic revolutionary poems of nineteenth-century national poet János Petőfi, 'Egy gondolat bánt engemet' [There's but one thought that bothers me]. What in Petőfi's poem, glorifying revolutionary heroics and death on the battlefield, is rejected as the least desirable of fates, 'to die on pillows, in bed' is here anticlimactically evoked as most wished-for among farcically improbable stories of deaths. [8]

The Finn parody also offers ample playground for linguistic carnivalization and for the eventual coming-into-being of additional meanings, language effects, of translatorial *Mehrwert*. Finn's catalogue of birds for instance is almost entirely made up of fanciful names ('maritime wren, green-lidded parakeet') playing on ornithological terms, with a fair share of sexual punning. Among these names Gaelic red herrings occur (*pilibeen*, *cruiskeen lawn*), turning the reader's expectations upside down and, at the same time, poking fun at an audience that enthusiastically embraces the cause of the ancestral tongue, while it has presumably lost touch with it to such an extent as to take these items of doubtful pedigree for winged specimens.[9] One resulting translation problem is the dilemma of whether to create analogous names in the target language (as did Gábor Csizmadia, highlighting the sexual pun in *pilibeen*), making these available to the Hungarian reader, or to preserve them as Gaelic red herrings. In other words, whether to suppress the foreignness of the *other* (unfamiliar) language and the text's hybridity, to appropriate it for the sake of driving the joke home, or to preserve this foreignness as an essential part of the joke and marker of context, substituting direct translation with an endnote. I chose to go for the latter (as well as in the case of Celtic terms occurring in the narrative, e.g., *ollavs*, *dun*, *duidi*n etc. where a Hungarian equivalent might have been used for the sake of greater fluency), since they function as signals of difference, hybridity, which have not only an important role in (re)creating the context but also in the multiple play with language(s). In the overall translation of the bird catalogue the joint version again chose to 'provect' the language games of the original, 'sinning' on the side of alliteration and sexual punning, arguably more explicit in the Hungarian version than in the original.

The poems recited by Finn are overtly devoid of any trace of parody, as if the mythological hero were allowed to speak in 'his' own voice; similarly, the verses in the Sweeny legend that he relates speak unequivocally in the voice of medieval Irish nature poetry, as a comparison with Seamus Heaney's *Sweeny Astray* reveals. The two translators produced an almost word-by-word translation of the original Sweeny poems in free verse with no dominant rhythm patterns, based on internal repetition and alliteration, following the original's rhetorical and stylistic 'anomalies' and occasional lapses into self-parody ('Just as it went *prestissimo*/The spear-shaft skyward,/You too, Sweeny, go madly-mad/Skyward', 65).

Among the other parodies of style and discourse in *At Swim-Two-Birds* we may find seventeenth-century Methodist epistles, newspaper reports, extracts from moral treatises, courtroom protocols, a nineteenth-century epic-descriptive poem of a sea voyage, a lengthy quote from the *Hebrew Bible* (*The Book of the Son of Sirach*) as well as a wide range of savoury low-brow entertainment books, mainly westerns. In conveying these the translator ought to consider the (nearest) equivalents of such traditions and discourses within the TL literary heritage, but rather than turning out bookish pastiches, had better make the best of all the linguistic and stylistic resources at his/her command – without, however, lapsing into indiscriminate wordplay for wordplay's sake. So much so that, in many cases, in reworking the successive versions along the stages of the translation we had to cut rather than add, following the 'less is more' principle.

The '*Memorandum of the respective diacritical traits of Messrs Furriskey, Lamont and Shanahan*' for instance is a lengthy exercise in academic clowning, its main source of humour being the use of pedantic Latinisms, (mock-) scientific terminology to classify and describe physical features and objects that are singularly banal and down-to-earth – thus situating form at the farthest possible remove from content:

> *Head*: brachycephalic; bullet; prognathic.
> *Vision*: tendencies toward myopia; wall-eye; nyctalopia.
> *Configuration of nose*: roman; snub; mastoid.
> *Unimportant physical afflictions*: palpebral ptosis; indigestion; German itch.
> *Mannerisms*: tendency to agitate or flick fingers together in prim fashion after conveying bread or other crumbling substance to mouth; tooth-sucking and handling of tie-knot; ear-poking with pin or match, lip-pursing (161).

The strategy on which linguistic comedy rests is, as in the case of 'Ithaca' and many passages from 'Eumaeus', delayed understanding – the reader first has to translate the foreign terms into a more 'homely' language. Hungarian, not being part of the family of Indo-European languages and therefore accomodating foreign terms (especially Latinisms and words of Greek origin) to a much less extent than English with its 'double' vocabulary, has obviously far less possibilities to play upon the difference of register, say, between 'palpebral ptosis', 'indigestion' and 'German itch'. The Hungarian translator here either performs the transfer that would be required of the reader – that is, makes intelligible at once what the English-language reader has to work out, thus also levelling the difference of register felt in the sequence – or, by preserving, as the two translators did, the Latin term, makes it markedly less accessible and therefore more 'scientific' than 'palpebral ptosis' would be in English. Without the intimidating Latin diagnostic (in Hungarian medical jargon the descriptive, homely Hungarian term being preferred) the banality of the symptom loses its inherently comic effect. The same refers to the botanical terms or to the foreign-sounding names of foods which on closer inspection turn out to be reassuringly plebeian.

The final Hungarian translation text is the product of a four-handed process of rewriting that started in the autumn of 2005 and has been going on for the past two and a half years. I learned about the existence of another rendering of the novel into Hungarian in the summer of 2005 when looking for a publisher interested in my own, by then complete, translation; exchanging our respective versions with Gábor Csizmadia, the idea arose to work them into one joint, 'corrected' text. It was I who carried out most of this work, going through the two initial translation versions and working them into successive stages of a translation-palimpsest; at the end of each of these stages we shared our thoughts and doubts about the current version which then served as a starting-point to a next stage of elaboration. Both Gábor and I have done extensive research on Flann O'Brien, being both PhD students – he, at Eötvös Loránd University, Budapest; and I, at Babeş-Bolyai University, Cluj, Romania. By a graceful irony of sorts we both happen to have tackled palimpsests in other contexts – Gábor holds a degree in classical archaeology, having specialized in provincial Roman civilization, while the author of the present paper is also a BA in art history, with a dissertation written on the mural cycles of the early medieval church of Santa Maria Antiqua in Rome, dated on the basis of a palimpsest-wall. My objective in writing a joint version from the two existing translations – a work not merely of collage and editing but rather, of continuous re-working of both translation versions together with the successive variants of the joint one – was to create a seamless text where each discourse parody appears as coherent, internally valid, yet allowing for internal hybridization. Throughout this process the two, continuously rewritten, translations read and reread each other, often resulting in the creation of a third, umpteenth text variant for one passage, sentence or another, rather than the substitution of one of the initial translation texts. Besides the SL text there were the two initial translation versions with their poignant differences and less conspicuous common denominators continuously playing upon each other, inscribing themselves on each other, making the work on the text more layered and complex, but also infinitely more instructive and rewarding. Cases when a lengthy passage was inserted unchanged from the one version into the joint translation were few; it was mostly words, turns of phrase, inflections from the one version changing, 'hybridizing' the syntax, phrasing, or rhythm of the other version to such an extent that in many passages of the final version it becomes well-nigh impossible to distinguish the one, or the other, initial translation text. My own translation prevails in the language, general tone of the frame narrative, in the Pooka and the Good Fairy and in the Orlick threads of narrative, as well as in most of the Sweeny prose; Gábor's translation predominates in most of the discursive parodies, he being the author of the Jem Casey *pomes*, as well as of the translation of the nineteenth-century blank-verse shipwreck saga, and it is he who holds the copyright to most of the puns and sparkles of wit. The most mixed language is that of the Ringsend cowboys whose staple Hungarian 'brogue' is imbued with turns-of-phrase taken from westerns and comics. Here one of the major problems and challenges was to find a common ground for our differing linguistic 'luggage': in my initial version the company speak something akin to rural Transylvanian dialect, while in Gábor's, urban slang with German and Yiddish inflections. The *querelle* of red-necks with citified pub-dwellers might be exemplified by the battle, in translating 'This is all my bum', of 'zseb szilvalekvár' ['this is all a pocketful of plum jam'] against 'nesze neked orrod alá szalámi' ['there's salami under your nose'], 'etesd a nénikédet' ['Go feed – i.e., tell this to – your nanny'] etc. These obvious differences had to be smoothed out without quite levelling them: so, in the present joint version Shanahan & Co. use both elements of Budapest lingo and a suave tincture of Transylvanian *couleur locale*, in a way that is in many respects akin to the Romanian translation. The primary fear usually voiced in connection with texts written/translated by more than one person is the loss of (stylistic, textual) unity, the emergence of lines of rupture. This issue must be viewed from a different angle with O'Brien's *At Swim-Two-Birds*, since the novel itself is willingly fragmentary, defying readerly expectations of (narrative, textual, stylistic) unity, made up, as it is, of pastiches and parodies of style ranging from school textbooks by the Irish Christian Brothers to *Portrait*-style aesthetic digressions. A joint translation, however, has the advantage that the (two) versions/-readings make each other visible *as* versions; this does not only mean that avoiding and recognizing translation mistakes becomes easier, but also that the co-translators bring into the process their own linguistic, stylistic background, which increases their knowledge of the SL text. Translation in collaboration may only be viable if in the process the translators become sufficiently detached from both their own work and that of the other, so as to detect not merely the errors proper (be they linguistic, cultural, stylistic in nature) but also the less conspicuous sites of incoherence, contextual/co-textual deviations, fissures in style or, on the contrary, places where one reading or the other forcefully domesticates, appropriates the original by virtue of a 'strong' stylistic solution (e.g., formulaic phrasings, stylistic patterns embedded in the TL). One of the greatest dangers in (joint) translation is the fascination with one's own, or the other's solutions to such an extent that these overwhelm the original; translatorial *Mehrwert* should never be allowed to dominate a text, however 'congenial' in style. It is in this respect also that resorting to yet other versions (e.g., translations into different languages) may help in making such 'appropriations' of the original visible.

One of the risks run in translating texts that push (linguistic, formal) experimentation to the extreme is precisely in their effect of 'defamiliarizing' the target language. A casual glance at the Hungarian translation versions of *Ulysses* (or indeed, most translations of the book) speaks volumes about the multiple strategies of domestication and back-normalizing adopted with Joyce's process-sentences – 'sents', dystax, grammatical, discursive anomalies and 'sintalks' against normative language use.[10] In the context of Hungarian publishing and reception it is still a pervasive practice that foreignizing, defamiliarizing uses of the language of writing are sacrificed for the sake of discursive normality and fluency. The charge of 'magyartalanság' [of a text being 'not Hungarian enough'] is among the most frequently invoked, and current translation practice relies rather heavily on domesticating language use – in translations of contemporary authors, of Anglo-Indian writers, of 'Inglish' for instance. It is all the more important for the translation of such experimental, parodic fiction as *At Swim-Two-Birds* to resist domesticating practice and explore valences of language (pedantry carried to self-parody, effects of style parodied to an extent comparable to 'Oxen of the Sun' in *Ulysses*) of which some may have to be created anew, inaugurated in the target language.

Joyce translations, as well as the two translations of *At Swim-Two-Birds* available to me have also greatly helped in shaping this joint version: the Romanian translation by Adrian Oţoiu, and the exemplary German translation, a joint work of Harry Rowohlt (translator of *Winnie the Pooh* and of the complete Flann O'Brien) and Helmut Mennicken. The comparison with translations into other languages has proven immensely instructive, especially regarding the solutions to convey the various registers and styles, foreignizing effects, the coping with obscure passages, puns, linguistic untranslatabilities. And, to no less extent, regarding the language effects of liberties taken in rendering, often recontextualizing certain parodies of style, hybridizing them with more or less established styles in the target language, resulting in curious mixtures of what might be described as translation fallacies and translatorial *Mehrwert*.

Coming to the title, after having toyed with different versions (reference to the novel in Hungarian was most often made as *A két madár-gázlónál* [at the ford of the two birds]), we chose to follow recent research which points out that *Snámh-dá-én* was an island *in* the river Shannon, rather than a placename *by* the Shannon. Consequently, the Hungarian title, in accordance with the title of the new German translation, is a word-for-word rendering: *Úszikkétmadáron*.

At Swim-Two-Birds is obviously a book of untranslatabilities, revelling in language games, there are thus too many puns and translators' cruxes to enlist. The most vicious of these, humiliating all translators (of the foreign-language versions accessible to me) is the one included in the epigraph and the title of the present paper. On the other hand, a most satisfying solution concerning one of the novel's key sentences – *Ars est celare artem* [Art is the concealment of art/of the artificial – with a byplay on the (Irish) pronunciation of 'ars'] – has been reached: Gábor Csizmadia's *Altest celare artem* [*Posterior* celare artem]. The immediate context of the fundamental law of poetics implied by the phrase, turned upside down with such unprecedented insolence in the book-web of *At Swim-Two-Birds*, is the musings of the novelist *emeritus* Trellis, while climbing up the stairs behind the plump skivvy Teresa on whose opulent posterior the presence of a corset, of the cheap industrially-tailored variety, is unequivocally perceptible. Its presence revealed, its *raison d'être* of creating a benign illusion is betrayed.

---

1 The translators wish to thank Ireland Literature Exchange, the Hungarian National Cultural Fund (Nemzeti Kulturális Alap) and the Hungarian Book Foundation (Magyar Könyv Alapítvány) for supporting the translation work.

2 On the issue of Hiberno-English as a language that incorporates translation, as well as on the linguistic politics of the writer in Hiberno-English – of whom James Joyce may be regarded as the epitome – see Michael Cronin, *Translating Ireland*: *Translation, Language, Culture* (Cork: Cork University Press, 1996). Cronin examines the 'linguistic schizophrenia' of the Irish, experienced in the language shift between two minor languages, Irish and Hiberno-English, yet the forceful dislocation in-between tongues is less relevant in this argument, for the writer who thus finds himself in permanent exile as translator, than the linguistic, poetic possibilities offered by the hybrid zone or battlefield ('bloodflield', *FW*) where the one language always *ghosts* the other. See also Katie Wales, *The Language of James Joyce* (London: Macmillan, 1992); Laurent Milesi, ed., *James Joyce and the Difference of Language* (Cambridge: Cambridge University Press, 2003).

3 Flann O'Brien, *At Swim-Two-Birds* (London: Penguin Classics, 2001): 12. Subsequent references are cited in the text.

4 On the problems and shortcomings of the two existing Hungarian translations of *Ulysses*, Endre Gáspár's 1947 version and what is regarded as the 'authoritative' Hungarian *Ulysses*, Miklós Szentkuthy's 1974 rendering, see András Kappanyos, 'Ulysses, a nyughatatlan' [Ulysses, the restless], *Átváltozások* 10 (1997): 44-54; András Kappanyos, 'Megint egy work-in-progress' [A work-in-progress again], *Filológiai Közlöny* 3-4 (2002): 245-50. Unfortunately the manuscript of the upcoming, corrected Hungarian translation, carried out by a team of Joyceans under the supervision of András Kappanyos, was not available to us at the time of finalizing the translation of O'Brien's novel.

5 Lawrence Venuti, *The Translator's Invisibility* (London: Routledge, 1995): 20.

6 Venuti's study calls for a new approach to translation that would resist the domestication work performed by bringing back the

cultural other as the same, the recognizable, the familiar, to the extent that 'translation serves an appropriation of foreign cultures for domestic agendas, cultural, economic, political' and acting against the 'fluent translations that invisibly inscribe foreign texts with [native] language values and provide readers with the narcissistic experience of recognizing their own culture in a cultural other' (15). On the other hand, as Venuti's critics point out, ultimately all translation, however foreignizing and minoritizing in intent, is inherently a domestication of a foreign language: if otherwise, it would be as linguistically foreign to the TL audience as to be unintelligible. Thus the 'foreignizing' strategies of liberating the 'remainder' of foreignness proposed by Venuti – e.g., literal translations into anachronisms, archaisms bordering on pastiche, foreign phrases, culturally foreign colloquialisms – can be viewed as merely different, more problematizing cases of domestication, or domestication made difficult, as these disruptions of norm would nevertheless have to belong to, and be recognizable in, the domestic major language. See Ida Klitgård, *Fictions of Hybridity: Translating Style in James Joyce's* Ulysses (Odense: University Press of Southern Denmark, 2007): 90-93.

7 See Sue Asbee, *Flann O'Brien* (Boston: Twayne Publishers, 1991): 4-5; *Alive-Alive O! Flann O'Brien's At Swim-Two-Birds*, ed. Rüdiger Imhof (Dublin: Wolfhound Press, 1985): 8-9.

8 The description of Finn's eyes in the original: 'To each of the two eyes in his head was there eye-hair to the fashion of a young forest, and the colour to each great eyeball was as the slaughter of a host in snow (15).' In the Hungarian: 'Mint növendék cserfaerdőé, olyan a szemét strázsáló szőrök sudársága, *mint hóban lemészárolt hadak, szeme pillantása.*' The translation plays on the pace and imagery of the Hungarian classic *Toldi*: 'Mint komor bikáé, olyan a járása,/Mint a barna éjfél, szeme pillantása', [appr., 'Like of a sullen bull's, so is his stride,/Like the gloomy midnight, so is his look']. Needless to say, playing upon literary echoes embedded in the TL is by far not unproblematic, being liable to slide into stylistic anachronisms and blurrings of context. In my own initial version the translation of one verse from a Finn poem ['I am a dark castle against bat-flutters'] shows a distinctive Endre Ady touch ('Vagyok ködvár denevérszárnycsattogásba bújva' [appr. 'I am a mist-castle clad in bat-flutters']. See Endre Ady, 'Vagyok fény-ember ködbe bújva,/Vagyok vesztegló akarat,/Vagyok a láplakók csodája/Ki fényre termett s itt maradt' ['I am a light-man in mists clad,/I am a will lingering awhile,/I am the wonder of marsh-dwellers/Born to light, entrapped to live here']), deriving from the first Hungarian

modernist poet's formulaic verse structuring, invariably opening with 'Vagyok – Vagyok' [I am – I am]. The verse, suppressed in the final version, shows a curious hybridization between Finn's robust imagery and the Ady poem's programmatic self-identifications, touched by Baudelairean *fin de siècle* decadence and early modernist nervousness. An additional irony of such squinting 'analogy' is that the Finn poems speak of the boundless, universal self-identifications and role-play of the 'God-big' Finn, whereas the Ady poem ['Vízió a lápon' – Vision Over the Marshland] magnifies the poetic self, the first-person singular embodiment of the 'modern' against the backwardness of a (mythical) Hungarian marshland. Translations are by the author.

9 Pilibeen, *pilibín*: the name of a common sea-bird, *Vanellus vanellus* – also: small man (Gaelic: diminutive of Philip) or thing; diminutive for male sexual organ. Cruiskeen lawn, *an crúiscín lán*: 'little full jug', title of a rollicking Irish drinking song.

10 I am using Fritz Senn's terms, launched in Senn's collections of critical essays *Joyce's Dislocutions*: *Essays on Reading as Translation,* ed. John Paul Riquelme (Baltimore: Johns Hopkins University Press, 1984); *Inductive Scrutinies. Focus on Joyce,* ed. Christine O'Neill (Dublin: The Lilliput Press, 1995).

11 | The Polishing of Heaney. Seamus Heaney's Poetry in Poland: Translations, Reception, Impact

Jerzy Jarniewicz

Bearing in mind the long-standing Polish-Irish cultural relations, it may be difficult to imagine that the first ever poetry book by an Irish poet in Polish translation was published as late as in 1987. It was, not surprisingly, a collection of poems by W.B. Yeats, who for many years remained the only Irish poet with his own book in Polish. True, a few Irish poets had been translated before, yet their poetry appeared only in anthologies or literary magazines, and, to add insult to injury, in most cases they were introduced as 'English poets'. The last, third volume of a monumental anthology *Poeci języka angielskiego* [Poets of the English Language] (1974), devoted to the poetry of the twentieth century, included only four Irish poets: Oscar Wilde, Yeats, James Joyce, and Louis MacNeice, with Wilde and MacNeice incorrigibly referred to as 'English poets'. In Poland, Irish poetry in English, subsumed into the history of English verse, had a long struggle to gain recognition of its identity. It took many years before the Polish reader realized the distinctness of Irish literature – written, admittedly, in the language of Shakespeare, but set in a different cultural and historical context, which could not be ignored in any serious discussion of its evolution.

If Yeats's book was the first individual collection by an Irish poet published in Poland, the next one was (predictably, perhaps) a poetry book by Seamus Heaney. *44 wiersze*, forty four poems in the translation of Stanisław Barańczak, appeared in 1995, soon to be followed by another collection, *Ciągnąc dalej* [*Keeping Going*] (1996) by the same translator, including poems from Heaney's *The Spirit Level* published almost simultaneously in Britain. Two years later *Kolejowe dzieci* [*The Railway Children*], another book of Heaney's poems, came out, this time, however, rendered into Polish by a different translator, Piotr Sommer. In 2003 Barańczak produced one more volume of his translations of Heaney's poems, *Światło elektryczne* [*Electric Light*], which was the Polish edition of *Electric Light* (2001). All in all, up till now there have been four collections of Heaney's poems in Poland, to which one should add two volumes of his essays: *Zawierzyć poezji* [*Crediting Poetry*] (1996) and *Znalezione-przywłaszczone* [*Finders-Keepers*] (2003). To appreciate fully the meaning of Heaney's presence in Polish, his publishing history should be measured against the number of books by other Irish poets produced in Poland: Yeats has by now three poetry books; each of five other Irish poets – Michael Longley, Derek Mahon, Ciaran Carson, Desmond Egan, and Paul Durcan – has a slim single volume. Thus, with anthologies excluded, Irish poetry of the whole twentieth century exists in eight books by authors other than Heaney. This makes Heaney the most widely published Irish poet of modern times, Yeats's true rival, with more books in Polish than all the other Irish poets of the last fifty years taken together.

Heaney's presence in Poland is due to the invaluable work of two poet translators, belonging to the same generation: Stanisław Barańczak (1946-) and Piotr Sommer (1948-). Though there have been a few other translators who had a try at 'Polishing' Heaney's poems, such as Tadeusz Sławek and Andrzej Szuba, their translations of individual poems have been sporadic, one-off ventures and appeared only in periodicals, whereas Barańczak and Sommer have offered an incomparably more substantial body of Heaney's work, supplementing it with competent critical and biographical commentaries. What is particularly interesting is that the two Polish translators of Heaney differed much, both in their choices and in their translation strategies. In consequence, without a risk of oversimplification, one could claim that there are two Polish Heaneys: the Sommer Heaney and the Barańczak Heaney. Since differences between them are naturally more interesting than similarities, the main focus of this article will be put on the two Heaneys' distinctive features.

Though the first book of Heaney's poetry published in Poland was by Barańczak, it was the pioneering, single-handed work of Piotr Sommer which introduced Heaney to Polish readers. His early translations of Heaney into Polish were published in literary magazines already in the mid-seventies, when Sommer was working on his ground-breaking anthology of contemporary British poetry, a work of many years that was eventually published in 1983, a year after its British equivalent, Andrew Motion and Blake Morrison's *The Penguin Book of Contemporary British Poetry*. On various occasions Sommer presented translations of Heaney's poems alongside other British and Northern Irish contemporary poets, without singling Heaney out. It seems that at the time Derek Mahon managed to draw livelier attention and greater critical acclaim – Polish reviews tended to concentrate on him more often than on the early poems by Heaney. In an essay from 1975, accompanying his translations of British and Irish poets, Sommer did not even mention Heaney's name; in another, written a year later, he ranked him with Mahon. When the anthology eventually appeared, Sommer's selection from Heaney's verse included 15 poems, mainly from the first four collections: the title poem from *Death of a Naturalist*, four poems from *Door Into the Dark*, five from *Wintering Out*, four from *North*, and one poem, 'Elegy' from *Field Work*. In the general preface to the anthology Sommer returned briefly to the idea of ranking Mahon and Heaney together as the two outstanding figures of Northern Irish poetry. At first he accentuated the differences between the two: Heaney, he wrote, 'delves passionately into the rural past, achieving his universal meanings by – to use Kavanagh's theory – thematic parochialism', whereas Mahon shows 'the *odi et amo* attitude in which he is indebted to MacNeice'.

After defining the differences between the two poets, Sommer showed their deeper affinities: 'Heaney's universalization of Irish themes has much in common with Mahon's branding the universal with Irishness'. In a short introduction to the selection of Heaney's verse in his anthology Sommer commented on the poems from the first two books, calling them 'poetry of nature', but was quick to add that these poems pointed to the parallelisms between the 'non-dramatic rural microcosm' and 'the external world of conflicts and tensions'.[1] Further on, Sommer remarked on the brutality of Heaney's metaphors, which to him was often linked with the sexualization of his landscapes, and with the dramatic, or even military aspect of the poet's language. One may assume that such a distinction between the internal and the external worlds, the seemingly peaceful and the overtly violent, corresponded with the diagnosis of contemporary Polish reality made by the Polish poets of the period. The rural tradition which Heaney examined in his early work might have recalled a similar rural movement in Polish literature, too, but what Sommer found most interesting in Heaney was the Irish poet's successful attempt to bridge the two worlds. It was not just a matter of refusing to idealize the past and to write nostalgic pastorals, but to bridge the anti-pastoral images of life in the countryside with the violence that far exceeds the boundaries of one's neighbourhood. Heaney's next two volumes met with Sommer's praise for their ambition to create a myth that extended the historical perspective by including the history of the whole of Northern Europe and, more interestingly, to 'refute the traditional yearnings of the Irish for the idyllic-pastoral past from before the English colonization'.[2] It is significant that Sommer pointed to the subversive aspect of the bog poems – contrary to some Irish and British readings of the sequence which criticized Heaney for dehistoricizing and mythologizing violence. And, if one is reminded of the historical context of the times in Poland, he did it not without reasons.

Heaney's introduction to Polish poetry and to the Polish language took place in the decade of the accelerating social and political tension, which culminated dramatically in the Gdańsk shipyard strikes of 1980, the foundation of Solidarity Trade Union, and the imposition of martial law a year later. Polish poets of the time, many of whom participated actively in the underground dissident movement, shared a number of the concerns that occupied also their Northern Irish colleagues: they were certain that as poets they could not remain blind to the external horrors of Polish realities, political pressures being too destructive to leave them unaddressed (in contrast to the terror in Northern Ireland, the Polish revolution was relatively bloodless; even the brutal introduction of martial law gave rise to hardly any acts of terrorism). On the other hand, to the more critical poets too obvious an identification with one of the sides of the conflict meant the curtailment of their sovereign power as poets. Politics was seen as the dangerous element encroaching upon the autonomous territory of poetry. This kind of danger was felt even by the most public, most civic of all the post-war Polish poets, Zbigniew Herbert, who on the one hand produced emblematic dissident poems of political and moral resistance, collected in his underground volume *Report from the Besieged City* (1985), and on the other hand questioned the poet's concern with topical, political issues. The former idea is best expressed perhaps in Herbert's poem 'To Ryszard Krynicki – a Letter', a poem directed to young poets, whose poetic diction was aimed at dismantling and compromising the official language of state propaganda:

> We took public affairs on our thin shoulders
> Recording suffering the struggle with tyranny with lying
> But – you have to admit – we had opponents despicably small
> So was it worth it to lower holy speech
> To the babble of the speaker's platform the black foam of newspapers[3]

It was thus almost inevitable that Polish poets living under pressure of immediate history turned to their Irish colleagues for a model of poetry that would – in Heaney's words – remain faithful to the song, while not giving offence to those who suffer. An interesting feedback occurred: when Irish poets of Heaney's generation read contemporary Polish poetry, looking for the ways in which historical issues could be addressed without sacrificing the poet's artistic autonomy, Polish poets of Sommer's generation read the works of their colleagues from Northern Ireland often for a similar reason: in order to find ways of merging public and personal themes and escaping the dangers of obvious politicization and the self-congratulatory posture of righteousness. Like Sommer, they admired the power of Heaney and other Irish writers to remain sovereign as artists and to be able to subvert communal dead certainties – national, cultural, political – irrespective of which side they were coming from. Heaney's introduction to Polish readers happened thus in a highly charged political and social context, first in the years of dissent and upheaval, then, after 1989, in the times of economic and cultural post-Communist transformation, when established modes of poetry were found dated and had to be revalued. In both cases, the external historical situation had an immediate effect on the literature of the period, affecting its themes and styles, spurring debates and necessitating changes in the ways poetry was produced, disseminated and understood. Translated into Polish, Heaney and a few other Northern Irish poets, were absorbed by, and implicated in, these historical conflicts: their introduction to Poland was not innocent. The Irish poet's work was seen as having relevance to the moment, relevance that far transgressed the purely aesthetic or literary concerns.

Sommer has returned to Heaney several times since his anthology, but his first book of Heaney's verse, *Kolejowe dzieci* [*The Railway Children*], was not published until 1998, already in post-Communist Poland. It included thirty-five poems and a selection of autobiographical essays from *Preoccupations*, providing an interesting cultural context for the fuller appreciation of Heaney's work by Polish readers. Heaney's new poems were praised by the translator for 'their metaphysical accuracy' which neither advertised itself, nor looked for grand words, but remained 'essentially demotic'.[4] And yet, in the nineties, when the book was published, Sommer seemed to be losing interest in Heaney, the process which he tried to articulate in his afterword called 'What interested me in Heaney when I started translating him?'[5] With its significant use of past tense, Sommer's article is a kind of translator's farewell not only to Heaney, but also to other Northern Irish poets, Longley, Mahon, Paulin, Carson, Muldoon, as if the translator believed that he had already learnt their lesson, absorbed their innovations, or that in the new situation in which Polish literature found itself after the fall of the Iron Curtain their poetry lost some of its importance. Sommer, however, was far from claiming that the quality of their poetry weakened. No, his waning interest in the poetry from the North had different reasons: this poetry seemed less important to him now, when he discovered the poetry of the New York school, and primarily the works of Frank O'Hara, whose poems he published in translation in 1987, to an unprecedentedly enthusiastic response among the young generation of Polish writers. Reflecting on the changes that Polish poetry of the post-1989 transition period had to undergo, the young Polish poets turned to the individualism and the colloquiality of O'Hara's verse, to his concern with the seemingly insignificant trivia of everyday existential situations and to the personal histories rendered in unassuming, semi-autobiographical anecdotes, often riddled with sequences of private names. They also listened closely to the rhythms and cadences of O'Hara's sentences in order to find Polish equivalents of his paratactic syntax and conversational flow, which they wanted to contrast with the rhetoric used by older Polish poets. The mid-nineties was a turbulent, revolutionary period in Polish verse during which young poets looked for alternative models and dictions elsewhere than in Ireland – in need of finding poetry that would be free from public concerns, would not have to assume high moral postures, or speak in the plural, or address collective experience.

At the same time, however, Heaney was discovered by Polish poets and critics of a more conservative, traditionalist attitude, who clung to the idea of the poet as an authoritative, priestly voice with moral responsibilities, performing public duties, guarding what Herbert called the 'holy speech' of poetry. With his rapidly growing reputation, with a shower of prestigious prizes and awards, Heaney became in the eyes of some readers more than a poet: an institution, much closer to the position that his Polish friend and poet, Czesław Miłosz, occupied. To put it crudely, Heaney, once an exemplary poet for the young, who were looking beyond the established traditions of Polish verse, was now, in other quarters, increasingly more associated with the generation of literary patricians: Miłosz, born in 1911, and Herbert, born in 1924, the two Polish poets conspicuously older than Heaney.[6] For a moment it seemed that Heaney in Poland was split between the two irreconcilable movements: the forward looking, innovatory, iconoclastic project and the conservative, established tradition marked by respect for cultural continuities and the sublimity of art.

It was then, in the late eighties, that the other Polish Heaney, the Barańczak Heaney, was born. The event was partly due to the significant changes in Heaney's poetic interests: in the second half of the decade Heaney turned towards Eastern European poets, towards traditions which had hitherto been absent from his verse or criticism. The most explicit sign of that important turn was a collection of critical writings, *The Government of the Tongue* (1988), which apart from essays on Irish, British and American poets, included highly original critical appreciations of a number of Eastern European poets: Osip Mandelshtam, Miroslav Holub, Zbigniew Herbert, and Czesław Miłosz. It is in this collection that Heaney voiced his concern about the conflict between the aesthetic and the ethical duties of the poet, but also declared his interest in translation as an indispensable, formative aspect of literature.[7] His previous collection of essays, *Preoccupations*, did not include a single essay on a translated poet, and the influences that helped to shape Heaney's verse had been so far coming exclusively from the English-language traditions (with a foray or two into the territory of the classics). By the mid-eighties, with the second volume of essays Heaney became international, both in his critical insights and in his own poetic enterprises. In both cases, this newly discovered importance of non-English traditions inspired the poet to reflect on the nature and functions of translation. And Heaney soon offered us such reflections, most significantly in the essay 'The Impact of Translation', where he famously declared that possibly 'the shortest way to Whitby, the monastery where Caedmon sang the first Anglo-Saxon verses, is via Warsaw and Prague'.[8] This declaration can be seen as a symbolic opening of the new stage in Heaney's Irish-Polish relations. In consequence, Heaney, who had already incidentally practised as a translator from Irish (*Sweeney Astray*) and in his collections included adaptations of Baudelaire (*North*) and Dante (*Field Work*), became now more deeply involved in translation, producing not only versions of individual poems by foreign poets such as Marin Sorescu (*The Spirit Level*) or Pushkin, Rilke, and Cavafy (*Electric Light*), but also book-length translations of Jan Kochanowski's *Laments* (co-translated with Barańczak, 1995), Leos Janáček's *Diary of One Who Vanished* (1999), and most famously perhaps *Beowulf* (1999). Barańczak's collection of forty four poems by Heaney was published shortly before Heaney's Nobel Prize in 1995, which made publishers decide quickly to make a second imprint, with a label announcing the award. Barańczak's book included poems from all Heaney's collections up till *Seeing Things* (1991). There is a significant shift noticeable in the choices made by the two Polish translators: whereas Sommer chose primarily Heaney's poems from the seventies, Barańczak concentrated on his later books. One of the reasons being of course the fact that Sommer started translating Heaney much earlier than Barańczak, before the great works of the eighties appeared. But one could also presume that the selections reflect a difference in the two translators' poetic tastes and assumptions about the role the Polished Heaney should play. Barańczak, most surprisingly, offered only four poems from *North* (as opposed to eight in Sommer), but made a generous choice from the book considered by many critics to be transitory, *The Haw Lantern* (1987). It is represented by eight poems as opposed to one in Sommer's book – a clear case of divergence between the two translators' critical stance. *The Haw Lantern* is reputed to be Heaney's most Eastern European collection, making use of the parabolic tradition in such poems as 'From the Frontier of Writing', 'The Republic of Conscience', or 'The Disappearing Island'. In Poland, in the late eighties, when the book came out, the parable was considered already slightly anachronistic and over-exploited as a poetic genre, having been associated with the poetry of Zbigniew Herbert, and then discredited by its overuse in Polish poetry during the martial law period.

Barańczak approached Heaney from a different angle than Sommer – the translator became interested in the Irish poet when he discovered Heaney's essay on Zbigniew Herbert, 'The Atlas of Civilization'. This particular essay was also, significantly, the first ever work by Heaney that Barańczak translated – poems followed much later. One of his interests, openly declared in his introduction, was to show Heaney as a careful, attentive and sympathetic reader of Polish poetry. In his introduction Barańczak said of the immediate understanding which linked the two poets, that it came into being not only because of 'the obligatory fondness that should bind the representatives of the two Catholic nations, wronged by history and consuming large amounts of potatoes (and potato products)'.[9] These words, their joking intention notwithstanding, by recalling national and cultural stereotypes, domesticated Heaney, brought the Irish poet to Poland. Thanks to Barańczak's accomplishments, Heaney in the eyes of Polish readers found his place among such doyen poets as Miłosz and Herbert.

At this moment one can attempt to compare the goals of the two Polish translators of Heaney. Barańczak tried to define the tradition in post-war poetry to which Heaney belonged, Sommer was interested in seeing Heaney as the poet who transcends any affiliation, who has to negotiate his identity and loyalties. Barańczak's Heaney was Polonized, or Polished, so that he could fit well in the company of modern Polish classics. Sommer's Heaney remained primarily an uprooted, unassuming, austere outsider, or more radically: a barbarian (Sommer linked Heaney with Tony Harrison and Douglas Dunn, the two 'barbarian' British poets).[10]

Two years later Barańczak published another book of Heaney's verse, *Ciągnąc dalej* [*Keeping Going*], this time the collection included almost exclusively the poems from one book, *The Spirit Level*, Heaney's first after the Nobel. Out of the original thirty-five poems Barańczak translated and included twenty-seven, adding however two more poems, 'The Party' and 'Audenesque'. The second title, which symbolically concludes the collection, is particularly interesting as it presents Heaney as the living classic who is in dialogue with the great masters of modern poetry: with Joseph Brodsky, to whom the poem is dedicated, and W.H. Auden, in whose style the poem is written, but also with Yeats, whose death was lamented in Auden's elegy.

The different approaches to Heaney and different uses made of Heaney can also be illustrated by a comparative analysis of the strategies of translations assumed by the two translators. A considerable number of Heaney's poems have been translated into Polish twice, by Sommer and Barańczak, thus providing us with a much-telling comparative material. Barańczak's translations are as a rule conspicuously longer than their Irish originals, the translator tending to keep all the details of the originals, even the ones which have slight semantic importance. In 'The Tollund Man', for instance, he translates the word 'tumbril' by its lexical definition, as 'cart on two wheels' ['*dwukołowy wózek*']; in Sommer's much more compact translation the word is rendered simply as 'cart'. It is true that tumbril is a 'two-wheeled, covert cart for carrying tools, ammunition, etc'. But the dictionary also reminds us that it was 'open cart used in French Revolution to convey victims to the guillotine; instrument of punishment'. Barańczak's focus on the two-wheeledness of the cart may puzzle the readers, who might justifiably ask about the relevance of that particular detail: why is it important that the cart is a two-wheeled cart? The detail seems contingent and irrelevant. Furthermore, of the two definitions of the word 'tumbril', it is the second, the cart as an instrument of punishment that matters more. The Polish language does not have a word with such historical connotations, so the translation of the phrase must involve semantic loss. Sommer's decision to render the word in the simplest possible way contributes to the general effect of the directness of the translated poem's language.

One of the characteristic features of Barańczak's translations is his tendency to introduce interpretations to the text of the poem: adding rather than omitting anything, careful to make the meaning of the poem transferable, as if in a belief that the translated poem should be a self-contained universe which – in order to communicate – does not demand information from other sources. Hence the first stanza of 'Personal Helicon' in Baranczak's translation ends with an explicit comment which is absent in Heaney's original: 'the wells were my world' [*'studnie były moim światem'*]. In Part II of 'Casualty' Barańczak says of the people, 'who were like brothers, who stand to fight,' whereas Heaney speaks only of those who 'were braced and bound / like brothers in a ring', without foregrounding the idea of struggle. Or, finally, in 'The Spoonbait' where Heaney speaks of 'the single drop that Dives implored', Barańczak adds a commentary: 'the single drop that the rich man from the parable implored'.

In comparison with Sommer's translations, Barańczak's Heaney is a much more formal poet. Barańczak retains rhymes, metric patterns, and stanzaic organization, though, of course, in many cases rather than transferring them directly to Polish he looks for their Polish equivalents. Sommer, on the contrary, lays stress elsewhere and is ready to dispose of rhymes or metric patterning altogether. His 'Digging' is a free floating colloquial piece. What is lost, however, is compensated for by the attention paid to the poem's diction. Whereas Barańczak, keen on keeping rhymes and metric patterns, sometimes has to twist the syntax, introducing inversions or complex structures, Sommer who does not have to look for rhymes can manage the syntax more freely and naturally. He introduces idioms and colloquialisms, simplifying the diction of the poem. Comparing the two strategies, one could claim that the two Polished Heaneys: Barańczak's and Sommer's, differ exactly in the translators' attitude to what they consider crucial in the poem. In the case of Barańczak, it is the form that has to be kept in translation as an absolute invariant; for Sommer it is the diction that matters most and has to be rendered most credibly, even at the cost of poetic organization. Thus Polish readers have Heaney the rigorous formalist, in conversation with the great modern masters of verse, and Heaney the poet of colloquial intonations and of precise detail. Heaney the classicist, and Heaney the barbarian. Heaney of the Republic of Poets, and Heaney the parochial wordsmith. Interestingly, the two Heaneys correspond to the two streams in the Polish poetry of the last twenty years.

Barańczak's greatest contribution to the popularity of Heaney in Poland is perhaps his collaboration with the Irish poet in the translations of Jan Kochanowski's *Laments* (1995), the sixteenth-century sequence of elegiac poems dedicated to the memory of the poet's two-year old daughter.[11] *Laments*, mythologized in Polish national consciousness and belonging to the absolute canon of Polish literature, had suffered unjust neglect and lack of recognition in the West. The new translation co-authored by an outstanding poet of the English language meant the rediscovery of the masterpiece for foreign readers, but also gave hope for old Polish literature becoming recognized as part of the world literary heritage. Though the initial impulse to translate Kochanowski came from Barańczak, the book was marketed as Heaney's and it was his name that came first on the cover. Indeed, one can see Heaney's strong impact on the whole project, if only in a few attempts at the Hibernicization of the English, a practice he would later develop in his rendering of the Anglo-Saxon *Beowulf* into English. In 'Lament I' among the synonyms of grief one comes across the word 'keen', which Terence Dolan's *Dictionary of Hiberno-English* defines as 'to lament, to wail shrilly over the dead; an act of lamenting; crying (of children)', and traces back to the Irish word *caoin*. Rather than sticking to the ideal of faithfulness the translators decided to produce translations which would be first and foremost successful poems in English. The thirteen-syllable Polish verse was thus rendered by what might be seen as its English equivalent, iambic pentameter. Rhymes which in the Polish originals are usually full and often based on the repetition of a grammatical ending, acquired in the translation a much richer variety of forms: we have imperfect, consonantal, assonantal, and refined rhymes, and sporadically even eye-rhymes. Since the translators did not stylize the language, nor did they archaize it, the diction is less stilted. To strengthen this effect, Heaney and Barańczak introduced informal, conventionalized phrases and idioms, sometimes even verging on the cliché, which they were not afraid to use to make the tone colloquial. Their English translations of the Polish Renaissance poems are thus clearer, more concrete, idiomatic, and decidedly modern.

The back cover of *Laments* carries a note written by Czesław Miłosz, who characteristically identified the cultural-political agenda behind the project: '[Kochanowski's] presence belies foggy notions common in the West about a barbaric Eastern Europe. And yet the Renaissance literature of Poland is virtually unknown in the West because of the lack of translations'. Miłosz voiced what many people in Poland agreed with: Eastern Europe, including Poland, had been largely ignored and misrepresented in the West, which associated it with barbarism and placed it beyond the pale of the civilized world. Heaney's and Barańczak's translations of *Laments* were thus perceived by Miłosz, and consequently by many readers in Poland, as an act of redress, an attempt to make up for the neglect that the cultural achievements of Eastern Europe had suffered. Heaney, as an Irish poet, was seen as particularly apt for such a task, as in the eyes of Polish readers he represented a history and tradition similarly neglected and marginalized. Heaney, with his genuine and generous interest in Polish poetry, with his Polish literary friends and frequent visits to Poland, was thus employed in the post-1989 process of reclaiming the country's past, of settling historical wrongs and correcting misconceptions. His work was seen as parallel to the revisionist histories of Poland and Europe written roughly at the same time by an Oxford-based historian of Welsh descent, Norman Davies, whose books, correcting the one-sided, Occidental visions of history, boosted the self-esteem of the newly independent Poland and satisfied its need for international recognition. One can say that in the second phase of his Polish history, Heaney acted, or was expected to act, as a public poet in Poland. By unofficial popular vote, and perhaps much to his own surprise, Heaney became in fact the cultural ambassador of Poland in the West – more so than the cultural ambassador of Ireland to Poland. As testified by a set of photographs reproduced in a cultural magazine, *NaGłos* (17, 1994), during his visit to Cracow Heaney was spontaneously approached by the people in the streets and given flowers. When Heaney went to Stockholm to receive his Nobel Prize, the Polish press reported that in the exhibition dedicated to the poet there was also a portrait of Jan Kochanowski – Heaney's success was thus seen as an occasion that promoted Polish culture, a triumph in which Poland also participated. In this role of the cultural ambassador Heaney has been active for many years and in many fields. In 2006 he became the patron of The Ireland-Poland Cultural Foundation in Dublin. In a note published on the Foundation's website he wrote: 'I am honoured to be Patron of this timely and promising venture. First and foremost, it allows me to be associated in a formal way with the country that produced one of the greatest bodies of literature in modern times and to signify my gratitude, personal and artistic, to the poets and poetry of twentieth century Poland.'[12]

An account of Heaney's presence in Poland should be supplemented by a note on two interesting, collectible publications belonging to the poet's vast bibliography and associated with his Polish cultural links. The first is a bilingual pamphlet, *From the Back of the North Wind. Three Poems*, produced in 2000 on the occasion of Heaney's visit to Poland, with poems selected by the author, including 'A Hyperborean', an elegy in memory of Zbigniew Herbert (a different version than the one published later in *Electric Light*); the second – a limited edition of a book, in memory of Czesław Miłosz, *The Door Stands Open. Czesław Miłosz 1911-2004*, conceived by Seamus Heaney and Cathal McCabe, published in 2005 by the Irish Writers' Centre in Dublin and printed by the Book Art Museum in Łódź, Poland, which includes two poems 'What Passed At Colonus' and the then uncollected 'Saw Music,' and an essay 'The Door Stands Open'.

The history of Heaney's presence in Poland, of the many competing translations of his poetry and their diversified reception, testifies to the richness of the Irish poet's work which has allowed different readings and resists simple classifications. Heaney's relations with Polish literature, including his friendship with Polish poets, and particularly with Czesław Miłosz, is an interesting example of fruitful reciprocal inspirations, with Heaney discovering creative impulses for his own work in Polish poetry and Polish poetry finding invigorating support in the works of Heaney.

---

1 Ibid., 146.

2 Ibid., 147.

3 Zbigniew Herbert, *Report from the Besieged City and Other Poems*, trans. John and Bogdana Carpenter (Oxford: Oxford University Press, 1987): 21.

4 Piotr Sommer, 'Co ciekawiło mnie u Seamusa Heaneya, kiedy zaczynałem go tłumaczyć' [What interested me in Seamus Heaney when I started translating him], *Kolejowe dzieci* [The Railway Children], by Seamus Heaney, trans. Piotr Sommer (Legnica: Fort 1998): 104.

5 Ibid., 94-104.

6 For a detailed account of Heaney's poetic dialogue with Czesław Miłosz and Zbigniew Herbert, see my essay 'The Way via Warsaw: Seamus Heaney and Post-War Polish Poets', *Seamus Heaney. Poet, Critic, Translator*, eds Ashby Bland Crowder and Jason David Hall (London: Palgrave Macmillan, 2007): 103-20.

7 The importance of translation for contemporary British and Irish poets is further discussed in my essay 'After Babel: Translation and Mistranslation in Contemporary British Poetry', *European Journal of English Studies* 6.1 (2002): 87-104.

8 Seamus Heaney, *The Government of the Tongue* (London: Faber and Faber, 1988): 41.

9 Stanisław Barańczak, 'Muzyka tego, co się dzieje' [The Music of What Happens], Seamus Heaney, *44 wiersze* [Forty Four Poems], trans. Stanisław Barańczak (Cracow: Znak, 1995): 18. My translation.

10 Sommer, *Antologia*, 18.

11 For a discussion of Heaney and Barańczak's translation of Kochanowski's *Laments,* see my review 'Of Bereavement and Affirmation', *Poetry Review* 81.1 (1996): 50-52.

12 Seamus Heaney, 'Definitions', www.irelandpoland.org/home.htlm.

12 | The Uses of a Disused Shed: Mahon's Poem in Hungarian

István D. Rácz

Discussing literary translation: from target to source

Contemporary Irish poetry can be assimilated into Hungarian culture only if good translations are available for a wide reading public. Although more and more Hungarians speak and read some English today, very few of them have the command that would enable them to read and enjoy poetry written in English. But even for those Hungarians who read English texts (both literary and non-literary) on a regular basis, good translations of poems can carry real aesthetic pleasure. My memory has inevitably preserved the Hungarian translations of a number of poems that I first read in my mother tongue, and I cannot help treating them as primary texts in my private intellectual history. Of course, one recalls Roman Jakobson's warning that poetry is untranslatable by definition, but also his remark that the recreation of a poem in another language is certainly possible.[1]

This raises the question of whether the translated poem belongs to the author of the original text or to the translator. Instead of entering the debate about the death of the author, I wish to suggest that a translated poem can be read in the contexts of two life works: the poet's and the translator's. If the translator is a poet in her/his own right (which is almost always the case), the two contexts will form a meaningful tension, since every life work in poetry (viewed as an organic whole,[2] as a huge text) is unique. Furthermore, a translated poem stands for the 'liminality' of the text: it cannot help representing a process rather than something completed and unchangeable. Although writing an original poem is also based on a series of choices, the reader will be much more aware of the translator's compulsion to choose than in the case of an original text. In other words, *translating* a poem is more obviously a matter of choosing from among various possibilities (words, grammatical structures, etc.) than *writing* a poem. Moreover, if the reader knows both the original and the translation, s/he will automatically enter a debate about the quality of the text in the target language. Reading a translated text includes not only interpretation but also evaluation.

All these theoretical problems, however, do not question the importance of translating poetry. To turn to a more practical side of the issue indicated in the subtitle: some contemporary Irish verse is available for Hungarian readers. Apart from Seamus Heaney (whose Noble Prize in 1995 drew attention to Irish literature in general), Ciaran Carson, Gerald Dawe, Paul Durcan, Desmond Egan, Adrian Fox, Michael Longley, Medbh McGuckian, Paula Meehan, and Paul Muldoon have also been translated.[3] Apart from Heaney and Egan, Derek Mahon is also represented in Hungary with a full volume of twenty-three texts, entitled after his poem 'The Sea in Winter' (A tenger télen). The poems were selected and translated by the poet András Fodor, who also added a postscript to the volume. But those who are interested in Mahon can also turn to an anthology of British (!) poetry, *Új kabát, utolsó esély* (entitled after a poem by Hugo Williams, 'New Coat, Last Chance'). This contains twelve poems by Mahon, all translated by the poet Eszter Tábor. Only three poems are included in both collections: 'Rage for Order', 'A Refusal to Mourn', and 'A Disused Shed in Co. Wexford'. In this paper I intend to discuss and compare the two translations of the last of these, probably Mahon's best-known text.

It has been suggested in a study on translation theory that the analysis of a translation should follow the same route from the source-language text to the target-language text that the translator used when writing the translation.[4] I see two problems with this suggestion: on the one hand, there is a danger that it may lead to a prescriptive analysis and a normative model; on the other hand, it isolates the text from the target culture. As I suggested above, the context of the translator's life work is just as significant as that of the original author. Therefore, I will make an attempt to go in the opposite direction; that is, I will start with the two translations as poems in their own right and as parts of two Hungarian poets' life works, and then explore how they are related to the source text.

Mahon the traditional poet: András Fodor's translation

Apart from the two dangers mentioned above, I have one more reason to use the Hungarian texts as my starting point. Translation has been a central part of Hungarian literary history since the late 18th century. Many of the major Hungarian writers were also outstanding translators and, moreover, their translations have generally been treated as integral parts of their life works. This can well be seen in the critical assessment of the older of the two translators I am discussing, András Fodor (1929-1997). His best critic, Miklós Csűrös, has concluded an essay about Fodor by pointing out the tripartite structure of his life work: an organic whole in which his original poetry, the essays, and the translations are equally important.[5] Fodor himself remarked in one of his reviews that if a poem is translated 'with proper linguistic and artistic force', it can result in 'a primary experience' for the reader.[6] In other words: ideally, a translated poem measures up to an 'original poem'. The uncertain term 'primary' (or 'original') can be interpreted in two ways if we follow Fodor's logic: it can mean the poem that has been translated or the translator's own poetry. On the basis of Fodor's rich life work one can risk the suggestion that his ambition was to create translations carrying aesthetic merits comparable to the original, but also forming a part of his own poetry. In the same essay he quotes Lőrinc Szabó's aphorism: nobody can make better translations than his/her own poetry.[7] Although he quotes Szabó to mention one notable exception immediately (László Kardos), this reference also reveals his ambition to write good poetry as well as good translations.

Szabó's opinion, of course, could generate fierce debates, even concerning his own achievement. Both his poetry and his translations have been canonized, but their evaluation keeps on changing. As a translator, he has been celebrated for the accuracy and the creative use of acoustic as well as visual effects; on the other hand, he has been criticized for making the translation 'rougher' than the original and 'full of anxiety'.[8] This way, he did the opposite of what his immediate predecessors, Mihály Babits, Dezső Kosztolányi and Árpád Tóth did. Nevertheless, the notion that his immense two-volume collection of translations (importantly, entitled 'Our Eternal Friends') represented the voice of humanity against an inhuman age in the 1930s and the 1940s is a consensus in Hungarian literary criticism. Fodor belonged to a different generation, usually referred to as *fényes szelek* ('glittering winds', after a once popular song). The members of this movement started their careers after the end of the Second World War, in an atmosphere of euphoria and ambition. Most of them were of lower-class origin, but educated in Budapest. The tension they felt between their former provincial (sometimes almost archaic) way of life and modern urban existence provided them with ample experience for lyric and dramatic verse. Their ambition was to write about the gap between two worlds and to play an important role in establishing a new, democratic culture. When they were bitterly disappointed in the new political system after the beginning of the communist dictatorship in 1949, their experience, as well as their poetry, became even more complex. Since they were concerned with their own personal problems and those of their society, original poetry, rather than translation, was of primary significance for them – Fodor being a notable exception with the equilibrium mentioned by Csűrös.

It much depends on the reader whether s/he will read the volume containing Mahon's poems in Hungarian as a representative of Irish poetry or as a part of the translator's oeuvre. Fodor's Hungarian collection of Mahon's verse is a slender book of translated poetry in the strict sense; nevertheless, some features of Fodor's own poems can be discerned in 'Elhagyott raktárhelyiség Wexfordban' (the Hungarian version of 'A Disused Shed in Co. Wexford'). The compound noun 'varjúpanasz' [crow's complaint] in the last line of stanza 2, for example, is typical of his method: he frequently constructs his metaphors out of familiar elements of nature, but extends them towards the human world. The original phrase, 'rooks querulous' is very nearly the same, except that it is two words. This example suggests that Fodor probably found an Irish poet whose verse offers affinity with his own.

Some more spectacular features of the poem reinforce this hypothesis. Mahon's 'A Disused Shed' is commonly known as 'the mushroom poem' not only because it describes a group of fungi, but also because Mahon makes them speak in the last six lines. The text ends as a dramatic monologue, in which the roles simulating reality are turned upside down: the mushrooms (originally the targets of the poet's gaze) become active speakers, and the poet figure becomes the listener. Importantly, the poem ends with the mushrooms' words, allowing the human voice no chance of comment or reply. The situation is grotesque; nevertheless, it suggests intimacy. Whenever one reads a dramatic monologue, the most obvious element of the reading strategy is that the reader puts him/herself into the place of the fictitious listener. In this text the listener is the implied poet; therefore, one intimacy simulates another. The intimacy between the mushrooms and the listener becomes the intimacy between the reader and the poet. As it usually happens in poetry, the implied poet has proved to be the mediator between the speaker and the reader: we listen to the words of the mushrooms through the poet as we construct him as a figure in the text.

Formally speaking, Mahon used an apostrophe, a device frequently applied in Fodor's poetry, too. In one of his best volumes, *Kettős rekviem* (Double Requiem, 1972) he uses the apostrophe to recall situations that he shared with two deceased friends. We read opening lines such as 'Kiszállsz az autóból. Nevetsz' ['You get out of the car. You laugh'],[9] 'Eljött a meghittség órája, / leül elénk a vastag szőnyegekre' ['The hour of intimacy has come, / and it sits down with us on the thick carpets'].[10] Even more often, he uses questions and answers implying the presence of a listener. As Miklós Csűrös suggests, one can observe the influence of W.H. Auden in this feature: the speaker addressing a fictitious listener.[11] But this is also a well-known feature of Mahon's poetry. As Eamon Grennan has written: 'The strangest impression made on me when I read any poem by Derek Mahon is the sense that I have been spoken to: that the poem has established its presence in the world as a kind of speech.'[12]

Of course, there are obvious differences between Mahon's dialogic texts and Fodor's apostrophes. Fodor always addresses an historical human being (more precisely: the artificially created portrait of a human being, usually a friend). Mahon, on the other hand, reverses the point of view; furthermore, the speaker is not necessarily a human being. Apart from the mushrooms in this poem, another appropriate example is the empty tins speaking in 'The Apotheosis of Tins'. If we read Fodor's translation of 'A Disused Shed', it is easy to see it as an extension of the method of apostrophe and, therefore, as a text enriching his own life work without violating its immanent logic. Fodor's basic value, human intimacy, has been preserved, but its essentialism has been questioned. The Irish fellow-poet added more to his own poetry than the translator may have realized at the moment. But what happened in this translation is symptomatic. In another essay Csűrös writes that although Fodor never identified the I with the other as openly as modernist poets usually did, in his own way he saw and represented the consequences of the disintegration of the personality.[13] The way Fodor as a minor poet[14] kept his mind open led not only to his flexibility and humility, but also to placing translation into the centre of his activity.

It is not without reason that I have written 'activity'. Fodor was famous for his sociability and his helpful attitude. In an interview he said that he was 'involved in the lives of at least a hundred people'.[15] This attitude is discernable in the way he translated the first three lines of the last stanza in Mahon's poem:

> A maguk néma módján mind esdeklenék,
> Tegyél az érdekükben valamit,
> Az ajtót legalább ne csukd be újra künt.

The second line in Mahon is: 'To do something, to speak on their behalf', and the next line starts with a concessive 'or'. Fodor contracted the two infinitives of the English line; Mahon's idea of speaking on the mushrooms' behalf has become an imperative of acting for them. Fodor's sentence 'Tegyél az érdekükben valamit' can be read as a commonly used phrase from the literary discourse during the communist era, when 'doing something for somebody' was a part of daily routine: giving someone the chance to publish her/his poems, helping a friend to get a flat or to put her child into a good school, and so on. The phrase has stuck in our minds, and so has the vision of a door closed in front of a humiliated person. Fodor must have found a familiar situation and well-known phrases in the Irish poem. The ironic thing is that the kind of 'acting for somebody' that I outlined above always meant speaking to someone in the right position. Nevertheless, Fodor kept the equivalent of the word 'do' and dropped 'speak' to emphasize efficiency. If interviews are read as parts of a writer's life work, the way this translation echoes Fodor's statement in a rather informal interview becomes evidence for cohesion, and helps us follow the immanent logic of a poet's work. As I indicated earlier in this paper, this logic is a construct of the reader; nevertheless, it is generated by the texts themselves.

Apart from being an author systematically organizing his texts to form a whole, Fodor was a very conscious translator, too. Csűrös has pointed out four particularly important features of his translations: the ambition to interpret the original at an intellectual level, the rationalist tendency to make all elements clear, the emphasis on pictorial effects, and the accurate recreation of metre.[16] In an interview Fodor himself said that he never gave up the principle of 'intact sounding' and insisted on achieving 'meaning'.[17] In his own verse he always made sure that his moments of intimacy should have meaning for the reader, too; in his translation we witness a systematic decoding and recreation of the original. The fourth last line of the poem ('Who have come so far in darkness and in pain') in his translation reads like this: 'Sötétbe, kínba hullva, hisz nekünk'. This is a perfect iambic pentameter, linking the poem with memorable Hungarian translations of Shakespeare, Milton, Browning, and others.

Terry Eagleton has emphasized the relevance of the corresponding line in Mahon's poem: '"Who have come so far in darkness and in pain" is not only an iambic pentameter but is meant to be perceptible as such. Even in this state of extremity, language continues to rebuff silence, to the point where the verse can venture what could almost be a piece of elegant, Audenesque wit or irony ... .'[18] Iambic pentameter is perhaps the most frequently used line in English poetry and is familiar to Hungarian readers as a synecdoche of English literariness. We know it from Mihály Vörösmarty's, János Arany's and Lőrinc Szabó's versions of

Shakespeare, to mention some well-known examples. Fodor followed in their wake when making the pentameter even smoother than it is in the original (it will be noticed that Mahon's first foot is an anapaest, which, of course, does not weaken the iambic character of the line, anapaest being another rising foot). To use Eagleton's reading: the pentameter also stands out as a pentameter for the Hungarian reader, suggesting eloquence or its parody. The next line in Mahon is a version of the iambic trimeter with an initial spondee followed by an anapaest and a final iamb ('We too had our lives to live'), which Fodor made very smooth, again, but his line is an iambic tetrameter catalectic, consequently suggesting an unfinished idea:

> Sötétbe, kínba hullva, hisz nekünk
> Is volna mit megélnünk.

The full stop at the end of the line forms a meaningful tension with the unfinished foot, that is, the feminine ending. (The best-known example of the meaningfulness of such unstressed ending is Shakespeare's 'To be, or not to be, that is the question' – metrically speaking, the last syllable is out of place.) To me, a possible implication is that the chain of ideas started by a human being (the poet figure) and continued by the mushrooms, is only seemingly completed. The poem (both in Mahon and in Fodor) is open-ended.

However complicated the relationship between the Irish poet and his Hungarian translator may be, the affinity is obvious. What Carol Rumens has written about Mahon is also true of Fodor: 'Mahon's work avoids self-pity. There are invariable undertones of irony and/or self-mockery, and a frequent bracing intellectual detachment. As the discipline of the metrical line permits the expression of emotion, so the sense of audience provides the self-awareness that lends wit and detachment to the tone.'[19] Both in Mahon's and Fodor's poetry the proportion of poems dedicated to or for somebody is so spectacular that no reading of their life works can dismiss the problem of its possible meaning. Once again, Carol Rumens's words are enlightening:

> [P]oetry in Ireland, as in Wales, retains some of its bardic characteristics as a sociable, even publicly accountable, art form. A poem may have a single addressee, or none, but it is

> hardly a private communication. The northern writers want to be heard and over-heard in poetry's agora.
>
> Mahon's dedicated poems can, however, seem intimate, as if they permitted the writer a confessional unmasking, a friendly but unanswering context in which to expose opinions and emotions and, of course, opinionated emotion, guilt.[20]

The intimacy of the situation in the poem, which creates tension between accidental overhearing and willing unmasking, is a particular feature that links Mahon's and Fodor's poems. More than that, it appears to be a manifestation of a general tendency that serves as a common denominator for Hungarian and Irish verse: the notion of poetry as a socially significant form of art.

Of course, it would be a mistake to put an equation mark between Mahon and Fodor: for all the similarities, they are two very different poets. Fodor rarely reversed the points of view of the speaker and listener, in other words: he hardly ever wore a mask in the sense as T.S. Eliot or Yeats used the term. When he did, the result was a playful, mildly ironic poem (one example is 'A feleség levele' [The wife's letter]). But this is exactly the reason why translating Mahon served as a means of enriching his own life work: the Irish poet enabled him to go further than he ever did in his own texts.

Mahon the experimental poet: Eszter Tábor's translation

The other poet who translated 'A Disused Shed' is much lesser known, although she is an extremely gifted author. Eszter Tábor was born in 1952, and has published only two slim volumes of her own poetry. She has also contributed to some volumes of verse with her translations, most significantly a selection of Emily Dickinson's poems, to which she also wrote a postscript (1989). Dickinson influenced her own poetry, too, but it is far from being derivative.

A comparison of the last two stanzas in her translation with Fodor's version calls the reader's attention to revealing differences. Stanza 5, lines 1-3 are a grammatically more accurate recreation of Mahon's words in Tábor's version:

> Fél évszázad magányban, sötétben,
> Szánalmas várakozás zárkattanásra
> Sarokvascsikordulásra. Mágusok, holdbéliek,
> Régi időkből ittfeledett sok poros fogoly...

In Fodor' version:

> Látogatók híján félszázadnyi sötétben –
> Szánalmas készülődés: kattan-e
> A zár, nyikkan-e ajtó. Mágus holdlakók,
> Volt-rezsim rízsporos bebörtönzöttei ...

The seemingly slight difference between 'zárkattanásra' in Tábor and 'kattan-e / A zár' in Fodor is in the syntax: Fodor turned Mahon's noun phrases 'cracking lock' and 'creak of hinges' into verbal predicates (finite forms), whereas Tábor kept the elliptical sentence structure. Her words, particularly the marvellously awkward compound 'Sarokvascsikordulásra' suggest passivity, even paralysis. The juxtaposition of 'Mágusok, holdbéliek' is more accurate than Fodor's 'Mágus holdlakók', which makes the first noun an adjective. One can also see two different interpretations of the word 'powdery' in Fodor's rational and realistic 'rízsporos' and Tábor's more daring 'poros'. Fodor's 'rízsporos bebörtönzött' is a simulated historical image; Tábor's 'poros fogoly' is symbolic and suggestive.

The difference in the translations of the next line is fundamental. In Mahon we read:

> Web-throated, stalked like triffids, racked by drought
> And insomnia...

Tábor:

> Hártyás torkúak, kocsányos triffidek, szomjúságtól
> És álmatlanságtól gyötörtek ...

Fodor:

> Pókhálós torkú, háromfele vált, aszott,
> Álmatlan nép ...

The simile that Mahon uses in the description of the mushrooms is 'stalked like triffids'. After the dedication of the poem to the novelist J.G. Farrell, which suggests that the image of the disused shed is derived from his representation of the devastated hotel ironically called the Majestic in *Troubles*, at this point Mahon creates an intertextual link with another narrative text: John Wyndham's science fiction novel, *The Day of the Triffids*. Terence Brown has written: 'The sci-fi aspect of the poem gives to it an eerie strangeness, as if the residually human, with its places, lives and histories, is an anachronism which nevertheless makes its claim on the present.'[21] Wyndham's novel was first published in 1951, and it also came out in Hungarian in 1990. It is obvious that Tábor knew the novel (or its film version) since she used the word that was not changed in the Hungarian title in Judit Gálvölgyi's version: *A triffidek napja*. The phrase 'kocsányos triffidek' is a calque, an exact translation of 'stalked triffids', which are fictitious man-eating plants in Wyndham's novel. In her own poem 'El idegen' (Away stranger) Tábor describes a plant:

> növény termett-e arra?
> hazánk jelképe lenne?
> egy szelíditett válfaj?
> ....
>
> hát erre-arra terjed,
> gyökértelenül elmegy[22]
>
> [did a plant grow there?
> could it be the emblem of our country?
> a domesticated type?
>
> ....
>
> so it spreads here and there
> it goes away rootlessly][23]

This could be the depiction of the triffids in Wyndham, but also the mushrooms in Mahon's poem. In her translation Tábor made a metaphor out of Mahon's simile, identifying the mushrooms with the triffids, both being a primitive threat to humankind in a decadent age.

Fodor, obviously, did not know the novel. He probably thought that triffid was either a misprint or an individual version of trifid, a word used in biology, or perhaps he only noticed 'tri-' as a prefix.

He was not very far from the real meaning: Wyndham also used the prefix 'tri-' to construct the word for the man-eater. As a rational translator, Fodor found the most convincing solution that one can imagine in a realist description. Tábor, however, got Mahon's message.

Not that his message can always be translated so easily. Who does he address in the first four lines of the last stanza, and how is the exclamation in line four related to the rest of the stanza?

> They are begging us, you see, in their wordless way,
> To do something, to speak on their behalf
> Or at least not to close the door again.
> Lost people of Treblinka and Pompeii!

Fodor's method is that of rationalization again: he identifies the victims of history with the mushrooms; in his interpretation, the mushrooms are begging us as the lost people of Treblinka and Pompeii would: 'Treblinka, Pompei mártírjaiképp', that is '*as* the martyrs of Treblinka and Pompeii'. But that is not the only possible meaning: the reader can link the exclamation with the phrase 'you see' in line one, or read it as an inorganic and irrational statement (almost like Conrad's 'The horror! The horror!' is in *Heart of Darkness*). Although neither of the two translators recreated the conversational phrase 'you see', Tábor reconstructed the ambivalence of the exclamation: 'Treblinka és Pompeji kárhozottjai!' is a phrase without any fixed referentiality, as it is in Mahon.

A similar difference can be observed in the translation of the punning penultimate line: 'You with your light meter and relaxed itinerary'. Fodor's phrase 'Te, fénymérős' refers to the situation that simulates reality in the poem. Tábor's 'Ti könnyű mértékűek' sounds like a moral judgment, but can easily be read ironically. The witty allusion to metre (a homophone of meter) in poetry has been dropped, but Tábor's version, once again, is more ambivalent and richer in meaning. Fodor's solution demonstrates that calques are not necessarily the best devices in literary translations.

Conclusion: from source to target

In a book about translation into English, Alan Duff quotes Leonardo da Vinci: 'He who can go to the fountain does not go to the water jar', and contextualizes it by claiming: 'The translator, if he is honest with himself, knows that his readers are those who cannot go to the fountain. Those who are free to choose, will prefer the original; those who are not, will "make do" with the translation'.[24] It may often be true, but not exclusively: Susan Bassnett mentions some examples of situations in which the translators counted on the reader's 'prior knowledge of the original'.[25] Although Bassnett's examples are from the sixteenth century, I am not at all sure that most of those Hungarian readers who will read Fodor's or Tábor's version are unable to read the original. Many of them will compare the two, perhaps all three. The attitude of sixteenth-century readers reading *in order to* compare a translation with the original and find pleasure in the mechanism of their own evaluative faculties may have a renaissance in the twenty-first century.

But the reader makes a mistake if s/he only wants to spot errors by contrasting Mahon's poem with the two translations. Masquerading as a translator, Horace Walpole wrote in his preface to *The Castle of Otranto*: 'It is natural for a translator to be prejudiced in favour of his adopted work.'[26] So it is, and one can add: the translator is 'prejudiced' by observing the other in the fellow-poet writing in a different language. Julio Cortázar has written that the poet sees an essence different from his/her own in any subject matter, and by taking possession of it s/he enriches her/himself ontologically.[27] It goes without saying that translating a poem is a case in point. The question is: how does contemporary Irish poetry in general and Mahon's poems in particular enrich those Hungarian poets who venture to make translations? I hope to have shown how Fodor's and Tábor's translations have enriched their own life works, but we can also put the Hungarian Mahon in a wider context. In the postscript of the anthology containing Tábor's translation, the editor, Péter Kántor, has written that in English and Irish poetry indirect speech, role-playing and the use of narrative elements is much more frequent than in Hungarian verse. Kántor is right, but one should add: the anthology was published in 1993, and these features have probably become much more common in Hungarian poetry in the past two decades.

The fresh water from Leonardo's fountain can be found not only in water jars, but also in newly discovered fountains, in a different field. The link between Irish and Hungarian poetry is not only in translation proper. Whenever Hungarian poets translate Irish poems, they gaze into another culture and experience its otherness. Apart from seeing Irish literature as a synecdoche of minority cultures, they also discover new forms and the full-fledged representation of general human dilemmas as well as their own very personal problems in Irish poems. If we read the translated texts as parts of a larger whole, as the Hungarian poets' life works, they help us realize, once again, that the still waters of poetry run deep.

---

1 Roman Jakobson, 'Fordítás és nyelvészet' [Translation and linguistics], *A fordítás tudománya. Válogatás a fordításelmélet irodalmából* [Translation Studies. Selections from the Literature of Translation Theory], eds István Bart and Kinga Klaudy (Budapest: Tankönyvkiadó, 1986): 21.

2 The emphasis falls on *viewed*. I use the term 'organic whole' as a textual unit constructed in the process of reading (determined by the reader's horizon of expectation) rather than something 'objective'. It does not exclude the possibility of other constructions or deconstructions as reading strategies, but my experience is that most readers perceive poems by the same author with the desire to interpret them as parts of a larger whole.

3 The periodical *Magyar Napló* (Budapest) published a collection of Irish poems in Hungarian translation in its January issue, 2005 (guest editor: Mária Kurdi). Another literary journal, *Korunk* (Kolozsvár/Cluj, Romania) also published an Irish issue in November 2007 (guest editor: Erika Mihálycsa). Desmond Egan's *Selected Poems*, edited and introduced by Csilla Bertha, came out in 2000. I am grateful to the editors for calling my attention to these publications.

4 A.D., Svejcer, 'A fordításelmélet mint interdiszciplináris tudomány' [Translation theory as an interdisciplinary field], *A fordítás tudománya. Válogatás a fordításelmélet irodalmából*, eds István Bart and Kinga Klaudy (Budapest: Tankönyvkiadó, 1986): 32.

5 Miklós Csűrös, 'Fodor András', *A költészet. A magyar irodalom története 1945-1975* ser [Poetry. The History of Hungarian Literature 1945-1975], ed. Miklós Béládi, vol. 2 (Budapest: Akadémiai, 1986): 816.

[6] András Fodor, 'A műfordító öröksége' [The heritage of the literary translator]. *Szülöttem föld* [My Homeland] (Budapest: Szépirodalmi, 1990): 252.
[7] Fodor, 'A műfordító öröksége', 253.
[8] Miklós Szabolcsi, *Költészet és korszerűség* [Poetry and modernity] (Budapest: Magvető, 1959): 144.
[9] András Fodor, *Pünkösdi hírnök. Válogatott versek 1944-1987* [The Whitsun Herald. Selected Poems 1944-1987] (Budapest: Magvető, 1989): 324.
[10] Fodor, *Pünkösdi hírnök*, 337. Rough translations are mine.
[11] Csűrös, 'Fodor András', 809.
[12] Eamon Grennan, '"To the Point of Speech": the Poetry of Derek Mahon', *Contemporary Irish Writing*, eds James D. Brophy and Raymond J. Porter (Boston: Iona College Press, 1983): 15.
[13] Miklós Csűrös, 'Fodor András és a Kettős rekviem' [András Fodor and 'Double Requiem'], eds Mátyás Domokos and András Lakatos, *Konok idő. Fodor András emlékezete* [Obstinate Time. In Memory of András Fodor] (Budapest: Nap Kiadó, 2003): 126.
[14] Needless to say, a minor poet can be a very good poet. However, as opposed to the two outstanding members of his generation, László Nagy and Ferenc Juhász, Fodor did not introduce any remarkable innovations into Hungarian poetry.
[15] Lajos Kelemen and Ádám Szeredy, eds, *'A működés több, mint a lét'. Fodor András emlékezete* ['Function is more than existence'. In memory of András Fodor] (n.p.: Berzsenyi Dániel Irodalmi és Művészeti Társaság-Kortárs Kiadó, 1997): 81.
[16] Csűrös, 'Fodor András', 813.
[17] Kelemen and Szeredy, 76.
[18] Terry Eagleton, *How to Read a Poem* (Malden, MA: Blackwell, 2007): 87.
[19] Carol Rumens, *Self into Song*, Newcastle/Bloodaxe Poetry Lectures ser. (Newcastle: Bloodaxe, 2007): 14.
[20] Ibid., 17.
[21] Terence Brown, 'Mahon and Longley: place and placelessness', *The Cambridge Companion to Contemporary Irish Poetry*, ed. Matthew Campbell (Cambridge: Cambridge University Press, 2003): 141.
[22] Eszter Tábor, *Külön óra* [Private hour] Lélegzet könyvek ser. (Budapest: Typotex, 1994): 56.
[23] Rough translation is mine.
[24] Alan Duff, *The Third Language* (Oxford: Pergamon Press, 1981): 1.
[25] Susan Bassnett, *Translation Studies* (London: Routledge, 1991): 109.

[26] Glenda Leeming, ed., *Three Gothic Novels* (London: The British Council, 1975): 41.
[27] Julio Cortázar, 'Poétikakísérlet' [An attempt to write a poetics], *Nagyvilág* 43. 7-8 (1998): 487.

Bibliography

Adler, Cyrus, ed., *Voice of America on Kishinev* (New York: Jewish Publications Society, 1904).

Alvarez, Roman, and M. Carmen-Africa Vidal, *Translation, Power, Subversion* (Manchester, UK: St. Jerome, 1996).

Andrews, Rachel, Review of *Festen*, *The Sunday Tribune* 26 December 2004: 33.

[anon.], and, Charles Frederick Henningsen, *Kossuth and "The Times" by the Author of "The Revelations of Russia"* (London: Charles Gilpin, 1851).

Asbee, Sue, *Flann O'Brien* (Boston: Twayne Publishers, 1991).

Babits, Mihály (B.M.), 'Költő, forradalom, és heroizmus' [Poet, Revolution, and Heroism], *Nyugat* 28.3 (3 May 1935): 259-60.

---, 'Teremtő utánzás' [Creative Imitation], *Nyugat* 31.6 (June 1938): 459-63.

---, *Az európai irodalom története* [The History of European Literature] (Budapest: Szépirodalmi, 1979).

---, *Kisebb műfordításai* [Minor Translations] (Budapest: Athaeneum, 1940).

---, *Pávatollak* [Peacock Feathers] (Budapest: Táltos, 1920).

---, 'Új klasszicizmus felé' [Towards a New Classicism], *Nyugat* 18.18 (1 October 1925): 17-20.

---, *Wilde Oszkár verseiből* [From the Poetry of Oscar Wilde] (Budapest: Athaeneum, 1916).

Balkányi, Magdolna, 'Az irodalmiság és színháziság viszonyáról' [On the Relation of Literariness and Theatricality], *Debreceni Disputa* 5.1 (2007): 8-13.

Barańczak, Stanisław, 'Muzyka tego, co się dzieje' [The Music of What Happens], *44 wiersze* [Forty-Four Poems] by Seamus Heaney, trans. Stanisław Barańczak (Cracow: Znak, 1995): 5-18.

Bassnett, Susan, 'Still Trapped in the Labyrinth: Further Reflections on Translation and Theatre', *Constructing Cultures: Essay on Literary Translation,* eds Susan Bassnett and André Lefevere (Clevedon: Multilingual Matters, Ltd. 1998): 90-108.

---, *Translation, History and Culture (*London and New York: Pinter Publishers, 1990).

---, *Translation Studies* (London: Routledge, 1991).

Battersby, Eileen, 'The Image Maker', *The Irish Times* 12 June 1997: 13.

Battlay, Imre, *Gulliver utazásai ismeretlen országokban Swift Jonathántól* [Gulliver's Travels into Unknown Lands by Jonathan Swift] (Pest: Bartalits Imre, 1865).

Beckett, Samuel, 'Act Without Words I', *The Collected Shorter Plays of Samuel Beckett* (New York: Grove, 1984): 41-46.

---, 'Catastrophe', *The Collected Shorter Plays of Samuel Beckett* (New York: Grove, 1984): 294-301.

---, *The Collected Shorter Plays of Samuel Beckett* (New York: Grove, 1984).

---, *Endgame* (New York: Grove, 1958).

---, *Waiting for Godot* (New York: Grove, 1954).

---, 'What Where?', *The Collected Shorter Plays of Samuel Beckett* (New York: Grove, 1984): 307-16.

Bell, Lian, ed., *Ireland PQ07* (Dublin: Ireland PQ07, 2007).

Beöthy, Zsolt. *Az irodalomtörténet elmélete* [The Theory of Literary History] (Budapest: Királyi Magyar Egyetemi Nyomda, 1940).

Berend, T., Iván, *History Derailed: Central and Eastern Europe in the Long Nineteenth Century* (Berkeley: University of California Press, 2003).

Berková, Alexandra, 'Tak mladý a už Angličan!' [So Young and Already English!], *Divadelní noviny* 14.14 (6 September 2005): 2.

Bertha, Csilla, 'The Hungarian of the West: Yeats's Reception in Hungary', *The Reception of W.B. Yeats in Europe,* ed. Klaus Peter Jochum (London: Continuum, 2006): 150-61.

---, and Donald E. Morse, *Silenced Voices: Transylvanian-Hungarian Plays,* Selected and Translated by Csilla Bertha and Donald E. Morse (Dublin: Carysfort Press, 2008).

Bertha, Zoltán, 'Páskándi Géza "filozófiai végjátéka"' [Géza Páskándi's Philosophical Endgame], *Sorstükör* (Miskolc: Felsőmagyarország Kiadó, 2001): 400-05.

Best, Joel, and Gerald T. Horiuchi, 'The Razor Blade in the Apple: The Social Construction of an Urban Legend', *Social Problems* 32.5 (June 1985): 488-99.

Bew, Paul, *Land and the National Question in Ireland, 1858-82* (Dublin: Gill & Macmillan, 1978).

Bibliography of the Theatre Institute (*Divadelní ústav*) *in Prague*, 28 August 2008. <http://www.divadelni-ustav.cz/kpsys_biblio.asp>.
Booker, Keith, *Flann O'Brien, Bakhtin and Menippean Satire* (New York: Syracuse University Press, 1995).
Brachfeld, Olivér, 'Spanyol nagyságok tündöklése és bukása' [The Rise and Fall of Spanish Notabilities], *Nyugat* 28.6 (June 1935): 518-19.
Brogyányi, Eugene, 'Introduction', *New Hungarian Drama*, ed. Eugene Brogyányi (Budapest: Corvina, 1991): 9-15.
Brook, Peter, Lecture at the Dublin Theatre Festival, 5 October 2007.
Brophy, James D., and Raymond J. Porter, eds, *Contemporary Irish Writing* (Boston: Iona College Press, 1983).
Brown, Terence, 'Mahon and Longley: place and placelessness', *The Cambridge Companion to Contemporary Irish Poetry*, ed. Matthew Campbell (Cambridge: Cambridge University Press, 2003): 133-48.
Buckle, George Earle, ed., *Letters of Queen Victoria, 1879-1885*, 3 vols (London: John Murray, 1928).
Bull, Philip, *Land, Politics and Nationalism: A Study of the Irish Land Question* (Dublin: Gill & Macmillan, 1996).
Burke, Patrick, 'Friel and performance history', *The Cambridge Companion to Brian Friel,* ed. Anthony Roche (Cambridge: Cambridge University Press, 2006): 117-28.
Bury, J.P.T., *France, 1814-1940*, 6th ed. (London: Routledge, 2003).
Cadden, Michael, 'Violence, Storytelling, and Irish Aesthetics. A Theatregoer's Guide to Martin McDonagh', *Princeton University Library Chronicle* 68 (2006-2007): 671-83.
Cărbunariu, Gianina, *Kebab,* trans. Philip Osment (London: Obern Books, 2007).
Chambers, Lilian, and Eamonn Jordan, eds, *The Theatre of Martin McDonagh. A World of Savage Stories* (Dublin: Carysfort Press, 2006).
---, Ger FitzGibbon, and Eamonn Jordan, eds, *Theatre Talk: Voices of Irish Theatre Practitioners* (Dublin: Carysfort Press, 2000).
Chekhov, Anton, *Dramaticeskie proizvedeniâ, 1889-1904*, 2 vols (Leningrad: Iskusstvo Leningradskoe Otdelenie, 1985).
Claeys, Gregory, 'Mazzini, Kossuth and British Radicalism, 1848-1854', *Journal of British Studies* 28. 3 (July 1989): 225-61.
Clark, Samuel, *Social Origins of the Irish Land War* (Princeton, NJ: Princeton University Press, 1979).
Clifford, James L., 'Gulliver's Fourth Voyage', *Quick Springs of Sense*, ed. Larry S. Champion (Athens: U. of Georgia Press, 1974): 33-49.
Cortázar, Julio, 'Poétikakísérlet' [An attempt to write a poetics], *Nagyvilág* 43. 7-8 (1998): 478-91.

Cronin, Maura, '"Of One Mind"? O'Connellite Crowds in the 1830s and 1840s', *Irish Crowds 1750-1920*, eds Peter Jupp and Eoin Magennis (Hampshire: Macmillan Press, 2000): 139-72.

Cronin, Michael, *Translating Ireland: Translation, Languages, Cultures* (Cork: Cork University Press, 1996).

Csorba, András, *Magyar-ír kapcsolatok 1867-ig* [Hungarian-Irish Relations to 1867] (Debrecen: Tisza István Tudományegyetem, 1944).

Csűrös, Miklós, 'Fodor András', *A költészet. A magyar irodalom története 1945-1975* ser. [Poetry. The history of Hungarian literature 1945-1975], ed. Miklós Béládi, 2 vols (Budapest: Akadémiai, 1986): 806-17.

---, 'Fodor András és a Kettős rekviem' [András Fodor and Double Requiem], eds Mátyás Domokos and András Lakatos, *Konok idő. Fodor András emlékezete* [Obstinate Time. In Memory of András Fodor] (Budapest: Nap Kiadó, 2003): 119-32.

Curtis, L.P., *Apes and Angels*, Rev. ed. (Washington, D.C.: Smithsonian Institute, 1996).

Czech-Irish Relations: A Bibliography of Books and Articles, ed. Daniel Samek, 7 September 2007 <http://ualk.ff..cuni.cz>

Czigány, Lóránt, *A History of Hungarian Literature from the Earliest Times to the Mid-1970s* (Oxford: Clarendon Press, 1984).

Davitt, Michael, *The Fall of Feudalism in Ireland, or The Story of the Land League Revolution* (London and New York: Harper, 1904).

---, *The 'Times'-Parnell Commission: Speech Delivered by Michael Davitt in Defence of the Land League* (London: Kegan Paul, 1890).

---, *Within the Pale: The True Story of Anti-Semitic Persecutions in Russia* (London: Hurst and Blackett; New York: Barnes & Co., 1903).

Deák, István, *The Lawful Revolution: Louis Kossuth and the Hungarians, 1848-1849* (New York: Columbia University Press, 1979).

Dolan, Terence Patrick, *A Dictionary of Hiberno-English* (Dublin: Gill & Macmillan, 1998).

Downie, J.A., 'The Political Significance of *Gulliver's Travels*', *Gulliver's Travels.* Norton Critical Edition, ed. Albert J. Rivero(New York and London: Norton, 2002): 334-52.

Driver, Tom, 'Beckett by the Madeleine', *Columbia University Forum* 4 (1961): 22-23.

Duff, Alan, *The Third Language* (Oxford: Pergamon Press, 1981).

Eagleton, Terry, *How to Read a Poem* (Malden, MA: Blackwell, 2007).

Egan, Desmond, *Selected Poems/Válogatott versek* (Budapest: Editio Plurilingua, 2000).

Eldred, Laura, 'Martin McDonagh's Blend of Tradition and Horrific Innovation', *The Theatre of Martin McDonagh. A World of Savage Stories*, eds Lilian Chambers and Eamonn Jordan (Dublin: Carysfort Press, 2006): 198-213.

Eörsi, István, 'A kihallgatás' [The Interrogation], *Kilenc dráma* [Nine Plays] (Budapest: Szépirodalmi, 1988).

Eötvös, József, 'Szegénység Irlandban' [Poverty in Ireland] *Reform és Hazafiság*: *Publicisztikai írások* [Reform and Patriotism: Publicistical Articles], eds István Fenyő, et al., 3 vols (Budapest: Magyar Helikon, 1978): 133-205.

Esslin, Martin, 'The Theatre of the Absurd', *The Tulane Drama Review* (May 1960). Rpt. *Essays in the Modern Drama*, ed. Morris Freedman (Boston: D.C. Heath, 1964): 320-34.

Fest, Sándor, *Angol irodalmi hatások hazánkban Széchenyi István fellépéséig* [English Literary Influences in Our Country Until István Széchenyi] (Budapest: Magyar Tudományos Akadémia, 1917).

Fitzpatrick, Lisa, 'Language Games: *The Pillowman, A Skull in Connemara*, and Martin McDonagh's Hiberno-English', *The Theatre of Martin McDonagh. A World of Savage Stories*, eds Lilian Chambers and Eamonn Jordan (Dublin: Carysfort Press, 2006): 141-54.

FitzSimon, Christopher, *The Boys*: *A Biography of Micheál MacLíammóir and Hilton Edwards* (London: Nick Hern Books, 1994).

---. *The Irish Theatre* (London: Thames and Hudson, 1983).

Fodor, András, 'A műfordító öröksége' [The heritage of the literary translator], *Szülöttem föld* [My Homeland] (Budapest: Szépirodalmi, 1990): 252-58.

---, *Pünkösdi hírnök. Válogatott versek 1944-1987* [The Whitsun herald. Selected Poems 1944-1987] (Budapest: Magvető, 1989).

Földi, Mihály, 'Chesterton ortodoxiája' [Chesterton's Orthodoxy], *Nyugat* 10.21-22 (November 1918): 709-10.

Foster, R.F., *Paddy and Mr Punch* (Harmondsworth: Penguin, 1993).

Friel, Brian, *Essays, Diaries, Interviews*: *1964-1999,* ed. Christopher Murray (London: Faber and Faber, 1999).

---, *Uncle Vanya*: *A version of the play by Anton Chekhov* (Loughcrew: The Gallery Press, 1998).

Furray, Julia, and Redmond O'Hanlon, eds, *Critical Moments. Fintan O'Toole on Modern Irish Theatre* (Dublin: Carysfort Press, 2003).

Fusco, Cassandra, '*Uncle Vanya* (1887-1998) "A contemporary Plea for Mercy and Grace"', *Etudes Irlandaises* 26.1 (2001): 33-53.

Gál, István, *Babits és az angol irodalom* [Babits and English Literature] (Debrecen: Tisza István Tudományegyetem Angol Szemináriuma, 1942).

Gallerová, Vlasta, 'PQ jako jedno velké divadlo' [PQ as One Big Theatre], *Lidové noviny* 21 June 2007.
Gálovits, Zoltán 'Szerelemmel elnyomott ősi város' [Ancient City Oppressed by Love], *Reggeli Újság* 21 Feb 2006 <http://elozo.szigligeti.ro> 3 Jan 2008.
Garvin, Tom, *The Evolution of Irish Nationalist Politics* (Dublin: Gill & Macmillan, 1981).
Gibbons, Luke,'Prefiguring the Past: Re-imagining the Archive in Irish Studies', *The Future of Irish Studies: Report of the Irish Forum*, eds Christina Hunt Mahony, Laura Lizzara, Elizabeth Malcolm, John P. Harrington, Ondřej Pilný, and Catriona Crowe (Irish Forum, Centre for Irish Studies, Charles University: Prague, 2006): 61-84.
Gide, André, *Oscar Wilde: in Memoriam (Reminiscences): De Profundis*, trans. Bernard Frechtman (New York: Philosophical Library, 1949).
Goldman, Márta, 'Belated Reception: James Joyce's Work in Hungary', *Comparative Critical Studies* 3.3 (2006): 227-48.
Gottlieb, Vera, 'Chekhov in Limbo: British Productions of the Plays of Chekhov', *The Play out of Context: Transferring Plays from Culture to Culture*, eds Hanna Scolnicov and Peter Holland (Cambridge: Cambridge University Press, 1989): 163-72.
Grant, David, Programme Notes to Brian Friel, *Fordítások* [Translations], Kolozsvári Állami Magyar Színház, 2001/2002.
Gregory, Lady Augusta, *Our Irish Theatre* (New York: Capricorn, 1965).
Grene, Nicholas, 'Irish Drama and the Occlusion of Influence', *Princeton University Library Chronicle* 68 1-2 (2006/07): 503-15.
Grennan, Eamon, '"To the Point of Speech": the Poetry of Derek Mahon', *Contemporary Irish Writing*, eds James D. Brophy and Raymond J. Porter (Boston: Iona College Press, 1983): 15-31.
Gyárfás, Endre, *Gulliver utolsó utazása: szatírák, humoreszkek és egy kisregény* [Gulliver's Last Voyage: Satires, Humorous Sketches, and a Short Novel] (Budapest: PolgArt, 2001).
Hamvai, Kornél, *Philadelphia, nincs más út*! [Philadelphia, There's No Other Way!] Playscript for Kaposvári Csíki Gergely Színház, 2001.
Haraszti, Éva H., *Kossuth as an English Journalist* (New York: Columbia University Press, 1990).
---, *Kossuth: Hungarian Patriot in Britain* (London, in association with Corvina Press: Budapest, 1994).
Harmon, Ken, *Done Up Like A Kipper* (London: Nick Hern Books, 2002).

Hartvig, Gabriella, 'Hungarian Gulliveriads: *Gulliver's Travels* in Faremido, Capillaria, and Kazohinia', *Reading Swift. Papers from the 5th Münster Symposium on Jonathan Swift*, ed. Hermann J. Real (Munich: Wilhelm Fink Verlag, 2008): 519-31.

Heaney, Seamus, 'Definitions', www.irelandpoland.org/home.htlm.

---, *The Government of the Tongue. The 1986 T.S. Eliot Memorial Lectures and Other Critical Writings* (London: Faber and Faber, 1988).

Heidegger, Martin, *Time and Being* (1931), trans. John Macquarie and Edward Robinson (Oxford: Blackwell, 1962).

Henningsen, Charles Frederick, and [anon.], *Kossuth and "The Times" by the Author of "The Revelations of Russia"* (London: Charles Gilpin, 1851).

Herbert, Zbigniew, *Report from the Besieged City and Other Poems*, trans., introd., and notes by John and Bogdana Carpenter (Oxford: Oxford University Press, 1987).

Hobsbawm, E.J., *Nations and Nationalism since 1780: Programme, Myth, Reality* (Cambridge: Cambridge University Press, 1990).

Hopper, Keith, *A Portrait of the Artist as a Young Post-Modernist* (Cork: Cork University Press, 1995).

Howe, Stephen, *Ireland and Empire* (Oxford: Oxford University Press, 2000).

Huber, Werner, 'From Leenane to Kamenice: The De-Hibernicising of Martin McDonagh?', *Literary Views on Post-Wall Europe*, eds Christoph Houswitschka, Ines Detmers, Anna-Christina Giovanopoulos, Edith Hallberg, and Anette Pankratz (Trier: Wissenschaftlicher Verlag, 2005): 283-94.

Hughes, Declan, 'Who the Hell Do We Still Think We Are? Reflections on Irish Theatre and Irish Identity', *Theatre Stuff*, ed. Eamonn Jordan (Dublin: Carysfort Press, 2000): 8-15.

Hutcheon, Linda, *A Theory of Adaptation* (New York and London: Routledge, 2006).

Ignotus, Hugó, 'Faj és művészet' [Racial Character and the Arts], *Nyugat* 22.11 (1 June 1929): 715-18.

Imhof, Rüdiger, ed., *Alive-Alive O! Flann O'Brien's At Swim-Two-Birds* (Dublin: Wolfhound Press, 1985).

Ionesco, Eugene, 'L'Impromptu de l'Alma', *Théâtre II* (Paris: 1958).

Jakobson, Roman, 'Fordítás és nyelvészet' [Translation and linguistics], *A fordítás tudománya. Válogatás a fordításelmélet irodalmából* [Translation studies. Selections from the literature of translation theory], eds István Bart and Kinga Klaudy (Budapest: Tankönyvkiadó, 1986): 15-22.

Jarniewicz, Jerzy, 'After Babel: Translation and Mistranslation in Contemporary British Poetry', *European Journal of English Studies* 6.1 (2002): 87-104.
---, 'Of Bereavement and Affirmation', Review of Jan Kochanowski's *Laments*, *Poetry Review* 86.1 (1996): 50-52.
---, 'The Way via Warsaw: Seamus Heaney and Post-War Polish Poets', *Seamus Heaney. Poet, Critic, Translator*, eds Ashby Bland Crowder and Jason David Hall (London: Palgrave Macmillan, 2007): 103-20.
Jordan, Eamonn, *The Feast of Famine: The Plays of Frank McGuinness* (Bern: Peter Lang, 1997).
---, ed., *Theatre Stuff* (Dublin: Carysfort Press, 2000).
---, Lilian Chambers, and Ger FitzGibbon, eds, *Theatre Talk: Voices of Irish Theatre Practitioners* (Dublin: Carysfort Press, 2000).
---, 'War on Narrative: *The Pillowman*, *The Theatre of Martin McDonagh. A World of Savage Stories*, eds Lilian Chambers, and Eamonn Jordan (Dublin: Carysfort Press, 2006): 174-97.
Joyce, James. *Ulysses*, trans. Endre Gáspár (Budapest: Nova, 1943).
---, *Ulysses*, trans. Miklós Szentkuthy (Budapest: Európa, 1974).
Kabdebo, Thomas, *Ireland and Hungary: A Study in Parallels with an Arthur Griffith Bibliography* (Dublin: Four Courts Press, 2001).
Kaffka, Margit [Mrs. Fröhlich], 'Papp Mariska: *Rög. Elbeszélések*' [Review of Clod: Short Stories by Mariska Papp], *Nyugat* 1.5 (1 March 1908): 290-91.
Kántor, Péter, ed., *Új kabát, utolsó esély. Kortárs brit költők* [New Coat, Last Chance. Contemporary British Poets] (Budapest: Európa, 1993).
Kappanyos András, 'Megintegy work-in-progress: a magyar Joyce-kiadás és a magyar anglisztika' [A work-in-progress again: the publishing of Joyce and the study of English literature in Hungary], *Filológiai Közlöny* 3-4 (2002): 245-50.
---, 'Ulysses, a nyughatatlan' [Ulysses, the restless], *Átváltozások* 10 (1997): 44-54.
Karinthy, Frigyes, *Capillária: Gulliver hatodik útja* [Capillaria: the Sixth Voyage of Gulliver] (Budapest: Kultúra, 1921).
---, 'Kosztolányi: "Readingi fegyház"' [Kosztolányi's 'Reading Gaol'], *Nyugat* 19.12 (16 June 1926): 139-54.
---, 'Levél H.G. Wells-hez' [Letter to H.G. Wells], *Nyugat* 18.14-15 (1 August 1925): 139-54.
---, 'Shaw Bernát *Caesarja*' [Bernard Shaw's *Caesar*], *Nyugat* 2.7 (1 April 1909): 393-94.
---, *Utazás Faremidóba: Gulliver ötödik útja* [Voyage to Faremido: the Fifth Voyage of Gulliver] (Budapest: Athenaeum, 1916).

---, *Voyage to Faremido. Capillaria,* trans. Paul Tabori (Budapest: Corvina Press, 1965).

Katz Clarke, Brenna Ferrar, and Harold Ferrar, *The Dublin Drama League* (Gerrads Cross: Colin Smythe, 1979).

Keating, Sara, 'All the World's a Set Design', *The Irish Times* 12 June 2007.

Kelemen, Lajos, and Ádám Szeredy, eds, '*A működés több, mint a lét*'. *Fodor András emlékezete* ['Function is more than existence'. In memory of András Fodor] (n.p.: Berzsenyi Dániel Irodalmi és Művészeti Társaság-Kortárs Kiadó, 1997).

Kékesi Kun, Árpád, *Tükörképek lázadása* [Rebellion of Mirror Images] (Budapest: Kijárat, 1998).

Killinger, John, *World in Collapse: the Vision of Absurd Drama* (New York: Dell, 1971).

Kilroy, Thomas, 'A Generation of Playwrights', *Theatre Stuff*, ed. Eamonn Jordan (Dublin: Carysfort Press, 2000): 1-7.

King, Carla, *Michael Davitt* (Dundalk: Dundalgan, 1999).

---, 'Michael Davitt and the Kishinev Pogrom, 1903', *Irish Slavonic Studies* 17 (1996): 19-43.

Király, György, 'Wundt', *Nyugat* 13.19-20 (October 1920): 988-89.

Klitgård, Ida, *Fictions of Hybridity: Translating Style in James Joyce's Ulysses* (Odense: University Press of Southern Denmark, 2007).

Knowlson, James, *Damned to Fame* (New York: Simon & Schuster, 1996).

Kochanowski, Jan, *Laments*, trans. Seamus Heaney and Stanisław Barańczak (London: Faber and Faber, 1995).

Koltai, Tamás, 'A Marconi-táncosok' [The Marconi Dancers], *Élet és Irodalom* (14 January 1994):12.

Komor, István, 'Magyar ostor, német vasderék' [Hungarian Whip, German Back of Steel], *Nyugat* 24.22 (16 November 1931): 524-31.

Kosok, Heinz, 'Cracks in the Jug: Recent Translations/Adaptations of Continental Plays by Irish Dramatists', *Drama Translation and Theatre Practice*, eds Sabine Coelsch-Foisner and Holger Klein (Frankfurt am Main: Peter Lang, 2004): 98-120.

---, 'Gulliver's Children: A Classic Transformed for Young Readers', *Proceedings of The First Münster Symposium on Jonathan Swift*, eds Hermann J. Real and Heinz J. Vienken (München: Wilhelm Fink Verlag, 1985): 135-44.

Kossuth, Lajos, *His Speeches in England* (London: Charles Gilpin, 1852).

---, *Kossuth in New England: a Full Account of the Hungarian Governor's Visit to Massachusetts with his Speeches and*

Addresses that Were Made to Him (Boston: John P. Jewett & Co., 1852).
Kossuth, Louis, *Memories of My Exile,* trans. Ferencz Jausz (London: Cassell, Patten, Galpin & Co., 1880).
Kosztolányi, Dezső, 'Bábel tornya. Úti jegyzet' [The Tower of Babel. Travel Note], *Nyugat* 18.16-17 (1 September 1923): 246-49.
---, 'Chesterton-könyvek' [Books by Chesterton], *Nyugat* 13.5-6 (March 1920): 331-32.
Kövér, Tamás, 'Ágendák és derogációk Európából' [Agendas and Derogations from Europe], *Sopron* 2 (1999): 89-92.
Kurdi, Mária, *Codes and Masks. Aspects of Identity in Contemporary Irish Plays in an Intercultural Context* (Frankfurt am Main: Peter Lang, 2000).
---, 'Transplanting the Work of "that rooted man": The Reception of John Millington Synge's Drama in Hungary', *Comparative Drama* 41.2 (Summer 2007): 219-41.
---, and Csilla Bertha, 'Hungarian Perspectives on Brian Friel's Theatre after *Dancing at Lughnasa', Druids, Dudes and Beauty Queens,* ed. Dermot Bolger (Dublin: New Island, 2001): 173-95.
Laczkó, Géza, 'Barbey D'Aurévilly', *Nyugat* 1.22 (16 November 1908): 387-88.
Laffan, Michael, *The Partition of Ireland, 1911-25* (Dundalk: Dundalgan, 1983).
Lázňovský, Matouš, 'Irská čerň a česká šed'? [Irish Black and Czech Grey?], *Svět a divadlo* 16.6 (2005): 24-30.
Leeming, Glenda, ed., *Three Gothic Novels* (London: The British Council, 1975).
Lefevere, André, 'Translation: Its Genealogy in the West', *Translating, History and Culture,* ed. Susan Bassnett (London and New York: Pinter Publishers, 1990): 15-28.
---, and Susan Bassnett, 'Where are we in Translation Studies?', *Constructing Cultures: Essay on Literary Translation,* eds Susan Bassnett and André Lefevere (Clevedon: Multilingual Matters, 1998): 1-11.
Lengyel, Laura, Mrs. Daniel, 'Swift Jonathán' [Jonathan Swift], *Nyugat* 22.5 (1 March 1929): 327-31.
Lipcsey, Ildiko, *Romania and Transylvania in the 20th Century,* trans. Peter Csermely (Buffalo: Corvinus, 2006).
'Literature/Children's books', 16 June 2008 <http://www.frankfurt.matav.hu/angol/kiadvanyok/eng/5.htm>.
Long, Joseph, 'Frank McGuinness in Conversation with Joseph Long', *Theatre Talk: Voices of Irish Theatre Practitioners,* eds Lillian Chambers, Ger Fitzgibbon, and Eamonn Jordan (Dublin: Carysfort Press, 2000): 298-307.

Loughlin, James, *Gladstone, Home Rule and the Ulster Question, 1882-93* (Dublin: Gill & Macmillan, 1986).

Lukeš, Milan, 'Irská zabijačka' [The Irish Butchery], *Svět a divadlo* 13.3 (2002): 61-70.

---, 'Šíleně šikovní s šikovně šílení Irové' [The Madly Skilful and Skilfully Mad Irish], *Druhý břeh* 1.3 (2003): 17-20.

Mahon, Derek, *Selected Poems* (London: Penguin, 2006).

---, *A tenger télen* [*The Sea in Winter*] (Budapest: Európa, 1992).

Marley, Laurence, *Michael Davitt: Freelance Radical and Frondeur* (Dublin: Four Courts Press, 2007).

Maume, Patrick, *The Long Gestation: Irish Nationalist Life, 1891-1918* (Dublin: Gill & Macmillan, 1999).

McDonagh, Martin, *The Pillowman* (London: Faber and Faber, 2003).

McGuinness, Frank, *Uncle Vanya*: A version by Frank McGuinness (unpublished manuscript).

Meany, Helen, Review of *Festen*, *The Irish Times* 30 January 2004: 12.

Mesterházi, Márton, 'Translations into Hungarian', *Brian Friel's Dramatic Artistry,* eds Donald E. Morse, Csilla Bertha, and Mária Kurdi (Dublin: Carysfort Press, 2006): 109-21.

Michael Davitt papers, Trinity College Dublin.

Mikulka, Vladimír, 'Martin McDonagh: Z Londýna do Prahy (přes Irsko)' [Martin McDonagh: From London to Prague (via Ireland)], *Kritická příloha Revolver Revue* 25 (March 2003): 30-42.

---, 'Tak trochu jiný McDonagh' [McDonagh Slightly Different], *Revolver Revue* 62 (2006): 238-41.

Milesi, Laurent, ed., *James Joyce and the Difference of Language* (Cambridge: Cambridge University Press, 2003).

Miller, Alice, *Child Abuse and Mistreatment* <http://www.alice-miller.com/index en.php>.

Moody, T.W., *Davitt and Irish Revolution, 1846-82* (Oxford: Oxford University Press, 1981).

---, 'Michael Davitt and the British Labour Movement, 1882-1906', *Transactions of the Royal Historical Society,* 5th ser., iii (1953): 53-76.

Mrożek, Slawomir, *Six Plays*, trans. Nicholas Bethell (New York: Grove Press, 1967).

Müller, Péter P., *Central European Playwrights within and without the Absurd* (Pécs, HU: JPTE TK Kiadói Iroda, 1996).

Newby, Andrew, *Ireland, Radicalism and the Scottish Highlands, c. 1870-1912* (Edinburgh: Edinburgh University Press, 2007).

Nikčević, Sanja, *Nova europska drama ili velika obmana* [New European Drama or the Great Deception] (Zagreb: Meandar, 2005).

O'Brien, Flann, *At Swim-Two-Birds* (London: Penguin Classics, 2001).
---, *Auf Schwimmen-zwei-Vögel, oder Sweeny auf den Bäumen*, trans. Harry Rowohlt and Helmut Mennicken (Zürich: Kein & Aber, 2002).
---, *La Doi Lebădoi*, trans. Adrian Oţoiu (Piteşti: Paralela 45, 2005).
Ortutay, Gyula, 'Kolumbusz Kristóf. Salvador de Madariaga könyve' [Review of *Christopher Columbus* by Salvador de Madariaga], *Nyugat* 34.2 (1 February 1941): 73-74.
Papházi, Tivadar, *Új Gulliver: Fantasztikus-utópisztikus regény* [New Gulliver: A Fantastic-Utopian Novel] (Budapest: Accordia kiadó, 2003).
Páskándi,Géza, 'The Avenger, the Gatekeeper, or It is Requested that You Wipe Your Feet', *Silenced Voices: Transylvanian-Hungarian Plays*, Selected and Translated by Csilla Bertha and Donald E. Morse (Dublin: Carysfort Press, 2008).
---, *Esszék, előadások, levelek: az absurd és az isten* [Essays, lectures: the absurd and God] (Budapest: Gondolat, 1995).
---, 'The Line', *Nine Plays*, trans. Eugene Brogyányi (Budapest: Szépirodalmi, 1988): 7-34.
---, 'Moment of Sincerity', *Nine Plays*, trans. Eugene Brogyányi (Kolozsvár [Cluj]: Polis, 1999): 75-82.
---, 'No Conductor', *Nine Plays*, trans. Eugene Brogyányi (Kolozsvár [Cluj]: Polis, 1999): 35-74.
---, *Todogar Jaur Kvárna: Filosozófiai végjáték* [Philosophical Endgame] (Budapest: Széphalom Könyvműhely, 1995).
---, 'World's Fair: A Post-exotic Absurdoid Play in Three Acts', *Nine Plays*, trans. Eugene Brogyányi (Kolozsvár [Cluj]: Polis, 1999): 180-239.
Passuth, László, 'Madariaga', *Nyugat* 19.7 (July 1936): 63-65.
Pataki, Ferenc, 'Nemzetkarakterológia?' [National Characterology?], *Magyar Tudomány* (February 1997): 169-79.
Peter, John, *Vladimir's Carrot: Modern Drama and the Modern Imagination* (Chicago: Chicago University Press, 1987).
Pilný, Ondřej, 'Grotesque Entertainment: *The Pillowman* as Puppet Theatre', *The Theatre of Martin McDonagh. A World of Savage Stories*, eds Lilian Chambers and Eamonn Jordan (Dublin: Carysfort Press, 2006): 214-23.
---, 'Martin McDonagh: Parody? Satire? Complacency?', *Irish Studies Review* 12.2 (2004): 225-31.
---, 'Proměny irského dramatu 1950-1999' [Transformations in Irish Drama 1950-1999], Conor McPherson, *Na cestě duchů* [*The Weir*] (Praha: Národní divadlo, 2000): 4-24.

Prohászka, Lajos, *A vándor és a bujdosó* [The Wanderer and the Exile] (Budapest: Minerva, 1936).
Ptáčková, Věra, 'Příběhy z jiného světa?' [Stories of Another World?], *Svět a divadlo* 13.3 (2002): 56-60.
---, 'Ti zvláštní Irové' [Them Strange Irish], *Svět a divadlo* 12.2 (2001): 59-64.
Rab, László, *A magyarok között: Gulliver sokadik utazása* [Among the Hungarians: Gulliver's Umpteenth Voyage] (Budapest: Népszabadság könyvek, 2005).
Rába, György, *Babits Mihály költészete, 1903-1920* [The Poetry of Mihály Babits, 1903-1920] (Budapest: Szépirodalmi, 1981).
Rácz, István D., 'Heaneys of the Mind', *Hungarian Journal of English and American Studies* 10. 1-2 (2004): 127-36.
Real, Hermann J., 'Gulliver's Travels into Remote Eighteenth-Century Germany', *The Novel in Anglo-German Context. Cultural Cross-Currents and Affinities*, ed. Susanne Stark (Amsterdam: Rodopi, 2000): 1-21.
---, *The Reception of Jonathan Swift in Europe*, ed. Hermann J. Real (London and New York: Thoemmes Press, 2005): 1-4.
Richtarik, Marilynn J., *Acting between the Lines: The Field Day Theatre Company and Irish Cultural Politics 1980-1984* (Oxford: Clarendon Press, 1994).
Rónay, György, 'Babits a fordító' [Babits the Translator], *Nyugat* 33.1 (January 1940): 48-51.
Rumens, Carol, *Self into Song*, Newcastle/Bloodaxe Poetry Lectures ser. (Newcastle: Bloodaxe, 2007).
Santino, Jack, ed., *Halloween and Other Festivals of Death and Life* (Knoxville: the University of Tennessee Press, 1994) <http://www.snopes.com/horrors/mayhem/needles.asp>.
Senn, Fritz, *Joyce's Dislocutions: Essays on reading as Translation*, ed. John Paul Riquelme (Baltimore: Johns Hopkins University Press, 1984).
---, 'Joycean Provections', *Inductive Scrutinies. Focus on Joyce*, ed. Christine O'Neill (Dublin: The Lilliput Press, 1995): 35-58.
Siklósi, Horváth Klára, *Siklósi Horváth Klára*, <http://www.siklosihorvath-knoll.hu>16 June 2008.
---, *Gulliver Bolgorogyban* [Gulliver in Bolgorogy] (Budapest: Littera Nova Kiadó, 1999);
---, *Gulliver in Joygorod*, trans. Ildikó Noémi Nagy (Budapest: Littera Nova Publishing, 1998).
---, *Gulliver legújabb kalandja Pinkwellben* [Gulliver's Latest Adventure in Pinkwell] (Budapest: Orpheus Könyvek, 2001).
Simpson, Alan, *Beckett and Behan and a Theatre in Dublin* (London: Routledge & Keegan Paul, 1962).

Singer, Isidore, ed., *Russia at the bar of the American People* (New York: Funk & Wagnalls, 1904).
Sloan, Robert, *William Smith O'Brien and the Young Ireland Rebellion of 1848* (Dublin: Four Courts Press, 2000).
Sommer, Piotr, ed., *Antologia nowej poezji brytyjskiej* [Anthology of New British Poetry] (Warsaw: Czytelnik, 1983).
---, 'Co ciekawiło mnie u Seamusa Heaneya, kiedy zaczynałem go tłumaczyć' [What interested me in Seamus Heaney when I started translating him], Seamus Heaney, *Kolejowe dzieci* [The Railway Children], trans. Piotr Sommer (Legnica: Fort, 1998): 94-105.
Šourek, Petr, 'Plačky nad rozlitými bojovými rybkami' [A Wake over Spilled Fighting Fish], *Nový prostor* 288 (20 August 2007): 26.
Sperber, Jonathan, *The European Revolution, 1848-1851* (Cambridge: Cambridge University Press, 1994).
Steiner, George, *After Babel: Aspects of Language in Translation* (Oxford: Oxford University Press, 1975).
Sugiera, Malgorzata, 'Beyond Drama: Writing for Postdramatic Theatre', *Theatre Research International* 29.1 (March 2004): 6-28.
Sütő, András, 'Advent in the Hargita Mountains', *Silenced Voices: Transylvanian-Hungarian Plays*, Selected and Translated by Csilla Bertha and Donald E. Morse (Dublin: Carysfort Press, 2008).
---, *The Wedding Feast at Suza*, trans. Csilla Bertha and Donald E. Morse (London: University of London Press, 1993).
Svejcer, A.D., 'A fordításelmélet mint interdiszciplináris tudomány' [Translation theory as an interdisciplinary field], *A fordítás tudománya. Válogatás a fordításelmélet irodalmából*, eds István Bart and Kinga Klaudy (Budapest: Tankönyvkiadó, 1986): 30-39.
Swift, Jonathan, *Gulliver's Travels*. Norton Critical Edition, ed. Albert J. Rivero (New York and London: Norton, 2002).
Szabó, Lőrinc, 'Tóth Árpád Wilde fordítása' [Árpád Tóth's Translation of Wilde], *Nyugat* 14.10 (16 May 1921): 790-93.
Szabolcsi, Miklós, *Költészet és korszerűség* [Poetry and modernity] (Budapest: Magvető, 1959).
Szász, Károly, *Kisebb műfordításai* [Minor Translations] (Budapest: Ráth Mór, 1872).
---, *Moore Tamás költeményeiből* [From the Poetry of Thomas Moore] (Pest: n.p., 1853).
Szász, Zoltán, 'A "mozi" felé' [Towards the 'Movies], *Nyugat* 1.21 (1 November 1908): 333-35.
---, 'Tűnj fel!' [Attract Attention!], *Nyugat* 1.24 (16 December 1908): 500-04.
---, 'Wilde Oszkár' [Oscar Wilde], *Nyugat* 12-13 (1 July 1908): 650-78.

Szathmári, Sándor, *Gulliver utazása Kazohiniában* [Gulliver's Travels in Kazohinia] (Budapest: Bolyai Akadémia, 1941).
---, *Kazohinia,* trans. Inez Kemenes (Budapest: Corvina Press, 1975).
Szentkuthy, Miklós, 'James Joyce', *A múzsák testamentuma* [The Testament of Muses] (Budapest: Magvető, 1985): 104-15.
Szerb, Antal, *Az angol irodalom kis tükre* [A Short History of English Literature], Hétköznapok és csodák [Weekdays and Wonders], ed. Csaba Pléh, 3 vols (Budapest: Magvető, 2002): 174-241.
---, 'A magyarság mitikus arca' [The Mythic Face of Hungarians] *Hétköznapok és csodák* [*Weekdays and Wonders*], ed. Csaba Pléh, 3 vols (Budapest: Magvető, 2002): 53-57.
---, 'Századvég' [*Fin-de-siècle*], *Nyugat* 27.10-11 (16 May-1 June 1934): 552-61.
---, *A világirodalom története* [The History of World Literature] (Budapest: Magvető, 1962).
Szini, Gyula, 'Három ibolyacsokor' [Three Bouquets of Violets], *Nyugat* 24.1 (1 January 1931): 60-61.
---, 'A mese alkonya' [The Twilight of Fable], *Nyugat* 1.1 (1 January 1908): 24-28.
---, 'Shaw margójára' [Marginalia on the Work of Shaw], *Nyugat* 4.3 (1 February 1911): 228-36.
Tábor, Eszter, *Külön óra* [Private hour], Lélegzet könyvek ser. (Budapest: Typotex, 1994).
Thurzó, Gábor, 'Szini Gyula emléke' [In Memory of Gyula Szini], *Nyugat* 33.5 (1 May 1940): 238-43.
Tolnai, Gábor, 'Arisztokratizmus és szecesszió' [Aristocratism and Art Nouveau], *Nyugat* 30.5 (May 1937): 332-38.
Tóth, Árpád, 'Babits műfordításai: *Pávatollak*' [The Translations of Babits: *Peacock Feathers*], *Nyugat* 13.3-4 (February 1920): 212-15.
Travers, Pauric, *Settlements and Divisions: Ireland, 1870-1922* (Dublin: Helicon, 1988).
Trensky, Paul I., *Czech Drama since World War II* (White Plains, NY: M.E. Sharpe, 1978).
Trenský, Pavel, 'Nihilistova přitažlivost' [The Attractivity of the Nihilist], *Svět a divadlo* 15.4 (2004): 40-52.
Trpišovský, Lukáš, 'SADOmasoDISCOkoláž', programme brochure for Enda Walsh, *Disco Pigs* produced by DISK – Divadelní studio DAMU, 2002: 25-28.
Tüskés, Tibor, '*Gulliver legújabb kalandja Pinkwellben.* Siklósi Horváth Klára regénye' [Gulliver's Latest Adventure in Pinkwell. A novel by Klára Horváth Siklósi], *Polísz* 62 (2001-2002): 90-92.
Tymocko, Maria, 'Connecting the Two Infinite Orders: Research Methods in Translation Studies', *Crosscultural Transgressions: Research Models in Translation Studies II: Historical and*

Ideological Issues, ed. Theo Hermans (Manchester, UK: St. Jerome, 2002): 15.

Upton, Carole-Anne, *Moving Target: Theatre Translation and Cultural Relocation* (Manchester, UK: St. Jerome, 2000).

Venuti, Lawrence, *The Translator's Invisibility* (London: Routledge, 1995).

Wales, Katie, *The Language of James Joyce* (London: Macmillan, 1992).

Wallace, Clare, 'Irish Theatre Criticism: De-territorialisation and Integration', *Modern Drama* 47.4 (Winter 2004): 659-70.

---, '"Pastiche Soup", Bad Taste, Biting Irony and Martin McDonagh', *Litteraria Pragensia* 15.29 (2005): 3-38.

Welch, Robert, *Changing States: Transformations in Modern Irish Writing* (London: Routledge, 1993).

Wesseling, H.L., *The European Colonial Empires, 1815-1919*, trans. Diane Webb (London: Pearson, 2004).

West, Michael, 'Authentic Fictions', *Irish Theatre Magazine* 4.16 (Autumn 2003): 15 -22.

Wilde, Oscar, 'Charmides', trans. Mihály Babits, *Nyugat* 4.8 (16 April 1911): 705-18.

---. *Dorian Gray arcképe* [The Picture of Dorian Gray], trans. Dezső Kosztolányi (Budapest: Genius, 1922).

---, *Dorian Gray arcképe* [The Picture of Dorian Gray], trans. Aladár Schöpflin (Budapest: Lampel, 1907.

---, *A páduai hercegnő* [The Duchess of Padua], trans. Dezső Kosztolányi (Budapest: Lampel, 1910).

---, 'A readingi fegyház balladája' ['The Ballad of Reading Gaol'], trans. Dezső Kosztolányi, *Nyugat* 19.12 (16 June 1926): 892-99.

—, 'A readingi fegyház balladája' ['The Ballad of Reading Gaol'], trans. Árpád Tóth, *Nyugat* 12.14-15 (June 1919): 954-73.

---, *Salome*, trans. Géza Battkay (Budapest: Révai, 1907).

---, *Salome*, trans. Dezső Kosztolányi (Budapest: Genius, 1923).

---, *Salome*, trans. Gyula Szini (Budapest: Lampel, 1903).

Woolf, Virginia, 'Modern Fiction', *The Gender of Modernism: A Critical Anthology*, ed. Bonnie Kime Scott (Bloomington: Indiana University Press, 1990): 628-33.

Yeats, William Butler, 'Szerelmesét halottnak kívánja' [He Wishes His Beloved Were Dead], trans. Mihály Babits, *Nyugat* 23.14 (16 July 1930): 140.

Žantovská, Kristina, 'Irský Inishmore na Smíchově' [The Irish Inishmore in Smíchov], *Svět a divadlo* 15.2 (2004): 43-47.

Zarek, Otto, *Kossuth*, trans. Lynton Hudson (London: Selwyn & Blount, 1937).

‘Zázrak a magie divadla’ [The Miracle and Magic of the Theatre], *Svět a divadlo* 11.1 (2000): 42-44.

Contributors

Csilla Bertha teaches at Debrecen University, Hungary. Her publications on Irish drama include *Yeats the Playwright* (in Hungarian); volumes co-authored or co-edited with Donald E. Morse: *Worlds Visible and Invisible, A Small Nation's Contribution to the World, More Real than Reality,* and, with also Mária Kurdi, *Brian Friel's Dramatic Artistry*. With Morse she co-translated *Silenced Voices*, a volume of Transylvanian-Hungarian plays (Carysfort, 2008).

Zsuzsa Csikai, an instructor in the Department of English Literatures and Cultures, University of Pécs, has completed her PhD dissertation on Irish adaptations and translations of Chekhov's plays. Her academic interests include Irish culture, literature and translation studies.

Gabriella Hartvig teaches eighteenth-century English and Anglo-Irish literature and reception studies at the Department of English Literatures and Cultures at the University of Pécs. Her publications include a monograph on the early Hungarian reception of Laurence Sterne (Budapest: Argumentum, 2000). She has also published essays in the journal *The Shandean* and contributed to the series 'The Reception of British and Irish Authors in Europe' on the receptions of Sterne, Ossian, and Jonathan Swift.

Jerzy Jarniewicz is a Polish poet, translator and literary critic, who lectures in English at the universities of Łódź and Warsaw. He has published nine volumes of poetry, six critical books on contemporary British, Irish and American literature (most recently studies of Seamus Heaney and Philip Larkin), and has written extensively for various journals, including *Poetry Review, Irish Review, Cambridge Review,* and *Krino.*

Carla King is a Lecturer in Modern History at St Patrick's College, Drumcondra, (Dublin City University). She studied at University College Dublin and University College London. She has published various works relating to Michael Davitt and other subjects, and is currently writing a biography of Davitt's later life.

Patrick Lonergan teaches at National University of Ireland, Galway. He reviews theatre for *The Irish Times* and *Irish Theatre Magazine.* His recent books include *Theatre and Globalization* (Palgrave, 2009), *The Methuen Drama Anthology of Irish Plays* (2008), and *Interactions – the Dublin Theatre Festival 1957-2007* (with Nicholas Grene, 2008).

Erika Mihálycsa is junior lecturer at the Department of English, Babeş-Bolyai University Cluj, Romania. She received her PhD from that university for a dissertation on the linguistic poetics of Joyce, Flann O'Brien and Beckett. She is also translator of British and Irish contemporary authors into Hungarian.

Donald E. Morse, Emeritus Professor, Oakland University, University Professor, Debrecen University, Fulbright Professor (1987–1989, 1991–1993) has published several books, including *The Novels of Kurt Vonnegut* (2003) and *Brian Friel's Dramatic Artistry* with Cs. Bertha and M. Kurdi (Carysfort, 2006) With Csilla Bertha, he published books on Irish Studies and translated contemporary Hungarian plays into English (*Silenced Voices: Five Hungarian-Transylvanian Plays,* Carysfort, 2008). He received an Honorary Doctorate (Debrecen University 1999) and the *László Országh Prize* (2006). Currently edits the *Hungarian Journal of English and American Studies.*

Péter P. Müller is Professor and Chair at the University of Pécs in the Department of Modern Literature and Literary Theory where he has taught since 1982. He is director of the Theatre Studies Programme there. From 1999 to 2004 he was director of the Hungarian Theatre Museum and Institute in Budapest. His books are, *The Dramaturgy of the Grotesque* (1990), *On Sopianae's Stages* (1992), *Central European Playwrights Within and Without the Absurd* (in English – 1996), *Dramatic Form and Publicity* (1997), *From Hamlet to the Hamletmachine* (2008), *From Rite to Media: Hungarian Drama at the Millennium* (in Croatian – 2009).

Ondřej Pilný is Associate Professor, Chair of the Department of Anglophone Literatures and Cultures, and Director of the Centre for Irish Studies at Charles University, Prague. He is the author of *Irony and Identity in Modern Irish Drama* (2006) and editor of *Global Ireland: Irish Literatures in the New Millennium* (with Clare Wallace), *Time Refigured: Myths, Foundation Texts and Imagined Communities* (with Martin Procházka), and an annotated volume of J.M. Synge's works in Czech. His translations include plays by Brian Friel, Martin McDonagh and J.M. Synge, and Flann O'Brien's *The Third Policeman.*

István D. Rácz is a reader in the Department of British Studies, University of Debrecen, Hungary. He has published books and studies on contemporary British poetry, including a monograph on Philip Larkin. He has co-edited a volume on Sylvia Plath and Ted Hughes. Currently he is working on a new monograph on Larkin's poetics.

Gabriella Vöő teaches American literature at the Department of English Literatures and Cultures at the University of Pécs. Her research interests include the reception of anglophone authors in interwar Hungary and she contributed to the series 'The Reception of British and Irish Authors in Europe' on the reception of H.G. Wells.

Index

C

D

E

F

G

N

O

V

W

Y

Carysfort Press was formed in the summer of 1998. It receives annual funding from the Arts Council.

The directors believe that drama is playing an ever-increasing role in today's society and that enjoyment of the theatre, both professional and amateur, currently plays a central part in Irish culture.

The Press aims to produce high quality publications which, though written and/or edited by academics, will be made accessible to a general readership. The organisation would also like to provide a forum for critical thinking in the Arts in Ireland, again keeping the needs and interests of the general public in view.

The company publishes contemporary Irish writing for and about the theatre.

Editorial and publishing inquiries to:
Carysfort Press Ltd., 58 Woodfield,
Scholarstown Road, Rathfarnham,
Dublin 16, Republic of Ireland.

T (353 1) 493 7383
F (353 1) 406 9815
e: info@carysfortpress.com
www.carysfortpress.com

HOW TO ORDER

TRADE ORDERS DIRECTLY TO:
CMD
Columba Mercier Distribution,
55A Spruce Avenue,
Stillorgan Industrial Park,
Blackrock, Co. Dublin

T: (353 1) 294 2560
F: (353 1) 294 2564
E: cmd@columba.ie

INDIVIDUAL ORDERS DIRECTLY TO:
eprint Ltd.
35 Coolmine Industrial Estate,
Blanchardstown, Dublin 15.

T: (353 1) 827 8860
F: (353 1) 827 8804
Order online @ www.carysfortpress.com

FOR SALES IN NORTH AMERICA AND CANADA:
Dufour Editions Inc.,
124 Byers Road, PO Box 7,
Chester Springs, PA 19425,
USA

T: 1-610-458-5005
F: 1-610-458-7103

Seán Keating in Context: Responses to Culture and Politics in Post-Civil War Ireland

Compiled, edited, and introduced by Éimear O'Connor

Irish artist Seán Keating has been judged by his critics as the personification of old-fashioned traditionalist values. This book presents a different view. The story reveals Keating's early determination to attain government support for the visual arts. It also illustrates his socialist leanings, his disappointment with capitalism, and his attitude to cultural snobbery, to art critics, and to the Academy. Given the national and global circumstances nowadays, Keating's critical and wry observations are prophetic – and highly amusing.

ISBN 978-1-904505-41-9 €25

Dialogue of the Ancients of Ireland: A new translation of Acallam na Senorach

Translated with introduction and notes by Maurice Harmon

One of Ireland's greatest collections of stories and poems, The Dialogue of the Ancients of Ireland is a new translation by Maurice Harmon of the 12th century *Acallam na Senorach*. Retold in a refreshing modern idiom, the *Dialogue* is an extraordinary account of journeys to the four provinces by St. Patrick and the pagan Cailte, one of the surviving Fian. Within the frame story are over 200 other stories reflecting many genres – wonder tales, sea journeys, romances, stories of revenge, tales of monsters and magic. The poems are equally varied – lyrics, nature poems, eulogies, prophecies, laments, genealogical poems. After the *Tain Bo Cuailnge*, the *Acallam* is the largest surviving prose work in Old and Middle Irish.

ISBN: 978-1-904505-39-6 (2009) €20

Literary and Cultural Relations between Ireland and Hungary and Central and Eastern Europe

Ed. Maria Kurdi

This lively, informative and incisive collection of essays sheds fascinating new light on the literary interrelations between Ireland, Hungary, Poland, Romania and the Czech Republic. It charts a hitherto under-explored history of the reception of modern Irish culture in Central and Eastern Europe and also investigates how key authors have been translated, performed and adapted. The revealing explorations undertaken in this volume of a wide array of Irish dramatic and literary texts, ranging from *Gulliver's Travels* to *Translations* and *The Pillowman*, tease out the subtly altered nuances that they acquire in a Central European context.

ISBN: 978-1-904505-40-2 (2009) €20

Plays and Controversies: Abbey Theatre Diaries 2000-2005

by Ben Barnes

In diaries covering the period of his artistic directorship of the Abbey, Ben Barnes offers a frank, honest, and probing account of a much commented upon and controversial period in the history of the national theatre. These diaries also provide fascinating personal insights into the day to day pressures, joys, and frustrations of running one of Ireland's most iconic institutions.

ISBN: 978-1-904505-38-9 (2008) €35

Interactions: Dublin Theatre Festival 1957-2007. Irish Theatrical Diaspora Series: 3

Eds. Nicholas Grene and Patrick Lonergan with Lilian Chambers

For over 50 years the Dublin Theatre Festival has been one of Ireland's most important cultural events, bringing countless new Irish plays to the world stage, while introducing Irish audiences to the most important international theatre companies and artists. Interactions explores and celebrates the achievements of the renowned Festival since 1957 and includes specially commissioned memoirs from past organizers, offering a unique perspective on the controversies and successes that have marked the event's history. An especially valuable feature of the volume, also, is a complete listing of the shows that have appeared at the Festival from 1957 to 2008.

ISBN: 978-1-904505-36-5 €25

The Informer: A play by Tom Murphy based on the novel by Liam O'Flaherty

The Informer, Tom Murphy's stage adapatation of Liam O'Flaherty's novel, was produced in the 1981 Dublin Theatre Festival, directed by the playwright himself, with Liam Neeson in the leading role. The central subject of the play is the quest of a character at the point of emotional and moral breakdown for some souce of meaning or identity. In the case of Gypo Nolan, the informer of the title, this involves a nightmarish progress through a Dublin underworld in which he changes from a Judas figure to a scapegoat surrogate for Jesus, taking upon himself the sins of the world. A cinematic style, with flash-back and intercut scenes, is used rather than a conventional theatrical structure to catch the fevered and phantasmagoric progression of Gypo's mind. The language, characteristically for Murphy, mixes graphically colloquial Dublin slang with the haunted intricacies of the central character groping for the meaning of his own actions. The dynamic rhythm of the action builds towards an inevitable but theatrically satisfying tragic catastrophe. ' [The Informer] is , in many ways closer to being an original Murphy play than it is to O'Flaherty...' Fintan O'Toole.

ISBN: 978-1-904505-37-2 (2008) €10

Shifting Scenes: Irish theatre-going 1955-1985

Eds. Nicholas Grene and Chris Morash

Transcript of conversations with John Devitt, academic and reviewer, about his lifelong passion for the theatre. A fascinating and entertaining insight into Dublin theatre over the course of thirty years provided by Devitt's vivid reminiscences and astute observations.

ISBN: 978-1-904505-33-4 (2008) €10

Irish Literature: Feminist Perspectives

Eds Patricia Coughlan and Tina O'Toole

The collection discusses texts from the early 18th century to the present. A central theme of the book is the need to renegotiate the relations of feminism with nationalism and to transact the potential contest of these two important narratives, each possessing powerful emancipatory force. Irish Literature: Feminist Perspectives contributes incisively to contemporary debates about Irish culture, gender and ideology.

ISBN: 978-1-904505-35-8 (2008) €25

Silenced Voices: Hungarian Plays from Transylvania

selected and translated by Csilla Bertha and Donald E. Morse

The five plays are wonderfully theatrical, moving fluidly from absurdism to tragedy, and from satire to the darkly comic. Donald Morse and Csilla Bertha's translations capture these qualities perfectly, giving voice to the 'forgotten playwrights of Central Europe'. They also deeply enrich our understanding of the relationship between art, ethics, and politics in Europe.

ISBN: 978-1-904505-34-1 (2008)   €25

A Hazardous Melody of Being: Seóirse Bodley's Song Cycles on the poems of Micheal O'Siadhail

Ed. Lorraine Byrne Bodley

This apograph is the first publication of Bodley's O'Siadhail song cycles and is the first book to explore the composer's lyrical modernity from a number of perspectives. Lorraine Byrne Bodley's insightful introduction describes in detail the development and essence of Bodley's musical thinking, the European influences he absorbed which linger in these cycles, and the importance of his work as a composer of the Irish art song.

ISBN: 978-1-904505-31-0 (2008)   €25

Irish Theatre in England: Irish Theatrical Diaspora Series: 2

Eds. Richard Cave and Ben Levitas

Irish theatre in England has frequently illustrated the complex relations between two distinct cultures. How English reviewers and audiences interpret Irish plays is often decidedly different from how the plays were read in performance in Ireland. How certain Irish performers have chosen to be understood in Dublin is not necessarily how audiences in London have perceived their constructed stage personae. Though a collection by diverse authors, the twelve essays in this volume investigate these issues from a variety of perspectives that together chart the trajectory of Irish performance in England from the mid-nineteenth century till today.

ISBN: 978-1-904505-26-6 (2007)   €20

Goethe and Anna Amalia: A Forbidden Love?

By Ettore Ghibellino, Trans. Dan Farrelly

In this study Ghibellino sets out to show that the platonic relationship between Goethe and Charlotte von Stein – lady-in-waiting to Anna Amalia, the Dowager Duchess of Weimar – was used as part of a cover-up for Goethe's intense and prolonged love relationship with the Duchess Anna Amalia herself. The book attempts to uncover a hitherto closely-kept state secret. Readers convinced by the evidence supporting Ghibellino's hypothesis will see in it one of the very great love stories in European history – to rank with that of Dante and Beatrice, and Petrarch and Laura.

ISBN: 978-1-904505-24-2   €20

Ireland on Stage: Beckett and After

Eds. Hiroko Mikami, Minako Okamuro, Naoko Yagi

The collection focuses primarily on Irish playwrights and their work, both in text and on the stage during the latter half of the twentieth century. The central figure is Samuel Beckett, but the contributors freely draw on Beckett and his work provides a springboard to discuss contemporary playwrights such as Brian Friel, Frank McGuinness, Marina Carr and Conor McPherson amongst others. Contributors include: Anthony Roche, Hiroko Mikami, Naoko Yagi, Cathy Leeney, Joseph Long, Noreem Doody, Minako Okamuro, Christopher Murray, Futoshi Sakauchi and Declan Kiberd

ISBN: 978-1-904505-23-5 (2007) €20

'Echoes Down the Corridor': Irish Theatre - Past, Present and Future

Eds. Patrick Lonergan and Riana O'Dwyer

This collection of fourteen new essays explores Irish theatre from exciting new perspectives. How has Irish theatre been received internationally - and, as the country becomes more multicultural, how will international theatre influence the development of drama in Ireland? These and many other important questions.

ISBN: 978-1-904505-25-9 (2007) €20

Musics of Belonging: The Poetry of Micheal O'Siadhail

Eds. Marc Caball & David F. Ford

An overall account is given of O'Siadhail's life, his work and the reception of his poetry so far. There are close readings of some poems, analyses of his artistry in matching diverse content with both classical and innovative forms, and studies of recurrent themes such as love, death, language, music, and the shifts of modern life.

ISBN: 978-1-904505-22-8 (2007) €25 (Paperback)
ISBN: 978-1-904505-21-1 (2007) €50 (Casebound)

Brian Friel's Dramatic Artistry: 'The Work has Value'

Eds Donald E. Morse, Csilla Bertha and Maria Kurdi

Brian Friel's Dramatic Artistry presents a refreshingly broad range of voices: new work from some of the leading English-speaking authorities on Friel, and fascinating essays from scholars in Germany, Italy, Portugal, and Hungary. This book will deepen our knowledge and enjoyment of Friel's work.

ISBN: 978-1-904505-17-4 (2006) €30

The Theatre of Martin McDonagh: 'A World of Savage Stories'

Eds. Lilian Chambers and Eamonn Jordan

The book is a vital response to the many challenges set by McDonagh for those involved in the production and reception of his work. Critics and commentators from around the world offer a diverse range of often provocative approaches. What is not surprising is the focus and commitment of the engagement, given the controversial and stimulating nature of the work.

ISBN: 978-1-904505-19-8 (2006) €35

Edna O'Brien: New Critical Perspectives

Eds. Kathryn Laing, Sinead Mooney and Maureen O'Connor

The essays collected here illustrate some of the range, complexity, and interest of Edna O'Brien as a fiction writer and dramatist... They will contribute to a broader appreciation of her work and to an evolution of new critical approaches, as well as igniting more interest in the many unexplored areas of her considerable oeuvre.

ISBN: 978-1-904505-20-4 (2006) €20

Irish Theatre on Tour

Eds. Nicholas Grene and Chris Morash

'Touring has been at the strategic heart of Druid's artistic policy since the early eighties. Everyone has the right to see professional theatre in their own communities. Irish theatre on tour is a crucial part of Irish theatre as a whole'. Garry Hynes

ISBN 978-1-904505-13-6 (2005) €20

Poems 2000-2005 by Hugh Maxton

Poems 2000-2005 is a transitional collection written while the author – also known to be W. J. Mc Cormack, literary historian – was in the process of moving back from London to settle in rural Ireland.

ISBN 978-1-904505-12-9 (2005) €10

Synge: A Celebration

Ed. Colm Tóibín

A collection of essays by some of Ireland's most
creative writers on the work of John Millington Synge, featuring Sebastian Barry , Marina Carr, Anthony Cronin, Roddy Doyle, Anne Enright, Hugo Hamilton, Joseph O'Connor, Mary O'Malley, Fintan O'Toole, Colm Toibin, Vincent Woods.

ISBN 978-1-904505-14-3 (2005) €15

East of Eden: New Romanian Plays

Ed. Andrei Marinescu

Four of the most promising Romanian playwrights, young and very young, are in this collection, each one with a specific way of seeing the Romanian reality, each one with a style of communicating an articulated artistic vision of the society we are living in. Ion Caramitru, General Director Romanian National Theatre Bucharest.

ISBN 978-1-904505-15-0 (2005) €10

George Fitzmaurice: 'Wild in His Own Way', Biography of an Irish Playwright

by Fiona Brennan

Fiona Brennan's...introduction to his considerable output allows us a much greater appreciation and understanding of Fitzmaurice, the one remaining under-celebrated genius of twentieth-century Irish drama. Conall Morrison

ISBN 978-1-904505-16-7 (2005) €20

Out of History: Essays on the Writings of Sebastian Barry

Ed. Christina Hunt Mahony

The essays address Barry's engagement with the contemporary cultural debate in Ireland and also with issues that inform postcolonial criticial theory. The range and selection of contributors has ensured a high level of critical expression and an insightful assessment of Barry and his works.

ISBN: 978-1-904505-18-1 (2005) €20

Three Congregational Masses by Seoirse Bodley

'From the simpler congregational settings in the Mass of Peace and the Mass of Joy to the richer textures of the Mass of Glory, they are immediately attractive and accessible, and with a distinctively Irish melodic quality.' Barra Boydell

ISBN: 978-1-904505-11-2 (2005) €15

Georg Büchner's Woyzeck, A new translation

by Dan Farrelly

The most up-to-date German scholarship of Thomas Michael Mayer and Burghard Dedner has finally made it possible to establish an authentic sequence of scenes. The wide-spread view that this play is a prime example of loose, open theatre is no longer sustainable. Directors and teachers are challenged to "read it again".

ISBN: 978-1-904505-02-0 (2004) €10

Playboys of the Western World: Production Histories

Ed. Adrian Frazier

'The book is remarkably well-focused: half is a series of production histories of Playboy performances through the twentieth century in the UK, Northern Ireland, the USA, and Ireland. The remainder focuses on one contemporary performance, that of Druid Theatre, as directed by Garry Hynes. The various contemporary social issues that are addressed in relation to Synge's play and this performance of it give the volume an additional interest: it shows how the arts matter.' Kevin Barry

ISBN: 978-1-904505-06-8 (2004) €20

The Power of Laughter: Comedy and Contemporary Irish Theatre

Ed. Eric Weitz

The collection draws on a wide range of perspectives and voices including critics, playwrights, directors and performers. The result is a series of fascinating and provocative debates about the myriad functions of comedy in contemporary Irish theatre. Anna McMullan

As Stan Laurel said, it takes only an onion to cry. Peel it and weep. Comedy is harder. These essays listen to the power of laughter. They hear the tough heart of Irish theatre – hard and wicked and funny. Frank McGuinness

ISBN: 978-1-904505-05-1 (2004) €20

Sacred Play: Soul-Journeys in contemporary Irish Theatre

by Anne F. O'Reilly

'Theatre as a space or container for sacred play allows audiences to glimpse mystery and to experience transformation. This book charts how Irish playwrights negotiate the labyrinth of the Irish soul and shows how their plays contribute to a poetics of Irish culture that enables a new imagining. Playwrights discussed are: McGuinness, Murphy, Friel, Le Marquand Hartigan, Burke Brogan, Harding, Meehan, Carr, Parker, Devlin, and Barry.'

ISBN: 978-1-904505-07-5 (2004) €25

The Irish Harp Book

by Sheila Larchet Cuthbert

This is a facsimile of the edition originally published by Mercier Press in 1993. There is a new preface by Sheila Larchet Cuthbert, and the biographical material has been updated. It is a collection of studies and exercises for the use of teachers and pupils of the Irish harp.

ISBN: 978-1-904505-08-2 (2004) €35

The Drunkard by Tom Murphy

'The Drunkard is a wonderfully eloquent play. Murphy's ear is finely attuned to the glories and absurdities of melodramatic exclamation, and even while he is wringing out its ludicrous overstatement, he is also making it sing.' The Irish Times

ISBN: 978-1-904505-09-9 (2004) €10

Goethe: Musical Poet, Musical Catalyst

Ed. Lorraine Byrne

'Goethe was interested in, and acutely aware of, the place of music in human experience generally - and of its particular role in modern culture. Moreover, his own literary work - especially the poetry and Faust - inspired some of the major composers of the European tradition to produce some of their finest works.' Martin Swales

ISBN: 978-1-904505-10-5 (2004) €40

The Theatre of Marina Carr: "Before rules was made"

Eds. Anna McMullan & Cathy Leeney

As the first published collection of articles on the theatre of Marina Carr, this volume explores the world of Carr's theatrical imagination, the place of her plays in contemporary theatre in Ireland and abroad and the significance of her highly individual voice.

ISBN: 978-0-9534257-7-8 (2003) €20

Critical Moments: Fintan O'Toole on Modern Irish Theatre

Eds. Julia Furay & Redmond O'Hanlon

This new book on the work of Fintan O'Toole, the internationally acclaimed theatre critic and cultural commentator, offers percussive analyses and assessments of the major plays and playwrights in the canon of modern Irish theatre. Fearless and provocative in his judgements, O'Toole is essential reading for anyone interested in criticism or in the current state of Irish theatre.

ISBN: 978-1-904505-03-7 (2003) €20

Goethe and Schubert: Across the Divide

Eds. Lorraine Byrne & Dan Farrelly

Proceedings of the International Conference, 'Goethe and Schubert in Perspective and Performance', Trinity College Dublin, 2003. This volume includes essays by leading scholars – Barkhoff, Boyle, Byrne, Canisius, Dürr, Fischer, Hill, Kramer, Lamport, Lund, Meikle, Newbould, Norman McKay, White, Whitton, Wright, Youens – on Goethe's musicality and his relationship to Schubert; Schubert's contribution to sacred music and the Lied and his setting of Goethe's Singspiel, Claudine. A companion volume of this Singspiel (with piano reduction and English translation) is also available.

ISBN: 978-1-904505-04-4 (2003) €25

Goethe's Singspiel, 'Claudine von Villa Bella'

set by Franz Schubert

Goethe's Singspiel in three acts was set to music by Schubert in 1815. Only Act One of Schuberts's Claudine score is extant. The present volume makes Act One available for performance in English and German. It comprises both a piano reduction by Lorraine Byrne of the original Schubert orchestral score and a bilingual text translated for the modern stage by Dan Farrelly. This is a tale, wittily told, of lovers and vagabonds, romance, reconciliation, and resolution of family conflict.

ISBN: 978-0-9544290-0-3 (2002) €20

Theatre of Sound, Radio and the Dramatic Imagination

by Dermot Rattigan

An innovative study of the challenges that radio drama poses to the creative imagination of the writer, the production team, and the listener.

"A remarkably fine study of radio drama – everywhere informed by the writer's professional experience of such drama in the making... A new theoretical and analytical approach – informative, illuminating and at all times readable." Richard Allen Cave

ISBN: 978- 0-9534-257-5-4 (2002) €20

Talking about Tom Murphy

Ed. Nicholas Grene

Talking About Tom Murphy is shaped around the six plays in the landmark Abbey Theatre Murphy Season of 2001, assembling some of the best-known commentators on his work: Fintan O'Toole, Chris Morash, Lionel Pilkington, Alexandra Poulain, Shaun Richards, Nicholas Grene and Declan Kiberd.

ISBN: 978-0-9534-257-9-2 (2002) €15

Hamlet: The Shakespearean Director

by Mike Wilcock

"This study of the Shakespearean director as viewed through various interpretations of HAMLET is a welcome addition to our understanding of how essential it is for a director to have a clear vision of a great play. It is an important study from which all of us who love Shakespeare and who understand the importance of continuing contemporary exploration may gain new insights."

From the Foreword, by Joe Dowling, Artistic Director, The Guthrie Theater, Minneapolis, MN

ISBN: 978-1-904505-00-6 (2002) €20

The Theatre of Frank Mc Guinness: Stages of Mutability

Ed. Helen Lojek

The first edited collection of essays about internationally renowned Irish playwright Frank McGuinness focuses on both performance and text. Interpreters come to diverse conclusions, creating a vigorous dialogue that enriches understanding and reflects a strong consensus about the value of McGuinness's complex work.

ISBN: 978-1904505-01-3. (2002) €20

Theatre Talk: Voices of Irish Theatre Practitioners

Eds Lilian Chambers and Ger Fitzgibbon

"This book is the right approach - asking practitioners what they feel." Sebastian Barry, Playwright

"... an invaluable and informative collection of interviews with those who make and shape the landscape of Irish Theatre." Ben Barnes, Artistic Director of the Abbey Theatre

ISBN: 978-0-9534-257-6-1 (2001) €20

In Search of the South African Iphigenie

by Erika von Wietersheim and Dan Farrelly

Discussions of Goethe's "Iphigenie auf Tauris" (Under the Curse) as relevant to women's issues in modern South Africa: women in family and public life; the force of women's spirituality; experience of personal relationships; attitudes to parents and ancestors; involvement with religion.

ISBN: 978-0-9534257-8-5 (2001) €10

'The Starving' and 'October Song': Two contemporary Irish plays

by Andrew Hinds

The Starving, set during and after the siege of Derry in 1689, is a moving and engrossing drama of the emotional journey of two men.

October Song, a superbly written family drama set in real time in pre-ceasefire Derry.

ISBN: 978-0-9534-257-4-7 (2001) €10

Seen and Heard: Six new plays by Irish women

Ed. Cathy Leeney

A rich and funny, moving and theatrically exciting collection of plays by Mary Elizabeth Burke-Kennedy, Síofra Campbell, Emma Donoghue, Anne Le Marquand Hartigan, Michelle Read and Dolores Walshe.

ISBN: 978-0-9534-257-3-0 (2001) €20

Theatre Stuff: Critical essays on contemporary Irish theatre

Ed. Eamonn Jordan

Best selling essays on the successes and debates of contemporary Irish theatre at home and abroad.

Contributors include: Thomas Kilroy, Declan Hughes, Anna McMullan, Declan Kiberd, Deirdre Mulrooney, Fintan O'Toole, Christopher Murray, Caoimhe McAvinchey and Terry Eagleton.

ISBN: 978-0-9534-2571-1-6 (2000) €20

Under the Curse. Goethe's "Iphigenie Auf Tauris", A New Version

by Dan Farrelly

The Greek myth of Iphigenie grappling with the curse on the house of Atreus is brought vividly to life. This version is currently being used in Johannesburg to explore problems of ancestry, religion, and Black African women's spirituality.

ISBN: 978-09534-257-8-5 (2000) €10

Urfaust, A New Version of Goethe's early "Faust" in Brechtian Mode

by Dan Farrelly

This version is based on Brecht's irreverent and daring re-interpretation of the German classic.

"Urfaust is a kind of well-spring for German theatre... The love-story is the most daring and the most profound in German dramatic literature." Brecht

ISBN: 978-0-9534-257-0-9 (1998) €20
